Raising the Grade

Raising the Grade

How Secondary School Reform Can Save Our Youth and the Nation

Bob Wise

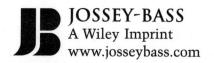

JOSSEY-BASS
A Wiley Imprint
www.josseybass.com

Published by Jossey-Bass
A Wiley Imprint
989 Market Street, San Francisco, CA 94103-1741—www.josseybass.com

Jossey-Bass books and products are available through most bookstores. To contact Jossey-Bass
directly call our Customer Care Department within the U.S. at 800-956-7739, outside the
U.S. at 317-572-3986, or fax 317-572-4002.

Jossey-Bass also publishes its books in a variety of electronic formats. Some content that
appears in print may not be available in electronic books.

Library of Congress Cataloging-in-Publication Data

Wise, Robert E., 1948–
    Raising the grade : how secondary school reform can save our youth and the nation / Bob
Wise.
        p.   cm.
    Includes bibliographical references and index.
    ISBN-13: 978-0-470-18027-3 (alk. paper)
        1. Education, Secondary—United States.   I. Title.
LA222.W57   2008
373.73—dc22   2007039590

Printed in the United States of America
FIRST EDITION
HB *Printing*   10 9 8 7 6 5 4 3 2 1

Contents

To two families:

First, my own. To Sandy, Robert, and Alexandra from whom I learn everyday how much more life means by being a part of yours.

And second, to the Gerard and Lilo Leeds family whose unwavering commitment has led the fight for every child to receive a quality education.

Acknowledgments

Gerard and Lilo Leeds founded the Alliance for Excellent Education in 2001. They and two of their sons, Dan Leeds and Greg Jobin-Leeds, have imparted outstanding vision and leadership to the organization over the years and inspired me since I joined the Alliance as its president in 2005. Along with the committed board of directors, they have helped me develop a deep and personal understanding of the vital importance to our nation of our high schools and their students. The generous financial support of the Leeds family has made possible much of the work of the Alliance.

I also owe a deep debt of gratitude to the many other funders of the research, policy development, and advocacy activities of the Alliance for Excellent Education. In particular, I want to thank the staff and leadership of the Bill & Melinda Gates Foundation, Carnegie Corporation of New York, and MetLife Foundation for their knowledge, guidance, and support of the many Alliance reports and events that have informed much of this book.

Although I have benefited from and am grateful to all these individuals and organizations, the views expressed in this book are my own. I am also solely responsible for any inaccuracies or errors.

I also want to acknowledge some who were directly involved and lent early encouragement, direct assistance, and constant support. Maya Rockeymoore made this book a reality and fostered its early development. Joe Williams got us started with a good foundation. Kim Hayes assisted in coordinating the entire process, "cracking the whip," and editing—and doing it all exceedingly well. The entire Alliance for Excellent Education staff—whose work is reflected in this book—are one of the most highly committed groups of individuals with whom I have been privileged to work.

Finally, I appreciate the spirit and generosity of the people of the state of West Virginia, who educated me, fought hard for quality education, and continue to give so much to others. My hope is that this book furthers the efforts that so many West Virginians and others have made, in so many ways, to improve life for all children.

Preface: Raising the Grade

I am writing this book to motivate you to demand federal action to improve our nation's high schools.

This is not just a book about education; it describes the very way of life that is being threatened by the failure of many of our secondary schools to provide a quality education to our nation's students. I share with you educational and economic statistics as well as show positive solutions that are already working.

We have a crisis in our high schools; we know what needs to be done; we have to display public will. This book seeks to build that will—hopefully yours.

If you sense something is wrong with our education system, believe there are serious implications for our nation if action is not taken, and question what can be done, then these pages are for you. I want to force examination of America's secondary grades with emphasis on high schools. Long ignored by policymakers, high school is the jumping-off point for every young person's future. Whether that destination is college, the workforce, or a life devoid of opportunities depends on the quality of the young person's secondary school educational experience.

A lifetime in the political world has taught me that ultimately all important decisions will be made by elected officials. I fervently believe that many of our high schools need attention and that our federal government must extend dynamic leadership and assistance to local school districts and states to support the most critical concerns.

For the record, there are some excellent high schools in the United States. There are many more that are mediocre but could be significantly improved with concerted effort. Then there is a toxic core, accounting for about one-half of all dropouts, that demand total transformation. The difference today from past eras is that no longer can we depend on a few to pull along the many. Both our students and our nation need every school—and its students—performing at the highest standard.

This book reveals what I wish I had known about education ten years ago. As a governor and U.S. congressman, I believe I improved education somewhat for the people I represent. But now I realize how much more I could have done—if only I had known then what I have learned in the past three years.

In this book, I frequently refer to my personal experiences, but they are not unique; every state faces similar problems. In many ways, West Virginia has made great strides educationally in the past twenty years. Indeed, every state can report some level of educational progress. But one major problem still before us is that despite progress made in particular areas of each state, our entire nation is being aggressively challenged in overall international comparisons.

Since leaving elected office in 2005, I have been president of the Washington, D.C.–based Alliance for Excellent Education, a nonpartisan and nonprofit organization whose mission is to promote high school transformation to make it possible for every child to graduate prepared for postsecondary education and success in life. For twenty-four years as an elected official, my vote was the final part of any major education policy process. Budgets, appropriation bills, major legislation—affecting everything from creating prekindergarten programs to continuing financial student aid in college—in some manner I had a role, sometimes minor and sometimes major, in creating federal as well as state education policy.

I was drawn to early childhood development initiatives. After all, giving a child a good start is obviously crucial to later success.

Preserving the federal Head Start program for three-to-five-year-olds, funding a statewide effort to offer prekindergarten for all four-year-olds, emphasizing the development of reading skills in the earliest grades—all of these initiatives were based on building a strong educational foundation in elementary school and earlier, so that every child would start middle school able to succeed.

I also found myself increasingly involved at the other end of the education policy spectrum, supporting opportunities for students to attend college once they finished high school. Increasing federal student financial aid opportunities, supporting funding for programs encouraging low-income students to attend college, and creating a major scholarship program in my state were all major activities. To encourage college-going aspirations, I personally conducted about a hundred public forums to inform parents and high school students about the numerous financial aid programs that could assist their entrance into college. For those who were ready for the academic coursework that higher education offered, these scholarship programs and financial aid forums were an important key to making a college education possible.

But I realize now that a crucial element was missing. I doubt that I visited one middle or high school for every ten appearances I made as an elected official at a day care center, elementary school, or college campus. In this case, what might have seemed indifference stemmed from ignorance. Unfortunately, it was shared by many education researchers, policy advocates, think tanks, journalists, and lawmakers who largely focused their attention on specific segments of education without recognizing the need to view the educational process as a K–20 (kindergarten through grade twenty, or graduate school) continuum.

Many of us incorrectly surmised that there was no need to focus on middle and high schools. By sixth grade, after all, kids should be educationally well on their way. The conventional wisdom was that success in the early grades from investing significant federal, state, and local resources would mean these students should be able to take it from there. Another prevalent attitude was that if a student was not succeeding by high school, then not much could be done anyway. To be honest, most of us find high school kids—boisterous and towering over us—to be intimidating, especially compared to the adorable faces that stare back at us in elementary schools. A trip to see first graders is always a wonderful political photo opportunity; they are always glad to see you and they usually end up saying the cutest things.

Clearly, I was not the only one guilty of educational indifference as it related to the importance of the middle and high school years. The federal government has traditionally targeted early grades for the overwhelming bulk of its resources. Until recently, almost no state had a reading program for grades six through twelve, despite mounting evidence that most middle and high schoolers cannot read at a sufficient level to do their course work. Because most school districts and states reported inaccurate—and overly rosy—graduation rates, few policymakers realized that the high school dropout rate had barely improved since my high school graduation ceremony forty years ago—despite our economy's unyielding demand for steadily rising skill levels.

As I prepared to leave elected office in the fall of 2004, I was sensing the hole in my education policy efforts. I visited major employers I had worked with through my career, especially during the last four years as governor; the venerable steel mill whose impending bankruptcy caused me to push through an unprecedented state loan to put it back on its feet; a new coal mine opening on the site of a long-closed operation; and one of the many chemical plants now being downsized. These industries were always the economic lifeblood of the community where I lived most of my life. A disturbing trend was beginning to stare me in the face.

When I was a high school student in the 1960s, anyone who dropped out of school could go to work for good wages in one of these industries. Over the next three decades, as I periodically visited these same companies and their successors, I noticed changes taking place: the inevitable reductions in workforce, introduction of new equipment, large glass-covered industrial dials with swinging needles giving way to digital numerical displays.

As I made one last round of visits before my retirement from public life, the economic and competitive challenges we had faced together dominated the questions I asked the employers. How well positioned were they to justify the great sums and employee sacrifices expended to make them competitive? Were they considering the potential downturn of the local marketplace and sales of their finished products if companies like theirs across the country laid off employees, leaving a void in consumer buying power? As I thought of industrial competition, I found myself returning to one question, time after time: what is the education level of these employees?

The owner of one newly opening coal mine rocked me most. Every miner had at least a high school education, he said, and most had postsecondary experience. Seeing my surprise, he observed, "We're not letting anyone underground with a half-million-dollar piece of technical equipment who does not have the credentials."

The response was the same at other industrial locations. The steel mill banked its entire future on installing an ultramodern electric arc furnace. Standing amid the gray-grime landscape of a steel mill, the CEO said any new hire would need postsecondary education as an employment prerequisite.

The answer was the same at a chemical plant I visited over several technological eras. A quarter-century earlier, when I campaigned in the biting cold dawn at its main gate and greeted the thousand-plus employees on their way in to work, the chemical manufacturing plant was a sprawl of tanks, pipes, and industrial buildings. Teams fanned out over the huge area, constantly monitoring fluid and gas pressures through an extensive system of tempered gauges or muscling steering-wheel-sized valves to make adjustments.

My last visit however, brought home the reality of what education policymakers have been missing for several decades. The large industrial structure is still there, but gone are the dials and valves as the instruments of manufacturing control. At this plant, the thousand workers now number fewer than two hundred. Instead of dispatching teams to patrol every point in the plant, the entire manufacturing operation is controlled by two to four workers sitting in climate-controlled comfort in front of myriad computer screens and keyboards. Like the generations before them, they are dressed in blue jeans, T-shirts, and ball caps, but no one sits in that room without postsecondary education.

The world has changed, and more changes come daily. Yet our American education system, by and large, has not kept pace with those changes. Almost every student in the twenty-first century needs at least some form of postsecondary education to ensure his or her place in the modern workforce. We are still preparing too many of today's students for yesterday's world of work.

As I began studying the problem in more depth with my colleagues at the Alliance for Excellent Education, the weaknesses of our nation's middle and high schools became crystal clear. Although the problem is severe, it is also clear that we have the ability to act today—at all levels—to make sure we get back on track.

In addition to wanting to share what I have learned about this crisis and how we can address it, I also wrote this book to try to make the case to the American public that all of us—regardless of where we live or whether or not we have children in the public schools—have a vital interest in seeing high schools greatly improved. I always knew the general importance of education to overall quality of life; what I did not fully appreciate was how directly we are all affected.

True education reform does not come without a major political effort—and 75 percent of the American public has no direct contact with the public school system. They are senior citizens and their children are grown; they are single; they are childless couples. So any building of political will must involve this overwhelming majority as well as make sure that the parents, constituting the other 25 percent, are similarly engaged.

Even those who live in a school district with positive outcomes—such as a high graduation rate and a large percentage of college-bound students—cannot avoid the cost of what is happening in the next district or downtown. The moral argument for giving all young people a quality education should be reason enough to act, but the economic case is even more compelling. Regardless of where we live, the quality of the high schools in our area directly affects our lives.

This book is about a crisis. It doesn't just state a problem but offers positive solutions that are already working. Above all, this book seeks to build the public will to change high schools as we know them.

I have learned much about our high schools since leaving public office. I hope this book brings you to the same realization: that the future of our children and our nation requires all of us to act—now.

Raising the Grade

1

AMERICA'S HIGH SCHOOLS

Ignoring Decades of Warnings

Sudden and dramatic catastrophes have always evoked a massive and comprehensive response from a united American population. The public and its leaders rally to confront the wars, terrorist attacks, floods, and natural disasters that threaten what we hold dear. But can this nation respond similarly to the type of crisis that equally challenges our way of life by affecting a large percentage of successive generations, year after year, only in insidious silence?

Fifty years ago (within the lifetime of many readers of this book), the entire United States of America found itself, overnight, stunned. Having lulled itself into believing it was the global technological leader, the nation awoke to the news on October 4, 1957, that the Soviet Union had launched *Sputnik I*, the first-ever unmanned satellite successfully launched to orbit the earth. Vice President of the United States Richard Nixon declared the development a "grim and timely reminder" that the Russians were on to something big and bold, while administration critics wondered how American dominance on the world stage could have fallen so quickly. Looking into the mirror that morning, Americans were forced to admit they had been fooling themselves about their technological prowess and world dominance. But American pride didn't allow the country's ego to stay wounded for very long. The national embarrassment promptly propelled the nation into the space race. NASA would be created by the end of the decade and federal funding for defense research and development would reach unprecedented levels. Federal support for scientific research also moved to the forefront of the nation's policy agenda. Funding for the National Science Foundation quadrupled in the year following the Russian launch, and it continued on a significantly upward trajectory through the end of the next decade. Calls went out through the American education system for stronger math and science instruction, so the nation would never again fall behind in the race against its Communist foes. Congress responded by passing the National Defense Education Act of 1958, a bill to improve math, science, and foreign language instruction in public schools, with special emphasis on subject matter reform at the high school level. For the first time, the federal government linked education to national security.

Seemingly overnight Americans realized they were no longer dominant in science; indeed, their own military security seemed at stake. Most important, America's leaders responded with alacrity to this perceived national crisis. They embraced education reform, along with other measures, as being central to the effort to regain international preeminence. Looking back, we see now that the nation chose to define itself by a strong response to the problem, rather than by the problem itself.

The launch of *Sputnik* created an immediate federal response. Fifty years later, could we expect a similar response to a news article such as this one?

7,000 Young Americans Disappear in Single Day

Washington, DC: Federal officials today confirmed that 7,000 teenagers vanished yesterday in broad daylight. Early reports indicate that no part of the country was spared loss; more than one-half of the missing are minority group members. "We don't know what happened to them," one urban official declared. "Yesterday they were here; this afternoon, they are gone."

Have you seen any such article in your newspaper or heard it blaring every three minutes on cable news? Yet this could be the startling headline every single school day in our nation. Before the last school bus pulls away from the westernmost school in Hawaii, almost seven thousand students will have dropped out of high school, effectively disappearing into a social and economic netherworld where there are few good opportunities and many bad outcomes. While *Sputnik* blazed across the national consciousness the disappearance of these young people—approximately 1.2 million annually—has gone unnoticed even though it poses an even more serious challenge to the continued economic and national security of our nation.

Fifty years after the onset of the *Sputnik*-inspired sense of urgency, America once again finds itself with an opportunity to both save and define itself in a rapidly changing world. Unlike *Sputnik*, which smacked the country hard and fast, America's struggling middle and high schools have slowly backed the nation into a corner. On the domestic front—our nation's ability to provide meaningful life opportunities for all of its citizens, regardless of demography—and in our ability to remain dominant in the evolving global economy, this country has arrived at an important turning point. How we choose to respond as a nation will determine whether we survive as a dominant global power, and whether our most disadvantaged members of society will have the ability and the chance to achieve anything resembling the American dream.

Unlike *Sputnik*, it is not as if we didn't know what was coming. The influential 1983 report A *Nation at Risk*[1] warned Americans about a "rising tide of mediocrity" in our public schools that, once again as in 1957, was deemed to threaten the nation's economic standing. I was a member of Congress when the report came out and recall the uproar it generated in the House of Representatives. The Congress considered and subsequently enacted numerous reforms, most aimed at improving education in prekindergarten and early elementary grades. The national goal was to make sure every child could read by third grade, so that learning to read in the early years would naturally prepare the way for reading to learn in the secondary years.

The underlying selling point in the report was that greater investment in the early years of the education system would inevitably lead to improvement in outcomes in the later years, with fewer children falling into the abyss of illiteracy and more completing high school and college. But more than two decades after the warning of *A Nation at Risk*, the overwhelming evidence shows that the theory of focusing on the front end and leaving the back end to take care of itself simply isn't working as well as we optimistically imagined. Even though the nation has seen improvements in elementary school performance in the following years, inadequate middle and high schools continue to jeopardize the future of too many students—and more crucially, the nation at large. The truth is that the majority of America's middle and high schools are failing dismally to educate all of their students well and prepare them for the rapidly evolving challenges and opportunities that await them when they leave school. Hundreds of thousands of current high school students can barely read at grade level on the eve of their high school graduation. Rather than highly engaging institutions of learning that serve as a stepping stone to success, many of our secondary schools have become warehouses of student failure. The American high school is in crisis.

The Crisis in America's High Schools

The problem isn't that our middle schools and high schools have changed. It is specifically that they *haven't* changed, at a time when the world around them and expectations for schooling are nothing like they used to be. The system that was designed for an earlier era has broken down under the strains of trying to meet the demands of an increasingly competitive society and a rapidly changing global economy.

Every year, more than one million students in this country drop out of high school without a diploma, leaving them unprepared for either meaningful work or postsecondary education. The nation cannot afford to allow this trend to continue. The opportunities these young people will miss throughout their lives have cumulative costs for them as individuals and also represent a significant loss for the country. Even if we don't have children in a neighborhood high school, this issue has a profound impact on the community and larger world we inhabit. Each of us needs to pay attention to the growing problems surrounding our secondary education system. Just about every social or economic issue in our nation intersects at some point with our education system—particularly our high schools—and too many of our high schools clearly are not up to the task.

A critical lack of investment in secondary school education is contributing to the social, political, and economic breakdown of generations of young Americans while at the same time undermining U.S. global competitiveness. Like watching a tornado relentlessly move toward us, we have stood largely transfixed for years and failed to take sufficient steps to protect our American way of life. At stake is not only our national economy, and whether or not our "two Americas" of haves and have-nots will continue to grow apart, but the future of the cherished democratic principles that require an educated and engaged citizenry. It is very difficult to vote if one cannot read the ballot. A legal system that requires a jury of peers to judge defendants cannot dispense justice if these jurors cannot understand basic legal concepts.

Currently, only about 70 percent of all American high school students graduate in the expected four years. The figures are even bleaker for students of color, as only 58 percent of Hispanic, 53 percent of African American, and 49 percent of Native American students graduate on time, compared to 76 percent of white students. As racial and ethnic minorities become a larger proportion of the American public, and if their low graduation rates remain the same, the national graduation rate will soon begin to fall as a growing number of minority students are left behind.

The results of those tragic figures are staring us in the face as a nation. Some of our largest employers are looking at long-term hiring projections and wondering if they can even survive within the current climate. This nation has historically thrived economically thanks to the talents and work ethic of its citizenry.

But what allowed us to thrive a generation ago is no longer good enough.

The achievement gap is already having an impact in terms of how we stack up internationally. Let's use a sports analogy. This proud country places high expectations on its Olympic athletes. When the United States men's basketball team won only the bronze medal in the 2004 Summer Olympics, newspaper articles called the team's performance a "humbling two weeks in Athens" and an "Olympic low point for U.S. men's basketball." Stu Jackson, the chairman of the U.S. Senior Men's National Committee, wasn't as critical, saying that the "rest of the world is getting better."[2] The same is true in education. However, while USA basketball has completely retooled its methodology for selecting players for the team in an effort to stay competitive, the nation still allows our high school students to be surpassed by much of the industrialized world in academics. International comparisons rank the United States a stunningly unimpressive eighteenth for high school graduation rates, a lackluster ranking of fifteenth for high school reading assessments among fifteen-year-olds in developed countries,[3] and an embarrassing twenty-fifth for high school math.[4] Were academic performance an Olympic competition, the United States would not even make it into the stadium.

It is worth noting that these rankings for high schoolers reflect average performance. Among countries examined by the Organisation for Economic Co-operation and Development (OECD), America finds itself with one of the largest gaps in the world between highest- and lowest-performing students.[5] This unacceptable performance gap will not be closed until we pay much more attention to the institutions that educate our nation's teenagers.

It isn't just about being able to compete, but whether or not American students will be able to survive and thrive at a time when education and skills mean more than ever in the emerging global workforce. Currently, a third of the nation's high school students will not graduate with a diploma; only about half of minority students will graduate. These students, who certainly face a doubtful future, have to go somewhere. Unfortunately, far too many end up unemployed, on welfare rolls, or even in prison. We cannot as a nation continue in this way.

Closing the gap is still possible, but our efforts must include renewed focus on how we meet the needs of modern-day high school students. This requires commitment, time, and perseverance. The solutions are not simple, and there is no silver bullet. Consider a few sobering facts:

- According to the Nation's Report Card (from the National Assessment of Educational Progress or NAEP, a national, voluntary measure of academic performance assessed periodically in fourth, eighth, and twelfth grades, providing a rigorous assessment of student achievement at the national, state, and local levels), less than one-third of eighth graders read at a proficient level. The figure is even more shocking for low-income eighth graders, of which just 15 percent read at a proficient level.[6] Millions of students will end up unprepared for college, work, or the many demands of adulthood.

- In a typical high-poverty urban high school, approximately half of incoming ninth grade students read at a fifth or sixth grade level.[7] By twelfth grade, average African American and Hispanic students read at the same level as white eighth grade students.[8]

- At America's four-year public colleges, nearly 20 percent of all entering students are required to take at least one remedial reading course.[9] Only about one-third of such students are likely to graduate within eight years.[10]

In short, all of the evidence indicates the United States is now in the midst of an "ongoing and silent Sputnik" moment, yet our political leaders and the nation remain mostly inattentive to the growing crisis. As has happened in similarly challenging periods, we must return to intensive education reforms—particularly centered on high schools—to ensure that the current international achievement gap does not become an insurmountable chasm. Although parts of this book contain facts and figures that can make the problem seem hopeless, I want to state emphatically that it is not too late for us to change our approach in ways that pay off for both our students and our society. High school is also not too late to prepare all our young people for the world that awaits them. Not only can proper reform and investment in our high schools protect and enhance our previous investment in the early grades but ample evidence exists that children can make important academic advances at any age, provided they are given the proper support. In short, it is not too late to do the right thing.

The good news is that we know a lot about how to renew and revitalize the country's middle and high schools, and to effectively reinvent how students are educated. Many schools and programs in communities scattered across the nation are successful at keeping children in school, raising their achievement level, and graduating them prepared for success. We know what needs to be done, but we must build the political will to make it happen.

High Schools and the Need for Twenty-First-Century Skills

When I was in high school in Kanawha County, West Virginia, my father owned a 1965 Chevrolet convertible. It was a wonderful piece of machinery, and when I close my eyes I can vividly remember what it was like to sit in the driver's seat with the top down as I pushed my way down the highway, mile after mile. I can remember the smell of the interior, the sound of the engine, and the feel of the wheel. At the time, it was a great car.

You can buy that same car today (which I did several years ago) and invest thousands of dollars to restore it to its glory. But aside from sentimental value as a showpiece, the vehicle would be considered useless by modern-day standards. The 1960s engine will be grossly inefficient, with more cylinders but less horsepower than today's version. Getting the car to pass vehicle emission tests would be a challenge. What are now commonplace fixtures, such as air conditioning, were virtually unavailable on the original model. The car will not only lack seat belts and air bags to protect its riders but will still have a rigid steering column that could fatally pin the driver on impact. Finding 1960s' commonplace leaded gas at the pump will now be impossible, and it goes without saying that Chevrolets of that era tended not to be outfitted with six-CD changers, cup holders, or DVD players to sedate the children on long road trips.

Like the American high school, that sexy old Chevy was a great vehicle for the era in which it was designed. But times have changed, along with the expertise and specifications, not to mention customer expectations, necessary to keep the car relevant in the marketplace. Likewise, any serious attempt to tackle today's education achievement gap must acknowledge the reality that our high schools themselves are antiquated. Arguably the nation's high schools actually are performing very well—for the era they were created to serve. Unfortunately, high schools in this country were created to meet the needs of an agrarian and emerging industrial society in 1907, not a digital and information-age economy of 2007. Despite a whirlwind of change in the last hundred years, for example, the structure of our middle and high schools has changed very little from a century ago, when only 10 percent of the population received a high school diploma.

If anything, my automobile analogy vastly understates how out-of-date our high schools have become. Essentially, we're still driving an antique vehicle that is far more at home in today's museum of automotive history than on a modern highway. The school calendar is designed around the agricultural life of yesteryear, and the expectations for students are stuck in an era when decent-paying factory jobs awaited even the lowest-performing students.

After World War II, there was still little change in our middle and high schools. As the Cold War escalated and *Sputnik* triggered the nation's newfound awareness that it needed to produce more scientists and mathematicians, schools developed tracking mechanisms to prepare the top 20 percent or so of students for college, and others were steered into the general (or increasingly vocational) track. That model of preparing the majority of students for the good jobs in manufacturing and other trades that were available for high school graduates, and even for dropouts, worked relatively well. But think back to my experiences with the steel mill or the chemical plant. Those jobs have gradually disappeared while the education level required to succeed in today's workforce has risen sharply.

Microsoft founder and philanthropist Bill Gates used the words "ashamed" and "appalled" when he discussed the state of America's high schools with the nation's governors in 2005. "When I compare our high schools to what I see when I'm traveling abroad, I am terrified for our work force of tomorrow," Gates said in his widely covered speech. "The key problem is political will."[11]

Our increasingly connected, globalized world of work has led to a significant shift in expectations for workers' skills and knowledge. Worries about outsourcing are no longer only about low-wage, low-skill workers. Accountants, medical technicians, insurance agents, and financial analysts' jobs are moving overseas or being taken over by increasingly powerful computer automation.[12]

A high school diploma is the very minimum credential that a worker needs these days. An increasing share of the ten million Americans who since 1971 earned a GED—by passing the General Educational Development test, which shows a person understands basic concepts and skills taught in high school—are finding that their failure to obtain an actual high school diploma has closed doors for them in the job market. The GED simply does not have the same economic return as the high school diploma. Students who obtain a GED may have a leg up on the average dropout in the workforce, but there are no guarantees, especially as expectations in the workplace rise.

The GED's main value is in providing the necessary credential to take the next academic step, which is usually entering community college. The discouraging reality is that the community college retention rate is much lower for GED recipients than for students with a high school diploma.

Obviously someone who has dropped out of high school should be encouraged to take every opportunity to resume his or her education, including earning a GED. But educators and policymakers must make keeping the student in school to earn a high school diploma the highest priority; any rationalization that tacitly supports students dropping out because they can earn a GED in the future is educational fool's gold.

One could compare having a high school diploma or GED to having a license to go deer hunting; it permits you to enter the forest but hardly guarantees you will get yourself a ten-point buck. You still have to go out and do the work. Unfortunately, "doing the work" with just a GED is growing increasingly difficult.

Experts predict that almost 90 percent of the fastest-growing high-wage jobs of the future will require some postsecondary education or advanced training.[13] By one estimate, the twenty-five fastest-growing professions have far-greater-than-average literacy demands, while the fastest-declining professions have lower-than-average literacy demands.[14] Even jobs that the previous generation of young workers considered basic, such as plant technician or auto mechanic, now require many of the advanced skills traditionally associated with a college-bound curriculum. Think of the last time you took your car in for servicing. In even a basic back-alley garage, the first act is to connect your car to a computer for a diagnostic check. The once self-described "mechanic" is now called a "service technician" and requires the higher level literacy, numeracy, and computer skills suggested by the title change.

In 1973, for example, 36 percent of Americans in skilled blue-collar and related careers finished high school; just 17 percent had some college experience or a degree. By 1998, 89 percent finished high school, while 48 percent of such workers had some college or a degree. The trend is similar in clerical and related professions. In a quarter century, the percentage of such workers not completing high school dropped from 14 percent to 4 percent, while the percentage with some college or a degree rose from 25 percent to 44 percent. Clearly, today's good jobs require high skill levels, a large and diverse knowledge base, and a commitment to lifelong learning.

Today's modern military, where high-tech computer skills are essential, dramatically demonstrates how far the needs have shifted over time. Armies have sought a technological edge from the dawn of time—evolving from the spear to the GPS-guided, nuclear-tipped cruise missile—but the U.S. war-fighting strategy over the last fifty years has recognized that the basic military survival of our nation depends on always maintaining technological superiority to counter a growing gap in manpower. U.S. strategists recognized that constantly superior technology was the only way to prevail against a seemingly endless supply of attacking Chinese army troops in the Korean War or face-off with countless Russian-designed MiG jet fighter planes over Eastern Europe. What the United States can not match one on one in numbers it must overwhelm with sophisticated technology, from "smart" bombs to computer-assisted infantry operations. But to have one U.S. soldier technologically equipped to take on five less-prepared foreign soldiers presumes one vital requirement: a military with the high skill demanded to operate in this increasingly complex environment. Even the U.S. armed forces have moved away from being the employer of last resort for the able-bodied uneducated to accepting few individuals who do not possess a high school diploma. Recently the manpower needs of the extended war in Iraq forced the U.S. Army to lower standards to permit more dropouts to enlist. No one questions the commitment or bravery of these new soldiers, but the lack of availability of qualified individuals demonstrates another reason to be concerned about the quality of our educational system.

This connection between education and national security was illustrated in 2002 in New York City when students at Brooklyn's Bushwick High School were surprised by the local naval recruiter's reaction to protests of a provision of the recently passed No Child Left Behind law that gave military recruiters access to high school campuses. Commander Edward Gehrke, in a letter to the editor that was printed in the *New York Daily News*, said Bushwick students needn't worry about recruiters because they likely couldn't pass the U.S. Navy's entrance exam and have "too many drug and/or police issues."[15] Gehrke took considerable heat for airing his comments publicly; however, military officials at the time said it reflected a growing concern about the pool of qualified applicants for military jobs. Bushwick High School has since closed and reopened in a partnership with the nonprofit Institute for Student Achievement as several smaller schools with specific academic themes.

The point is that this is a technological army, and the military requires men and women capable of being thoroughly trained to use technology correctly and efficiently. Unquestionably the skill level required for most military positions has risen considerably in recent years.

For both manufacturing and the military, competition in the final decades of the twentieth century pitted the basic strategy of more people and less technology against that of fewer people using greater technology. The United States began hemorrhaging jobs in the textile, apparel, and shoe industries to Mexico and developing Asian nations, where low wages meant several low-skilled workers could do the work of one much more highly paid though probably low-skilled U.S. worker. For some domestic companies, the response was to invest in advanced manufacturing technology for U.S. operations that would offset the cheaper labor competition abroad. Others conceded the competition to foreign manufacturers. Economists and academics assured us that even though these low-skilled jobs were lost, the United States would still be dominant in high-skilled jobs, assuming we maintained our technological superiority in both design and level of skill.

I saw this industrial migration first-hand in West Virginia during the late 1980s and early 1990s, as several apparel and shoe factories began moving offshore. Even paying low wages, those operations were an economic mainstay in relatively isolated rural communities served only by a narrow two-lane road. For the business owners, the trade-off for remoteness (a decade later, to these businesses "remote" was more concerned with limited Internet access) was a reliable workforce, high productivity, and a low wage base. Education attainment and high-skill levels were not an issue.

For one mountain community in my state, the international competition was particularly jarring. Originally, their shirt factory was one of several that the parent company operated in the United States. One by one, other factories closed as their operations moved offshore, however, the innovative workers at this one found a niche that kept the doors open. They began inspecting the shirts manufactured in Mexico or the Philippines and correcting the many mistakes and imperfections, such as a dropped stitch or a missing button.

But the point came when even this high productivity and attention to detail could not offset the wage disparity of much cheaper foreign operations. In desperation, a committee of employees visited the governor's office to ask for my help. Representatives of the two hundred workers—ranging in age from thirty to fifty-five, some with a high school diploma, probably none with a college degree—spoke passionately about what the six-and-seven-dollar-per-hour jobs meant for their ability to raise a family. In many rural communities, there is a tight-knit family structure that values above all else having the children and grandchildren able to live nearby as they grow up. But keeping them at home requires some economic opportunity. Besides a few convenience-store jobs, there were no other steady employment opportunities in this rural area. Some drove thirty to fifty miles in each direction, every day, over twisting mountain roads to work at the shirt factory. For many, this was the only job they had ever had.

I visited the plant and met with management to offer incentives or assistance. But the economic forces rumbling thousands of miles away from rural West Virginia were inexorably in play.

The plant closed. I still wonder where those workers went and what they did.

These workers, many in their late forties and early fifties, were the cross-over generation in terms of both their personal needs and those of society. For many, a high school diploma—much less a rigorous curriculum—was not a prerequisite to a stable life in the community. Their parents had worked in the shirt factory without needing much education; they could do so as well. Wages weren't high by many standards, but neither was the cost of living.

Whether a rural or urban community, low-income neighbors and families are used to sharing and being resourceful. Failure to have a high school diploma does not mean someone is not smart. One could say that many low-income people have a Ph.D. in innovation: stretching the grocery dollar beyond expectation with soups and leftovers, keeping old automobiles running beyond any reasonable mechanical life, figuring out a way to maintain a business's equipment when a massive new investment could cost jobs, or recognizing that truckloads of imported shirts would need inspection.

But while these workers were running sewing machines and stitching seams, our society crossed over to a new era in education. Recent reports by the National Council on Education and the Economy and the Educational Testing Service thoroughly document the movement to a status where the rest of the world's education has improved such that today the United States is increasingly competing for what used to be our constant triumph: the high-skilled, high-paying job.

For those rural West Virginia workers and their millions of counterparts across the country, the shelter of a low-wage, low-skilled job has been ripped away. Without the formal education required for other entry-level positions, most are unlikely to obtain significant employment.

With more jobs in all sectors requiring increased skill levels, the United States is fast reaching the critical tipping point where there are more unprepared workers than those equipped to compete and contribute. Many of our corporations will face serious decisions about whether or not they are better off relocating someplace where skilled workers can meet their demands. Absent a critical mass of skilled workers, jobs will continue to relocate abroad, overall U.S. productivity is likely to decline, and the American standard of living will surely fall precipitously in the coming decades. The projections are devastating. A nation that has prided itself since inception on being able to hand the next generation a better quality of life than it experienced could be forced to confront an unhappy reality: the good times have ended.

It bears repeating: this is a fate that can be avoided. Let's use an analogy of two cars: the 1964 Ford Mustang and its 2007 namesake. Placed next to each other, the two look much the same—a sporty, two-door body on four wheels—but the similarity ends with the appearance. Vast differences exist inside those two machines. The modern engine has a computerized fuel ignition system; the mechanical carburetor is gone. Today's ubiquitous processing chips and software were nonexistent in the early model. Astonishingly, the car today has more computing power to drive to the grocery store than was available for the first lunar landing.

When the highly acclaimed state-of-the-art Mustang was rolled out in the 1960s, only slightly more than one half of the American public had a high school diploma. Our economy was humming, with 30 percent of those graduating from high school going to college. A high school diploma was not required to land a job in the factory producing this breakthrough automobile.

Just as our cars have changed to meet increasing performance demands, so has our nation's economy. Today 60 percent of current jobs require postsecondary education.[16] Of course, being fortunate enough to be hired for a job making cars (or designing software) requires postsecondary education. Our cars have changed; so have society's economic and technological demands. Have our high schools kept pace? Like the Ford Mustang, today's high school may physically resemble its 1964 predecessor, with a traditional school building, athletic fields, kids streaming in and out. But what is happening inside *should* be vastly different.

Unfortunately, performance statistics indicate high schools are not keeping up with cars or the economy's demands. In a society where postsecondary education is becoming an acknowledged necessity for a successful future, seeing a third of our students dropping out and another third not ready for college simply doesn't meet modern standards. No one today would accept a new car whose cruising speed is sixty miles per hour, one that has no modern safety equipment, and that will last only fifty thousand miles. Likewise, what is happening—and not happening—in our high schools must be rigorously examined.

It is time for America to trade in its older high school model for a newer one with the capacity to be first in its class.

About This Book

Chapter Two takes up the many hidden costs associated with failing schools and high school dropouts, including lost taxes, increased need for social services and even prison, remediation costs, and lower overall productivity for the nation.

The third chapter in this book examines what happens to those who are left behind by our antiquated high schools, the role that demographics plays in determining a student's destiny, the politics of class and how it relates to education, and the less-than-stellar academic performance in the suburban schools that so many of us believe are nearly flawless.

The fourth chapter takes us inside the nation's dropout factories, and the charade that passes for our nation's graduation rate.

Chapter Five explains why the strengthening of adolescent literacy in our American high schools demands a national response.

Chapter Six illustrates the elements of a successful school, from an engaging and rigorous curriculum to skilled teachers and a safe learning environment.

The seventh chapter briefly examines the past and current roles that the federal government has played in high schools, with the following chapter discussing recommendations for a new role.

Chapter Eight looks at how all of us can build the public will so that we end up with more successful schools of the type outlined in earlier chapters, which includes activities we should be coordinating and addressing in our local communities to fight for these American schools. Also examined is what the federal, state, and local governments can do to share in this commitment.

2

THE HIGH COST OF HIGH
SCHOOL NEGLECT

"Carl," a dropout that the Alliance caught up with in Dallas, told us the only thing that interested him when he was in school back in the seventies was football. He eventually dropped out, his professional football career never took off, and now he has a job—ironically—cleaning up after the local high school football team. Making it as a dropout has been difficult, especially since he is basically illiterate. "I wouldn't have gotten my driver's license if someone hadn't read me the test," he said.

As a forty-five-year-old, Carl decided he needed to go back and at least earn a GED, so he could have options. "There's a lot of kids who are still in school, and I wish I could reach them," Carl said. "School wasn't for me, but nowadays everyone needs to get an education if they want to survive."

Looking back, Carl told us there was one thing that might have helped him in his academic career: a teacher willing to push him harder. "If I would have had a strong teacher, and strong one-on-one help, I would have stayed in school."

Almost thirty years later, the reasons for dropping out remain the same for Carl's present-day counterparts. The authors of *The Silent Epidemic: Perspectives of High School Dropouts*, a major report issued in March 2006 by Civic Enterprises in association with veteran pollster Peter Hart for the Bill & Melinda Gates Foundation, surveyed and conducted focus groups with high school dropouts aged sixteen to twenty-five in two dozen diverse locations. For 47 percent of those surveyed, boring and uninteresting classes were the primary motivation for dropping out. Fifty-six percent of the respondents suggested that having someone within the school to turn to for school-related problems would have been a strong factor in preventing them from dropping out; 62 percent said that schools needed to do more to help students with problems outside the classroom.[1]

Indeed, the responding students also reported giving warning signs that were never addressed by the school staff. Fifty-nine percent to 65 percent began missing class a year before dropping out; 32 percent had repeated a grade before leaving school. Clearly, having an adult directly and regularly engaged with at-risk students is one major antidote to this "silent epidemic."[2]

To reverse the trend, the vast majority of the survey's respondents recommended improvement of the curriculum with the inclusion of real-world applications to make school more relevant. The same high percentages of those surveyed urged creation of a support system for struggling students—yet another means of calling for at least one adult in the school to take responsibility for constant interaction with each student and ensuring the student's needs are met.[3]

There are millions of other individuals like Carl in cities and towns across our nation, people who believed years ago that they could make it without a solid academic foundation, only to learn in recent years that the ground is caving in around them. Seventy-four percent of the high school dropouts in the Civic Enterprise's survey agreed with Carl that they would have stayed in school had they known what dropping out would mean to the rest of their lives.

High school dropouts suffer more than just the individual economic and social destruction of lost opportunities. Faced daily with the realities of idleness and little income, these jobless or underemployed dropouts too often wander into serious trouble. There is an important connection—one that people often do not like to talk about—between low-quality high schools and our nation's criminal justice system. Lower educational attainment increases the likelihood that individuals, particularly males, will be arrested or incarcerated.

Unfortunately, an increasing number of female dropouts are also becoming involved in the criminal justice system. Consider the case of "Tanya". On the surface, she was a somewhat typical public school student in Tallahassee, Florida, in the 1980s. Her attendance was decent, and she even seemed interested in some classes (art, English, American history). But she struggled in math, and even in the courses she liked she had trouble seeing what value there was in obtaining knowledge. As she progressed through middle school, she continued to attend her classes, but like many teenagers she was living in the here-and-now and didn't understand why school really mattered. Her eye was not on her future, and no one—at home or at school—was reminding her that there was a connection between her schoolwork and her future.

"I couldn't even think past whatever day that was," Tanya, now in her early thirties, told us. "I didn't even think about what I wanted to be when I grew up. I was too busy worrying about whatever my friends were thinking and what was going on at home."

Like many students, her home life was strained at times. She was raised by a single mom, with whom she often battled. She got little reinforcement at home about the value of school. She had few meaningful relationships with any adults, inside school or out. Academically, she is able to pinpoint the precise moment when she fell behind in math; it was in third grade. Her teacher that year wasn't very good at math either, she recalled, and she never mastered the basics. "I really should have been left back in third grade, but I got pushed through," Tanya said. "You can't learn the harder stuff in the above grades if you haven't learned the stuff in the lower grades."

She was going through the motions, and her schools seemed just fine with that. In ninth grade, not having much reason to be there, she started regularly skipping her last class of the day, a study hall. By tenth grade, lured by the desire to spend more time with her boyfriend, she dropped out entirely.

Since leaving school, her life has been difficult. She said she hasn't had any good jobs, sometimes lived in housing projects without basic amenities and found herself, and her two kids, in an abusive relationship. Eventually she was convicted of robbery and landed in prison. She talked to us by telephone from a Florida Department of Corrections facility, where she recently earned a GED.

"If I would have stayed in school, I would have been able to get an education so I could get a job that is better than flipping burgers," Tanya said. "If you don't have a high school diploma, you don't get a good job and you don't get any money."

Tanya's story is tragic, and unfortunately it is more common than it should be across America. We have failed to make the necessary connection between students and their schoolwork; it is no wonder so many students fail to understand how important a good education is to securing their own future. As Reginald Weaver, president of the National Education Association, put it in 2007: "We're paying the price, folks . . . socially, economically, and politically, for a generation that is more likely to be incarcerated than be in college."[4]

One group of researchers looked at state prisoners' education level in 1997 and found that "male inmates were about twice as likely as their counterparts in the general population to not have completed high school or its equivalent." In contrast, four times as many males in the general population had attended some college or other postsecondary classes as those in prison.[5] Of black males who graduated from high school and went on to attend some college, only 5 percent were incarcerated in 2000, and only 1 percent of white males were incarcerated.[6] High school dropouts dominate the prison population regardless of the type of inmate counted. Researchers found, for example, that about 75 percent of the nation's state prison inmates were dropouts, along with 59 percent of federal inmates and 69 percent of those in county jail.[7]

The increased likelihood that dropouts will be associated with criminal behavior also comes with considerable costs beyond the obvious matter of the criminal serving time. The greatest cost, of course, is usually borne by the victim of an actual crime. But the rest of us pay as well. Research shows that in general terms higher educational attainment reduces crime by juveniles and adults. One theory behind this phenomenon suggests that as educated students shift into well-paying jobs, the opportunity costs associated with getting caught committing a crime are more likely to keep an individual on a straight-and-narrow course.

Specifically looking at "high cost" crimes such as murder, rape, violent crime, property crime, and drug offenses, Henry Levin and associates (Levin, a noted economist and researcher at Teachers College, Columbia University, and a team of academic colleagues in 2007 calculated a range of costs associated with absorbing poorly educated dropouts into society) estimated that an improved graduation rate had the potential to reduce the overall crime rate by 10–20 percent. Using Bureau of Justice Statistics data and survey information, the researchers calculated the costs of these crimes in terms of policing, government programs to fight crime, and state-funded victim costs, as well as costs associated with trials, criminal sentencing, and incarceration. They concluded that the average saving per new high school graduate was $26,600, mostly from lower incarceration costs but also from substantial savings from lower criminal justice system costs.[8]

The Alliance for Excellent Education applied the methodology developed by economists Lance Lochner of the University of Western Ontario and Enrico Moretti of the University of California Berkeley to estimate that if the male high school graduation rate were increased by just 5 percent, annual crime-related savings to the nation would be approximately $5 billion. The benefits vary from state to state: South Dakota (at the low end) would save $1.6 million, Oklahoma (near the middle) would save $63 million, and California (at the high end) would save almost $753 million annually.[9]

Obviously, dropping out of school does not automatically mean that a person becomes a criminal. To be sure, the vast majority of dropouts, even though struggling to achieve the American dream, never resort to a life of crime. Yet however the numbers are calculated, the larger message remains the same: individuals with a lower level of education are more likely to commit crimes and be jailed than their better-educated peers.

It isn't just a crime issue, however. Even if they beat the odds and aren't part of the prison pipeline, many of the students dropping out of our failing schools are sentenced to a life of poverty, with wages significantly below those of their peers who have earned a high school diploma or attended some postsecondary education institution.

On the basis of what we know about the steadily increasing skill demands of the workplace, it should come as no surprise that many of today's employers are hesitant to hire applicants who lack basic skills or who can't read, write, or do arithmetic at even the most fundamental level. As a result, the employment rate for undereducated dropouts is staggering. Between October 2005 and October 2006, only 51.4 percent of the nation's high school dropouts were considered employed.[10] Think about that: nearly one out of every two high school dropouts is essentially not gainfully employed. They have fallen through the economic floor of our society. It is nearly impossible to imagine the future of those nonworking dropouts being anything but bleak.

Without the high school diploma, few young people will achieve their dreams; most will constantly be running frantically to stay ahead of their nightmares. The first goal is to have every student graduate from high school, but policymakers must also recognize that graduation itself cannot be the sole objective. The quality of education behind the diploma is an equally important goal. Offering opportunities for these new graduates to receive a lifetime of further education is also essential.

Clearly the employment outlook significantly improves for those who walk across their high school commencement stage. Indeed, 76.4 percent of high school graduates who did not continue into postsecondary education were employed in the nation's workforce.[11] This is a positive statistic for many high school grads, and those seeking employment, but what this percentage does not tell us is the salary expectations associated with these positions, or the skill levels required. As Chris will tell you, these are factors of employment that forced him to reassess the value of his high school degree.

Chris got by for years with just a high school diploma, working as a waiter and bartender in the Bronx. But by the time he turned thirty-one, he realized he had hit a wall. He had a fiancée to support, and as a family they understood that if their two young children were going to have any sort of meaningful opportunities in life they would have to go to college someday.

Suddenly the pressure of feeding a family, putting a roof over their heads, and trying to save for the future began to appear impossible, short of a major career change. His monthly tally for bills was more than $1,700. He and his fiancée were bringing in only slightly more than $500 per week.

"That's not food, babysitting, transportation," Chris told a reporter from the *Washington Post*.[12] By the time he and his fiancée's income is counted, there is little left over for anything else. "It only gives us $400 to spend for the month," he said.

Something had to give.

"I realized there isn't much of a future in that," Chris said. But without a college degree or advanced training, Chris's options were limited.

Like millions of Americans, Chris was walking around with a high school diploma that used to be worth a whole lot more than it is today. Completing high school certainly opens up more doors than dropping out, but the rapidly changing workforce makes it very difficult for workers with just a high school diploma to survive and thrive, much less support a family. Chris did what an increasing number of high school graduates are finding necessary in the new economy: he went back to school to participate in a specialized training program, called Per Scholas, that prepares workers for new careers as computer technicians. The training opened new doors for Chris, and he has his eye set long-term on someday running his own computer consulting business. "Not that I'm lazy, but who wants to work hard all their life?" Chris said. "I want to work smart."

Increasingly, American workers with only a high school diploma are finding themselves working harder and longer while struggling to provide the basics for themselves and their family. It is important to remember people like Chris, because their struggles are part of the bigger picture showcasing the need for us to rethink the entire high school experience. Though some level of retraining will be inevitable in all career fields in the future, the key is to make sure those opportunities aren't wasted learning basic skills that should have been learned in middle school and high school. Retraining opportunities will work best when workers are adding to their knowledge base, not creating it from scratch.

What Happens to Those Underserved?

The failure of our present system of secondary education can be seen on two equally destructive fronts: in the form of dropouts whose futures include very little hope for prosperity, and in the form of actual graduates, who put in their time in high school but nonetheless emerge unable to compete long-term in the growing economy without intensive training or additional education. By identifying struggling students early, addressing their needs, keeping them engaged, and continuously challenging those who are succeeding, we can begin to address these problems.

We know, for example, that hundreds of thousands of eighth graders will each year enter high school lacking basic literacy skills (not to mention basic math skills and a working knowledge of the scientific method, American history, civics, and so on). These students will be considered "at-risk" from the moment they set foot on the high school campus. That is, they are at risk of never making it to graduation. Many will grow frustrated with an outdated high school that doesn't feel relevant to their future lives, and many will never become engaged academically in their high school setting because they don't have the basic skills to be productive students. The sense of hopelessness and disenfranchisement they feel in high school will only be magnified when they leave school early and face the realities of modern life. Too many of these students, failed by the education system, will face bleak prospects in the future.

Even students who do graduate with a high school diploma are not necessarily guaranteed the future they may have thought awaited them. For Chris, a high school degree was not enough to sustain a viable lifestyle for him and his family. Moreover, many students who do choose to continue their education and enroll in institutions of higher learning are quickly jolted by the realization that the K–12 education they fought so hard to complete did not adequately prepare them for the academic rigor they are soon confronted with.

College-Readiness and Remediation

All of the studies on dropouts and the hopelessness and detachment from economic and civic life that they face have the potential of diverting our attention from another problem that looms just as large. Many of our students who do make it through high school and leave with a diploma are themselves not adequately trained to be able to lead a productive life in a rapidly expanding global economy. Our nation's high school graduates do seem to understand that some sort of postsecondary education is crucial to their futures, even if they aren't adequately prepared for higher-level academic work. The U.S. Department of Labor's Bureau of Labor Statistics estimated that 65.8 percent of high school graduates from the class of 2006 nationwide enrolled in colleges or universities.[13] Unfortunately, this doesn't mean they were prepared to handle college-level academic work. Far from it.

Of those American students who earn a high school diploma, only about half are up to the job of being a college student. A recent study of high school juniors and seniors taking the ACT college entrance exam, for example, showed that only about

50 percent were prepared for college-level reading assignments in core subjects such as math, history, science, and English.[14]

When the increased demand for postsecondary education is coupled with the poor preparation many students receive in high school, it is perhaps not surprising that higher education institutions are being forced to offer, and often require, remedial courses to large numbers of students. These classes have the sole objective of teaching precollegiate subject matter. Richard Lee Colvin, the executive director of the Hechinger Institute on Education and Media at Teachers College, wrote in a 2005 op-ed piece:

> These are the students who met every high school requirement, scoring higher grades than most of their classmates in courses the academic establishment said would prepare them for the future.
>
> That was a lie.
>
> Yes, these students have the required credentials. But they don't have the skills. They won't comprehend what they read in college well enough to jump into classroom discussions. They can't write analytically. They'll find college-level math over their heads. The California State University system this year required 58 percent of its freshmen to take remedial classes in math or writing, or both, while acknowledging that such classes do a lousy job of helping laggards catch up. In fact, those who take one remedial class are twice as likely to drop out of school, and those who take two rarely finish.
>
> Free and open to all, the public school system tricks students into believing they've been well educated, then shoves them into higher education, where learning is rationed by cost and capacity. And despite the decades-long effort to beef up academic demands and the tens of billions of dollars spent to open college doors to students who can't pay on their own, the percentage of U.S. college students who eventually earn degrees has been about the same since the 1970s.[15]

Across the nation, a National Center for Education Statistics (NCES) report estimated that 42 percent of community college freshmen and 20 percent of freshmen in four-year public institutions enroll in at least one remedial course.[16] We're talking about nearly a third of all college freshmen having to take courses to learn basic skills they were supposed to have mastered in high school. Remember, these are supposedly our best and brightest high school students. Community colleges already bear the greatest share of the remediation burden, and trends indicate that their responsibilities in this arena are likely to grow. Nearly a dozen states, for example, have passed laws preventing or discouraging public four-year institutions from offering remedial courses to their students, thus having the effect of concentrating unprepared students in community colleges.[17]

Analyses of students' preparation for college-level work show the weakness of core skills such as basic study habits and the ability to understand and manage complicated material. The lack of preparation is also apparent in multiple subject areas; of community college freshmen taking remedial courses, 35 percent were enrolled in math, 23 percent in writing, and 20 percent in reading.[18]

Sadly, the very same students who need remediation are more likely to leave college without a degree. Research shows that the leading predictor that a student will drop out of college is the need for remedial reading. Although 58 percent of students who take no remedial education courses earn a bachelor's degree within eight years, only 17 percent of students who enroll in a remedial reading course receive a B.A. or B.S. within the same time period.[19]

Even more alarming is the fact that just 11 percent of all college freshmen are African American and 7 percent are Hispanic, although these populations make up 14 and 17 percent of the eighteen-year-old population, respectively.[20] Their completion rate is even lower. In 2005, just 40.5 percent of African American students and 47 percent of Latino students enrolled in college graduated within six years, compared to 59.5 percent of white students.[21] What we see from these statistics, in part, is the result of disproportionate level of college readiness among student subgroups, as illustrated in Figure 2.1.

Figure 2.1 College Readiness by Race, 2002

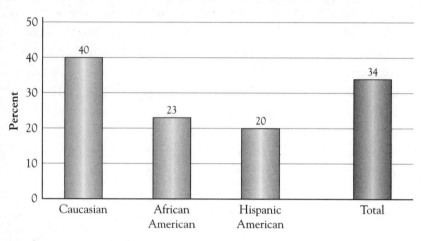

SOURCE: Greene, J. and Winters, M.

Not even high school teachers are particularly optimistic about what their students will be able to accomplish once they go off to college. Though 71 percent of students plan to go to a four-year college, only 52 percent of parents and 32 percent of teachers think the student will actually enroll.[22] In a wide-ranging survey of American teachers in 2007 by the National School Boards Association, nearly one in four teachers in urban schools said most of their students "would not be successful" at a community college or university. An additional 18 percent of teachers said they weren't sure.[23] This is a particularly gloomy assessment from those who work with our young people every day, and it illustrates a significant "expectation gap" between students and those charged with educating them.

The numbers seem to match what many of us have been hearing anecdotally for years. Anyone who knows a college professor teaching undergraduates has undoubtedly heard the instructor lament the sorry state of preparedness among students—like the art history professor who spends half a semester teaching her students how to write a basic term paper, so that in the second half of the semester they can actually begin writing about art history.

I know another professor who was assigned to teach a course called Challenges in Government and was assured by college administrators that the students taking the course were advanced enough to at least name the three branches of government. What happened? You guessed it. The professor, teaching this high-level course, was required to start the semester by having to reteach the three branches of government—a lesson his students were supposed to have been taught in grade school.

With so many of our students seeming to be so similarly unprepared, however, it is difficult to pin the blame solely on the students themselves. With this much remediation required for basic academic skills from coast to coast, it is obvious that our outdated high schools must shoulder a good deal of the blame. These "academic do-overs" for college students come at a tremendous cost to taxpayers. The Alliance for Excellent Education conservatively estimated that the nation would realize an additional $3.7 billion annually in combined reduced expenditures and increased earnings if more students who graduated from high school were actually prepared for community-college-level work.[24] Moreover, if the nation's high schools and colleges raise the graduation rates of Hispanic, African American, and Native American students to the level of white students by 2020, the potential increase in personal income across the nation would add, conservatively, more than $310 billion to the U.S. economy.[25]

Once again, this highlights how important it is that we transform our high schools to ensure that we get the job done right the first time.

A number of components contribute to the high price that colleges, students and their families, and taxpayers pay to get students up to speed for postsecondary education. Colleges must pay faculty to teach the remedial courses; furnish the classroom space; and supply a variety of support services, including counseling, administrative support, parking, facilities maintenance, and so on. Because of tradeoffs required by limited space and resources, schools must often reduce the number of nonremedial courses offered to students, higher-level courses that would impart greater benefits to the community and its economy.

Through tuition, students and their families directly pay about one-fifth of the overall cost of remediation. This relatively small portion totals approximately $283 million in community college tuition alone, but it is not the only cost. Another factor is students' time, which could be more productively spent taking college-level courses that advance their goals and increase their earning potential. Because many colleges offer no credit for remedial courses, students are expending energy in study that, though necessary, delays the quest for a degree.

Taxpayers are conservatively estimated to pay a billion dollars a year to cover the direct and indirect instructional costs of community college remedial courses through the subsidies community colleges receive from state and local governments. These tax dollars are in addition to the taxes allocated to support communities' secondary schools. Thus, taxpayers are essentially paying twice for the coursework and skill development students are expected to receive in high school.

Businesses, in particular, are bearing the financial brunt of having to train workers in basic skills they should have learned in high school. By one estimate—the result of a survey conducted in cooperation with 113 employers across the state (on the condition of anonymity)—businesses in Michigan spend approximately $40 million per year teaching their workers how to read, write, and perform basic math functions.[26] The next time you go shopping for a new American-made car, consider that the sticker price may include not just the cost of building the car but also the cost of reeducating a workforce that was failed by its high schools. Even more important, consider that the lack of a quality education in parts of Michigan, as well as other parts of the country, is contributing to the slow collapse of our own national manufacturing industry—particularly the automobile industry.

Clearly, businesses are important stakeholders in our education systems, and they rise or fall with the quality of the education that is being delivered to American students. How important is a better educated workforce for American corporations? Many of our nation's major corporations annually petition for growing numbers of H1B visas (the official U.S. work visa for international professionals and students) to enable skilled foreigners to move to the United States and keep the company competitive, while retaining headquarters on American soil. Even American manufacturing companies, formerly regular employers of high school dropouts, cannot adequately staff positions; more than 80 percent of those surveyed in 2005 reported a moderate-to-severe shortage of qualified workers.[27]

Who Pays for Poor Schools? The Rest of Us

Two significant groups are affected when students are failed by our out-of-date high schools. Perhaps the stories of Carl, Tracey, and Chris make it obvious that the first group is the students themselves. To identify the second group, however, we need only look in the mirror. It is the rest of us. Our society struggles with a growing population of dropouts and the undereducated. Poorly prepared for the realities of adulthood and the modern workforce, they struggle to make ends meet and participate in the economic and civic life of our nation. Far more likely to be tax-takers than taxpayers, the high school dropout and the academic underachiever will not be the skilled worker, active consumer, or engaged citizen vital for the survival of our communities. We all pay the price when our students don't succeed.

Even those dropouts who do find work often end up struggling to survive at the bottom end of the income spectrum (Fig. 2.2).

The average high school dropout in 2005 earned just $17,299 per year in income, according to the U.S. Census Bureau. For high school graduates, the average income that year jumped to $26,933, while workers with a bachelor's degree earned $52,671. Just as most dropouts struggled in their high school work, their inability to earn family-sustaining wages in the new economy means they

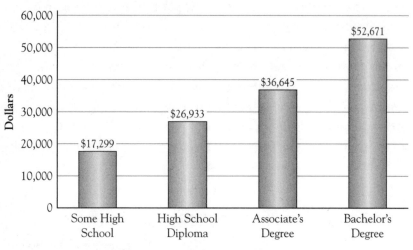

Figure 2.2 2005 Average Income by Educational Attainment

Source: U.S. Census Bureau, 2006

are likely to continue struggling through life as well. Without drastically transforming how our middle and high schools prepare our students for life in the so-called real world, the prospects for radically altering this vicious cycle seem hopeless.

Poverty-level wages often lead to increased likelihood that these students will require some, or even multiple, forms of public assistance. Their health and well-being hang in the balance, in large part because we as a nation have failed to provide them with the kind of education they need to position themselves for success.

Because of their frequent inability to earn higher wages owing to a lack of basic literacy skills, dropouts are highly vulnerable to poverty and other risks that undermine their quality of life. The Alliance for Excellent Education, from projections developed by Elena Gouskova and Frank Stafford at the University of Michigan Institute for Social Research, determined that citizens of the United States would have an additional $74 billion in accumulated wealth if all heads of household graduated from high school—and this does not include the significant value of home ownership.[28]

Accumulation of some degree of wealth is critical because it softens the blow if a family faces sudden unemployment, illness, or another kind of financial emergency. That financial cushion is often out of reach for high school dropouts, making them acutely vulnerable to bad luck. It is not difficult to imagine how frustrating it is for low-skilled, undereducated adults not only to live from paycheck to paycheck but to live one setback away from financial ruin.

By extension, dropouts are also far less likely than their adequately educated peers to exercise the full measure of their citizenship. The National Conference on Citizenship, a nonprofit organization created by Congress, found in 2006 that high school dropouts were significantly less likely than better-educated Americans to vote, trust government, do volunteer work, or go to church. As the conference chairman, John Bridgeland, put it, "High school dropouts are nearly voiceless in a system that fails them."[29]

High School Diploma: Economic Benefits

The long-term costs of our current systemic failure with regard to how our high schools prepare students for the workforce and for the pressures of adulthood are indeed tremendous. But so are the savings we would realize from every student that we prevent from slipping through the cracks. It is important to understand that investment in fundamental reforms has the potential to more than pay for itself over the not so long run. It bears repeating: the investments I am talking about involve much more than money. More important, we must invest in a wholesale rethinking of the high school experience itself. As the data here suggest, either we are going to pay the price now or our students and society at-large will pay an even greater price in the years to come.

There are other ways the rest of us pay a significant price when we tolerate failing schools and an excessively high dropout rate. Henry Levin's economic study further demonstrates the costs to society. Some of the costs are real, such as the cost of arresting a dropout for committing a crime and processing the person through the justice system. But some of the costs represent opportunity costs, or lost opportunities, on the part of the nation to reap the income and property taxes incurred by a person who earns the increased wages associated with a better education and attainment of higher skills. The researchers estimated that every dropout who could be converted to a high school graduate would, on average, generate economic benefits to the public sector of $209,100 over a lifetime.[30] Multiply this by more than one million students who leave high school each year without a diploma, and you're looking at staggeringly high figures.

For example, let's look at the lost tax revenue associated with dropouts who enter the workforce and are confined to the lowest-level wages (Table 2.1). The researchers estimated, for example, that the difference in lifetime earnings between a male high school dropout and a college graduate was between $950,000 and $1.387 million. This is income the dropout could have used over the course of his or her life to purchase goods (triggering the sales tax), buy or improve a home (triggering the higher property tax), and so on. It also represents income the state and federal governments will not be able to tax, because it has never been earned.

Table 2.1 Extra Lifetime Tax Payments Per Expected High School Graduate

| | Tax payment Extra lifetime contribution per expected high school graduate | |
	Male	Female
White	$202,700	$109,100
Black	$157,600	$94,300
Latino	$119,000	$85,000
Other	$168,600	$96,700
Average	$139,100	

NOTES: An expected high school graduate is one who probabilistically either: terminates education after graduation; completes some college; or completes a BA degree. Discount rate is 3.5%.
SOURCE: Levin, Belfield, Muennig, and Rouse (2007).

Using a formula that estimates taxes on earnings for income, sales, and local property taxes, the researchers estimated that each high school graduate would generate an additional $139,100 in taxes over the course of his or her life. The amounts vary by race and by gender, but for each subgroup they are significant.

Then there is the cost of health care and the impact that low-wage jobs associated with failing schools bring to the equation. Individuals with higher educational attainment tend to enjoy improved health status and a lower rate of mortality than high school dropouts.[31] These higher-earning, healthier individuals are also less likely to use public programs such as Medicaid, and they more often have steady employment that furnishes health insurance. A dropout, for example, on average receives $60,800 in Medicaid and Medicare payments or services over a lifetime up to age sixty-five. A high school graduate receives $23,200, and a college graduate just $3,600.[32]

Levin and his team concluded that because higher education not only led to higher income (which reduced enrollment in all means-tested medical programs, such as Medicaid), it also led to a smaller probability of a worker being disabled on the job, further reducing the role of public medical assistance or disability costs. When all of the costs and figures are accounted for, the average saving to the public health system for each dropout who can be converted to a high school graduate is $40,500. The Alliance for Excellent Education, for example, estimated that if the approximately 1.2 million young people who drop out of school in the United States every year earn diplomas instead, states could save more than $17 billion on medical expenses over the course of these young people's lifetime.[33]

For welfare and other forms of public assistance, Levin and colleagues noted that half of the nation's recipients of Temporary Assistance for Needy Families (TANF) have less than a high school diploma; that a disproportionate number of the 1.6 million people who receive housing assistance are high school dropouts; and that receipt of food stamps, a program serving 9.6 million nonelderly adults, was almost double for high school dropouts what it was for graduates. Another team of researchers calculated that over a lifetime 64 percent of adult dropouts will use food stamps at least once, compared to 38 percent of high school graduates.[34]

Levin and his team of researchers concluded that being a high school graduate is associated with a lower probability of TANF receipt by 40 percent, of housing assistance by 1 percent, and of food stamps by 19 percent. Understandably, these figures are slashed even further for college-educated students, who tend to earn even more than someone with a high school diploma. Because many of these government programs are designed to be of short duration (and because men, the largest percentage of dropouts, also tend to be less likely to be eligible for government assistance), the dollar figures associated with converting dropouts to graduates is not as significant as some of the other areas we have seen, but worth noting nonetheless. The average cost saving per new graduate is estimated at about $3,000 over the lifetime of the graduate, the researchers estimated.

Putting it all together, from health care to taxes to welfare, the Levin team estimated that each new graduate will, on average, generate economic benefits to the public sector of $209,100—leaps and bounds above what it would reasonably cost to give that same student a better education in a high school that is geared for the realities of modern life.

As staggering as these figures are on a national scale, what do they mean for each community? As an astute state senator who was also a self-made millionaire in retailing frequently reminded me, "Wise, if you can't get it to the folks in the 'little white houses,' you aren't communicating." Creating public pressure to reform high schools requires that every community leader and businessperson see the direct economic impact played by the high school in his or her community.

Let's start with the individual earnings chart previously shown. A high school dropout, if working, makes nearly $10,000 less than a high school graduate; a four-year college graduate earns three times what the dropout does, the equivalent of over a million dollars more during a working life. Assume you are a local car dealer, realtor, or banker. Whom do you want walking into your office Monday morning? More directly, who is able to walk in and pay for a car, buy a house, or take out a loan?

A high school dropout strolling into an automobile dealer's showroom most likely ends up in the far end of the used car lot, paying cash for a ten-year-old clunker. The high school graduate with some postsecondary education is able to finance a new car. For the realtor down the street, the dropout is, at best, a renter. Every increment of education represents a home buyer with increasing capability to assume a higher mortgage. For the banker next door, the dropout is a credit disaster: no loans to start a business or upgrade a home; no investing in a 401(k) or IRA to finance a retirement. The dropout is more likely to frequent the payday lender than the banker. Only those with higher education will have disposable income to make investments that benefit both them and the bank.

From furniture to restaurants to clothing, an area's high schools have a direct impact on the community economic well-being. With the exception of pawn shops, payday lenders, and dollar stores, every business in a community grows as the education level increases.

The Levin report, of course, concludes with the wise warning that this is about more than just money: "A society that provides fairer access to opportunities, that is more productive and with higher employment, and that has better health and less crime is a better society in itself." Further: "It is simply an added incentive that the attainment of such a society is also profoundly good economics."[35]

Conclusion

To one in public life, it is easy to overlook the individual and societal impact of failing high schools. Until recently, overstatement of the graduation rate has obscured the true scope of the dropout problem. This statistical sleight of hand is compounded by the reality that dropouts usually disappear from our immediate sight, dwelling in society's shadows and flitting across our consciousness only when seen behind the counter at the fast food restaurant, in another menial occupation, or hanging out on school days at the shopping mall.

When I visited high schools while in public office, I was not aware of who was *not* present: those who had already dropped out. Those who were on a path to dropping out usually weren't the students brought in to meet with the visiting dignitary. I still remember one teacher writing a letter criticizing my visit to her high school because I conducted a discussion in the school library with the advanced students. "Why didn't you meet with the students who might not be as engaged in your presentation but who represent a larger part of the student population?" she raged. A fair question, and I realize that the justification "But that is whom the principal arranged for me to see" was not satisfactory.

In America today, more than ever, the lack of a high school diploma and the basic skills offered by an adequate education translates to immediate hopelessness. America's promise of upward mobility becomes nearly impossible to fulfill when dropouts walk away from their education or students graduate without the skills needed to succeed in college, work, and life. Indeed, as *Time* magazine stated in an April 2006 cover story on the nation's high school dropout epidemic: "Dropping out of high school today is to your societal health what smoking is to your physical health, an indicator of a host of poor outcomes to follow, from low lifetime earnings to high incarceration rates to a high likelihood that your children will drop out of high school and start the cycle anew."[36]

But even those of us lucky enough to be on the receiving end of a quality education, who have picked up the skills necessary to excel in the workforce and participate in the civic life that our nation affords, end up paying a severe price for the vast number of our high school students who slip through the cracks every day. Even if you don't have children of your own, the community high school that you pass on your way to work affects you and the nation at-large more than you might realize. The next time you see a group of ten high school students hanging out at the local shopping mall, remember that only about seven out of ten of them will make it to graduation (or five of ten if they are students of color). Remember the profound impact that a diploma has on future wages and the taxes those workers will pay, including the essential contribution they will make to the solvency of Social Security. Remember that many of those students who graduate from high school do so unprepared for serious, high-paying work in the modern world. These are the future workers who will be determining our nation's economic prosperity as well as supporting the baby boom generation shortly. Who can be comfortable with this future?

3

DEMOGRAPHY AS DESTINY

Race and Class Inequities

When I was in a suburban West Virginia high school in the 1960s, the student body was made up of two main groups: the "hill kids" and the "creekers." The hill kids came from middle- to upper-middle-class neighborhoods and attended the same feeder schools growing up. The creekers were from lower-income families in a more rural part of the region. When our respective high schools consolidated into one school, the hill kids and the creekers suddenly found themselves as classmates. Even though we were all West Virginians and from the same region, we really came from two different worlds, and it showed itself in profound ways in our classrooms.

The high school that absorbed the creekers was primarily a college-prep high school geared toward meeting the needs and expectations of what had been its middle-class base. But for much of their academic careers, the creekers had been pushed along on what was essentially a vocational-technical track. It became clear to me after some time that my high school was actually one school with dual expectations. That is, the college-prep school was set up in a way that worked well for its students who were in the college preparatory curriculum but offered far less to those students who were tracked into a different course of study and preparation. Rarely were these students exposed to the high expectations that they were capable of college-level work, instead being largely directed to general classes or shunted to vocational education. We shared the same building, but not the same expectations or educational experience. Over the course of their academic careers, the hill kids and the creekers received vastly different educations—a difference with roots in nothing more than the area of the county where they happened to have been born and raised.

In this case, these differences had to do with the social class to which the family belonged. Such differences, and the fragile politics of class as it relates to education, continue to play out in ways large and small in communities all across America. In Oakland, California, for example, we found similar differences in educational experiences for kids from the "hills" as opposed to others from the "valley." The phrase "other side of the tracks" is ingrained in our culture and reminds us that many of our communities all over the nation have operated this way for years, with students in the "right" neighborhoods seemingly aided in their pursuits by having higher expectations and more resources given to them in their schools.

I saw the "hiller-creeker" divide revealed in a discussion recently with a prominent member of the U.S. Congress. Interested in introducing legislation addressing a specific high school reform issue, he invited my organization to meet with him. As I always do when meeting with elected officials, I took a list, developed by Johns Hopkins University researchers, of the high schools in his state that had less than 60 percent promoting power, indicating that almost one-half the students starting the ninth grade would not graduate four years later.

Let's call the most glaring example on his list "Bellwether High School," where almost one-half of its students will not graduate and the dropouts are heavily African American. I handed him the list as I began my presentation on the needs of low-performing high schools.

The federal legislator never heard me. As soon as he saw the name, Bellwether High School, his eyes shone with pleasure and he called to his young legislative assistant, "Look! Bellwether High School. This is where I went to school. What a great college-prep program it has."

Still awash in youthful memories, he turned to his assistant and said, "And you went there, too. Doesn't it have a great program?"

She echoed his enthusiasm, recounting the high percentage of her friends who had taken Advanced Placement (AP) courses and gone on to select colleges. I was never able to return to my critical point: that almost 40 percent of the students in Bellwether High School were not graduating.

The vastly different perceptions of Bellwether High School between its well-educated elite and the rest of its students reminded me of the same disconnect I felt one day going from a meeting atop a Wall Street skyscraper to a Harlem gathering—the same city, but worlds apart. To the white, upper-middle-income student, Bellwether High School had offered a quality education. The classrooms were a world of high expectations, stimulating teachers, and AP or International Baccalaureate (IB) curricula. Ninety-five percent of the congressman's friends graduated, with almost everyone going on to college. Meanwhile, black and brown students flowed through the halls at every class change, but no one was noticing how many were quietly disappearing each month. Looking back to his high school days, this decent and intelligent young lawmaker apparently never saw the other school *down the hall*, where poverty, low expectations, and lackluster teaching dominated many classrooms.

The obscure nature of these "one school with dual expectations" institutions makes it difficult for elected policymakers to even identify them. The solid outcomes of the majority often mask the failing results of a sizable minority. Recently, I visited East Palo Alto High School in California, a reform high school operated by the Stanford New Schools Corporation, with assistance from Stanford University. In this newly created school, three hundred primarily black and Latino high school students are beating the overwhelming odds of their socioeconomic circumstances and trying to break the cycle of poverty. Their test performance shows improvement, and a large percentage are college-bound. These three hundred students benefit from clear targeting of resources and an effort to create a positive learning outcome.

Just a few minutes away is a high school almost four times the size. For three-quarters of that largely middle-income student body, high school is an equally positive experience. Their performance results in a relatively high graduation and college-going rate. But for almost several hundred of the school's students—about the number in the entire East Palo Alto student body—the same recognition or targeted interventions do not exist. Their need for help is obscured by the overall school results. Here are two groups of equally at-risk students, but the East Palo Alto contingent receives necessary attention and the second group does not.

The phenomenon of dual expectations within the same school can be observed annually in the *Newsweek* magazine annual ranking of "100 Best High Schools in America." Excitedly, every district superintendent flips pages to see if one of her schools made this prestigious list; community leaders gain bragging rights if a local school is named. Yet the primary consideration is the percentage of a school's students taking AP or IB program courses, divided by the number of graduating seniors.

Certainly the percentage of students taking advantage of a large number of rigorous course offerings is an important measurement of a school's positive direction. However, a June 2007 *Washington Post* article revealed that relying on only one factor to make comprehensive judgments can overshadow differing outcomes in the same school. The article highlights three high schools that made *Newsweek's* best 100 list but ironically failed to make Annual Yearly Progress (the measure of annual school performance) under the No Child Left Behind Act (NCLB) standards. These schools were found to have a low overall graduation rate, and at least two of them showed a distressingly large achievement gap between white and black students.

We see schools all over America where half of the enrollment seems to be getting a great education and heading off to college, while the rest of the school seems actively enrolled in what is essentially a dropout factory. Even in the mildest cases, you see small groupings of students benefiting from the kind of rigorous curriculum that is used in AP or IB courses while the rest of the school is consigned to lesser-quality academic substance and lowered expectations. On a national level, it is a reminder that the range of educational quality that we give our children is similar to health care. Just as some of the best health care in the world and some of the worst can be found right here in America, so too can you find some of the best schools in the world and some of the worst. Ironically, these stark disparities can often be seen within the same school districts—and even within the same school.

Because our nation's public schools are largely funded on the basis of local property values and assessments, which depend on the income and wealth of taxpayers in the area immediately surrounding a school, we see unequal funding patterns that exacerbate the inherent material and social differences between the haves and have-nots. State and federal funds are also distributed unequally. In the case of federal funding, the targeting of resources—namely, Title I dollars intended to go to the schools with the highest percentage of low-income students—is not nearly as sharp as it needs to be. Ostensibly federal funding generally attempts to compensate for disparities in other state and local funding by ensuring that schools with the fewest resources and greatest needs receive the most assistance. However political compromise sometimes makes these boosts for local districts uneven. As the Government Accounting Office noted in 2002:

> States with similar numbers and percentages of poor children did not always receive similar Title I allocations. The same was true of school districts. State and district funding levels differed because factors other than numbers of poor children are included in Education's formula calculation, for example, the amount a state spends on education. At the school level, more dollars were targeted to schools with higher percentages of poor children. However, funding per poor child still varied at the school level, reflecting the flexibility districts have in setting priorities and allocating funds to individual schools, such as to target funds to elementary schools rather than to middle or high schools.[1]

Just looking at the state level, for example, one sees that a state such as Vermont in 1999–2000 received $1,150 for each low-income student, while New Mexico received only $520 for each one. Even when policymakers try to get it right, the end result appears to be uneven funding for education across the spectrum.

Unfortunately, when all is said and done, we end up with a system where the most advantaged students attend the best-funded schools, and those without do without.

It is worth noting that the differences aren't always the fault of schools or school districts, though it is in the schools where we most clearly see the impact. Housing patterns and race and class segregation play a role. Even in schools and communities that appear to be integrated on the outside, a closer look reveals that students tend to be separated by income and race into different programs and classes. Districts that boast gifted and talented programs, for example, often see a higher representation of middle-class white students in these programs than their lower-income, minority classmates. You needn't look much further than the lunchroom at a supposedly integrated school to see forms of socially imposed segregation at play. Students sit together, both by personal choice and because of their academic groupings. It is seldom difficult to tell the educational haves from the have-nots.

The April 2006 *Time* magazine cover story quoted students at Shelbyville High School in Indiana complaining that the "rich kids" at the school seemed to be having a completely different school experience. "The rich kids always knew how to be good kids," a student named Sarah was quoted as saying. "So I guess it's natural the schools wanted to work with them more than with the rest of us."[2]

The federal NCLB law has also exposed what were long-hidden problems in some of our nation's predominantly white, well-resourced suburban schools. Proud parents and real estate brokers initially scoffed at the federal suggestion that not everything was as perfect as Garrison Keillor, the host of the show *A Prairie Home Companion*, mockingly stated in his description of the fictitious Lake Wobegon, where "all the women are strong, all the men are good-looking, and all the children are above average."[3] But a closer look beneath the surface revealed weaknesses in how many schools are teaching student subgroups such as special education students, minorities, and English language learners (ELLs), and the schools' inability to show required academic progress for these groups of students. Despite the graduation rate in many of these schools being over 90 percent and the white students boasting math and reading proficiencies at or above average, their minority and economically disadvantaged classmates are scoring below proficient in math and reading—a difference of twenty to thirty points in many cases. A public school that is unable to reach and teach *all* students is a school that is not doing its job.

Despite the oft-stated claim that every child has an equal opportunity to reach for the stars academically, and that the once widely-used "tracking" of students has been abandoned, there are clear differences in classroom preparedness and resources for various subgroups. These differences often translate into negative effects on academic achievement, graduation rate, and college attendance and graduation. Even as kids in my hometown, forty years later, still refer to themselves as hill kids or creekers, the reality is that race and class issues continue to play a role in influencing the quality of education students receive nationwide.

Many of today's high schools have proven to be stunningly unprepared to meet the nation's racial, cultural, and class shifts over the course of the last generation. Failing inner-city high schools today tend to have mostly poor, minority students; but visitors at many of these schools often need only to look at the faded pictures of its former sports teams on display in dusty trophy cases to understand that these schools were once highly touted, and once highly middle-class. The schools that were built to serve one population at a time when the workforce had lower expectations haven't evolved to meet the needs of a changing student population and higher employment expectations. Our middle and high schools, particularly those in neglected areas, must be transformed to offer any hope to either the students or the nation's economic readiness.

By requiring schools to separate, or "disaggregate," student assessment data by variables such as race and special needs status, NCLB placed a much-needed emphasis on the problem, but solving it will require significant work—particularly in middle and high schools where the federal law falls short. As California Superintendent of Public Instruction Jack O'Connell observed in 2007: "Too often the struggles of the African-American student, the English language learner, and the learning disabled student were hidden by overall school achievement gains. . . . That day is past. Today we are holding ourselves accountable for the results of all children."[4]

This focus on the needs of diverse learners couldn't come a moment too soon as demographic trends change rapidly. The U.S. Census Bureau projects growth in the overall U.S. population from just over 282 million in 2000 to almost 336 million in 2020. The same projections show that the minority population, particularly Hispanics and Asians, will grow at a considerably faster pace than the overall population. By 2020, the U.S. population will be 61 percent white, 18 percent Hispanic, 14 percent African American, 5 percent Asian, and around 3 percent Native American and all others.[5] By 2050, the U.S. Census Bureau projects that these nonwhite groups will make up 50 percent of the nation's population (Fig. 3.1).

The obvious trend lines of our nation's fast-changing demographics clearly demonstrate the growing crisis. A rapidly rising minority population coupled with an excessive education achievement gap mandates comprehensive action that affords all citizens the right to participate fully in an information age economy. Currently more than one-half of the approximately six million students, grades seven through twelve, who are at risk of dropping out of school every year are students of color. Remember, on entering ninth grade about half of poor urban students read at only a fifth or sixth grade level.

Figure 3.1 Projected Population Growth by Subgroup from 2000 to 2050

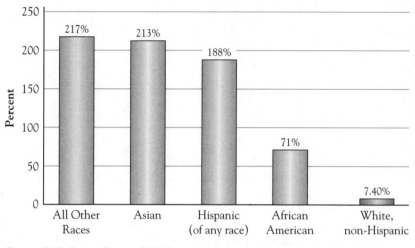

SOURCE: U.S. Census Bureau (2004).

The education gap that exists between white and minority students is the result of both economic disparity and inequality. Lack of resources and fewer qualified teachers are just two facets that contribute to the problem. The results can be seen in high school graduation: only 58 percent of Hispanic, 53 percent of African American, and 49 percent of Native American students graduate on time, compared to 76 percent of white students.

A half century ago, Brown vs. Board of Education was America's wake-up call to the malevolence of 'separate but equal' in our schools and was a massive step forward; a half-century later, our nation must now confront the harsh truth that many minority students are still receiving a lesser education in the public school system than their nonminority peers. Consider this:

- Schools serving a majority of minority students and serving high-poverty areas are five times more likely than other schools to have what Johns Hopkins University researchers describe as weak "promoting power." Schools with weak

promoting power promote 60 percent or fewer of their freshmen to senior status within four years.[6]

- Schools serving a concentration of low-income students (who
  are often disproportionately minority) have three times as
  many uncertified or out-of-field teachers teaching English and
  science as do higher-income schools.[7]

- Eighty percent of the nation's high schools that produce the
  highest number of dropouts can be found in just fifteen states,
  and the majority of high schools with weak promoting power
  are located in northern and western cities and throughout the
  southern states.[8]

The problem is at its worst in our inner cities and as it relates
to how we educate African American males. The *New York Times*
bluntly stated in 2006 in a special report on the status of black
men: "Finishing high school is the exception, legal work is scarcer
than ever, and prison is almost routine, with incarceration rates
climbing for blacks even as urban crime rates have declined."[9]

Longstanding educational practices have contributed to the
plight of many of our undereducated citizens. In the case of black
males, for example, a strong case has been repeatedly made that
as a group they have been both underrepresented in gifted-and-
talented programs and overrepresented in special education programs. The same systems that have played a role in essentially
predicting the destiny of these students must be altered to foster
meaningful opportunities for all students, whether male or female,
black or white.

It isn't hard to find successful and brilliant black males who were
told they were essentially retarded when they were children. I am
reminded of a story often recounted by my former colleague, U.S.
Congressman Elijah E. Cummings, of Baltimore, a Phi Beta Kappa
graduate of Howard University, former speaker pro tem of the
Maryland State House of Delegates, former chairman of the Congressional Black Caucus, and current chairman of the U.S. House

Transportation and Infrastructure Subcommittee on Coast Guard and Maritime Transportation. He speaks movingly of being labeled a special education student and forced to take remedial courses until he reached the sixth grade, at which time he boldly approached his teacher to request the opportunity to test out of his assigned courses. Like Congressman Cummings, many African American men had to fight to remove these special education labels, but how many others—and their parents—accepted what the schools were telling them and forever fell short of their destiny?

Uprooting these long-established systemic inequities must be a crucial part of our efforts to reinvent our middle and high schools. Improving the quality of the education we give our young people is the most cost-efficient way to make sure that all Americans have the opportunities that generations of our citizens have cherished.

If unaddressed, the chronic achievement gap between minority and white students has even greater future ramifications. As minority populations become a larger percentage of the population while maintaining the same low achievement and graduation rates, the national graduation rate will soon begin to fall as a growing number of minority students are left behind. Because the country's economic strength is inextricably tied to the level of education of its citizens, American high schools must significantly increase the percentage of minority students who receive a high school diploma or risk further weakening the nation's economic condition. Just as important, the increasing national dropout rate is very likely to correspond with an increasing number of minorities who are unable to enjoy the best that America has to offer its citizens.

Another great concern should be the fate of our nation's English language learners (ELLs). In 2000, our public schools enrolled roughly three million ELLs, or 7 percent of the total enrollment. This represented an increase from two million ELL students in 1993.[10] These children are the fastest-growing segment of the nation's student population, with enrollment soaring in every part of the country, including states that have not traditionally

Figure 3.2 English Language Learners (ELLs), the Fastest-Growing Population in U.S. Schools

Rate of total K–12 and ELL enrollment growth, 1992–2003

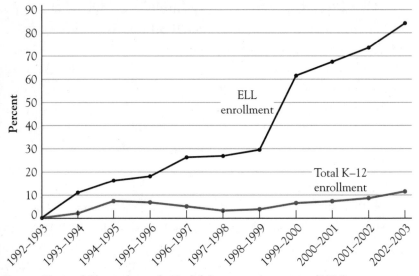

SOURCE: National Clearinghouse for English Language Acquisition (2004).

seen large ELL populations such as Nebraska, Tennessee, North Carolina, and Georgia. They are also among the nation's lowest-performing students and are the least likely to complete high school (Fig. 3.2).

ELLs score well below the national average on the reading portion of the National Assessment of Educational Progress (NAEP), with only 4 percent of eighth grade ELLs reaching the proficient or advanced level in 2007. Additionally, ELLs graduate from high school at a much lower rate than their native English-speaking peers. For ELLs who say they speak English with difficulty, the dropout rate rises to 51 percent.[11]

From the laser beam of attention that NCLB has aimed at performance for various student subgroups, there is a general understanding nationally of the importance of closing the educational achievement gap. Less recognized, however, is the fact that the segment of the population that is the least well educated is also the fastest growing. Unaddressed, this circumstance alone will mean significant reductions in the knowledge and skill level of the U.S. workforce. It will also mean dramatically lower personal income, leading to a reduced tax base for the nation and the states.

The Alliance for Excellent Education recently calculated that our nation's economy will lose $329 billion in income over the lifetime of the students who failed to graduate with their class of 2007.[12] This gap between the haves and the have-nots—graduates and nongraduates—will continue to grow. The stunning potential economic benefit to the nation and the states of turning life around for underserved youths through improved schooling should be a wake-up call to the importance of reforming America's high schools now. The nation truly needs the economic and social contributions these young people can make.

But as shown by some of the statistically detailed assessments of even the highest rated schools under NCLB, solving the national secondary school problem will involve transforming almost all of our high schools, at least to some degree, to bring them up to date with the modern-day realities of the economy and workforce. Scholars who have compared the results of state test scores with the results of students in those same states on the nationwide NAEP test have concluded that many of our states have lowered the standards and expectations for our students. One state, for example, recently reported 89 percent of its eighth grade students as scoring "proficient" on the state-administered reading test, while the federal NAEP examination, the closest form of national measurement, rated only 26 percent reading in the proficient category (Fig. 3.3).

This disparity is unfortunately far too common in many states. One southern mother, for example, was shocked to learn that the passing grade on her middle-school-aged son's end of year algebra test did not necessarily ensure his preparedness for high school math. In fact, his teacher informed her that the state's students were only required to answer less than half the questions correctly to pass—deeming them "proficient"—and in some grades the passing percentage was closer to one-third. Despite its sharp discrepancies

Figure 3.3 Eighth Grade Reading "Proficiency," 2007

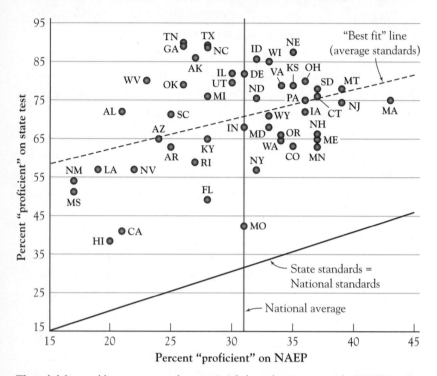

The solid diagonal line represents the states' eighth graders' scores on the NAEP assessment. The dots represent eighth graders' scores on their states' assessment. The farther the dot is from the line, the greater the difference between that states' standards and assessments and NAEP.

SOURCE: Alliance for Excellent Education with assistance from Goodwin Liu (2007) 8th Grade Reading, 2007.

between state-administered and national tests, the state is one of just a few that have recently taken steps to begin raising the standards on grade three through eight math assessments.[13]

On the state level, Connecticut is known for having some of the best systems of public education in the nation. Yet in July 2007, only 29.5 percent of African American fourth graders and 27.5 percent of Hispanic fourth graders met the Connecticut Mastery Test (CMT) goals in reading for that year, compared with 69.5 percent of white fourth graders.[14] As U.S. Education Secretary Margaret Spellings noted in 2004 when the CMT results were released for that year— the scores were slightly lower, but the achievement gap was just as appalling—"I think it is un-American, I would call it, for us to take the attitude that African-American children in inner cities are not going to be able to compete."[15]

The Connecticut achievement gap, however, reminds us of just how pervasive the problem is. Not only must there be massive measures to raise the achievement level for traditionally under-served black and Latino students, but even the 69.5 percent of Connecticut white fourth graders reading at grade level reveals the 30.5 percent who are not. These students too are at great risk of being left behind in the new economy.

4

DROPOUT FACTORIES

Behind the Graduation Rate Charade

Lafayette High School was once the pride of Bensonhurst, Brooklyn. Back in the 1950s and 1960s it was considered a wonderful place for lower-middle-class students to get the kind of education that would open the doors to the American Dream.

Some twenty alums went on to become major league baseball players—more than any other school—including standout pitcher Sandy Koufax. Television personality Larry King, actor Paul Sorvino, singer Vic Damone, and artist and author Maurice Sendak were proud graduates of Lafayette. To say you graduated from Lafayette really meant something.

But that was then. Today, Lafayette is a classic case of the old-model car trying to transport its students on modern-era six-lane interstate highways. Sadly, this Model-T wasn't up to the task. As the world around it quickly changed in the 1970s and 1980s, Lafayette failed to keep pace. The demands of the workforce changed, requiring more and more from high schools such as Lafayette. Not only did the school not keep pace, it found itself falling far behind.

By the turn of the twenty-first century, Lafayette High School was a dangerous mess. The school itself was built for four thousand students back when America was focused on creating schools that could prepare all students for all things. More recently, it became one of almost two thousand high schools in America known as "dropout factories." Predominantly serving low-income and minority communities, these are chronically low-performing high schools where fewer than 60 percent of ninth graders are enrolled as twelfth graders four years later.[1] In the case of Lafayette, thugs roamed the halls of the once-proud school committing acts of violence against classmates and teachers, lighting bulletin boards on fire, and engaging in acts of behavior that are pretty good indicators that academics is not their primary focus.

In the fall of 2002, an Asian student who was on track to be the senior class valedictorian was beaten unconscious by other students outside the school. "The school isn't safe, that's clear," the student, Siukwo Cheng, said at the time.[2] Students were frequently taken to the local hospital for injuries they suffered at the hands of other students. Drugs and weapons were as common as math books. One student wrote a poem about the hopelessness she felt at Lafayette and had it published in the *New York Daily News*. Another student appeared on the television show *The People's Court* to settle a dispute with a classmate, only to find the television personality judge to be incredulous about the dangerous and unproductive climate inside the school.

To be sure, the challenge of educating the Lafayette students had changed over the years. New students came from China, Mexico, Pakistan, and a host of other countries, and some thirty languages were spoken in the homes of this diverse student body. The preponderance of lower-middle-class white students in the 1950s gave way to a majority of culturally and racially diverse students (70 percent) whose low socioeconomic status qualified them for free and reduced-price lunches, a common measurement for poverty in schools.

Like many of America's struggling high schools, Lafayette had what observers often call a "ninth grade parking lot." That is, there are far more ninth graders than any other grade because students enroll and are then slow to earn enough credits to become tenth graders. In 2005, for example, there were 1,011 ninth graders, 467 tenth graders, 277 eleventh graders—and only 216 seniors on track to graduate from the troubled school.[3] Not only was earning a diploma a long shot at Lafayette, but just making it to tenth grade proved to be a significant challenge for thousands in this generation of Lafayette students.

This is the case in schools across the country, where ninth grade serves as a bottleneck for many students who begin their freshman year only to find that their academic skills are insufficient for work at the high school level. Unfortunately for these students, lack of academic success in ninth grade coursework is highly predictive of eventually not graduating and is more telling in this regard than demographic characteristics such as race, ethnicity, or poverty level, or even academic success in earlier grades.[4] In many cases, these high-risk freshmen are not given the support they need to make the transition to high school, catch up, and succeed in ninth grade courses, which would give them hope and confidence for continuing their high school experience.

What happens to these students? In the best cases, in high schools with resources dedicated to helping struggling students through the ninth grade transition (such as the Baltimore Talent Development High School), these students receive the targeted support they need to catch up and have a successful high school career. In other cases, these students are required to repeat the ninth grade year. The jury is out on the benefits and consequences of holding students back; in cities with the highest dropout rates up to 40 percent of ninth graders repeat and only 10 to 15 percent of those repeaters go on to graduate.[5] In the worst case, struggling freshmen see no hope or purpose in their academic future and walk out the school building door for good. More than one-third of all dropouts nationwide are lost in their ninth grade year.[6]

Also true to form, a majority of Lafayette's students entered their freshman year already having struggled academically. More than half (54.4 percent) of the incoming ninth graders were considered overage for their grade, meaning they had been held back at least once in elementary or middle school. Only 18.5 percent of the freshman class tested at the "proficient" level in reading as eighth graders; 21.6 percent were "proficient" in math.

As sad as these statistics are, they have enabled researchers to use these and other similar warning signs to identify potential dropouts. In Philadelphia, researchers used four educational indicators—low attendance, bad behavior marks, failing math, or failing English—to identify 50 percent of all eventual dropouts as early as sixth grade. In Chicago, two educational indicators— earning enough credit in ninth grade to move on to tenth grade and receiving no more than one failing mark during ninth grade— were used to predict 85 percent of eventual dropouts.

These findings are important for two reasons. First, using data of this kind to develop "early warning systems" can help educators identify potential dropouts and get them back on the road to success. Second, the importance of these educational indicators contradicts the long-held myth that demographic or family factors are a guaranteed ticket to academic success or failure—otherwise known as the "bigotry of low expectations," as President George W. Bush has termed it. In other words, high expectations and a good education, rather than the color of a student's skin or the size of the parents' bank account, can matter most in determining whether or not a student will stay in school and earn a diploma. Craig Jerald, an education researcher, then writing for the Center for Comprehensive School Reform and Improvement, put it this way in a 2006 issue brief titled "Dropping Out Is Hard to Do":

> For many years, researchers focused primarily on identifying personal or family factors that dropouts tend to have in common. Several decades worth of studies have documented that dropouts are more likely to be poor, minority, and male; come from single-parent families with a mother who dropped out of high school or have parents who are less involved in school; and have adult responsibilities themselves like jobs or spouses.
>
> However, while students with those characteristics *are more likely* to drop out, the most immediate causes for leaving school are educational. Recent research has found that both poor academic performance and educational disengagement are reliable predictors of whether students will leave high school without a diploma. Students who earn failing grades and low test scores, who fall behind in

course credits, and who are held back one or more times are much less likely to graduate. The same is true for students who exhibit high absenteeism, poor classroom behavior, and bad relationships with teachers and peers. Disengagement from school and poor academic performance often are closely related, with each reinforcing the other.[7]

In 2004, Lafayette spent $11,106 per student, slightly less than the $11,282 on average spent at New York City high schools.[8] Unlike most city schools, however, one of the few problems Lafayette didn't have was overcrowding. In fact, many students did whatever they could to get out of the school, seeking "safety transfers" because they feared for their lives. Some worked political connections in Brooklyn to find a seat anywhere but at Lafayette.

Despite these changing realities of more crime and violence and less learning and graduation, Lafayette continued to bask in the glow of its past reputation. Even when things started to get bad, a new principal would be brought in and the community seemed to express faith that any previous isolated incidents would be properly dealt with. As late as the 1990s and early 2000s, as more and more data began to reveal that all was not well at Lafayette, school officials and politicians maintained that the school was doing just fine. In one semester seven students were transported to local hospitals from beatings, but these were isolated occurrences, school leaders argued at the time. Students were still graduating, and they were still learning; so the defense went.

But the evidence eventually got to be too much. In June 2004, the New York City Department of Education entered into a consent decree with the U.S. Department of Justice, which found evidence of "severe and pervasive peer-on-peer harassment of Asian students." Suddenly, everything that happened in the school was under a microscope. City officials installed a new principal for the 2005–06 school year, but the problems that had plagued Lafayette for years proved to be too much to overcome. It became abundantly clear that too many students were enrolling in Lafayette and leaving with very little to show for it other than grief and fear. In December 2006, the New York City Department of Education at long last announced that Lafayette would close its doors. In its place would be several smaller schools-within-a-school, a last-ditch effort to turn around what had become an educational disaster. By the time something was done to rectify the problem, thousands of students had passed through the doors and eventually left unprepared for the adult world.

This was and still is the case in other chronically low-performing high schools across the country. By the time you add up the students being left behind in the Lafayettes in every state and the pockets of dropouts hidden in larger, otherwise successful schools, it totals about 1.2 million students each year—seven thousand students each school day—walking out the door unprepared for the adult world.

Graduation Rate Charade

With statistics like these, it seems improbable that the downward spiral of a school such as Lafayette would have remained acceptable and unaddressed for so long. Unfortunately, as with many high schools across the country, the dropout crisis that rapidly unfolded at Lafayette was hidden behind misleading and contradicting statistics that muddied perception of the school's success. Consider this:

- In the 2004–05 New York State School Report Card, Lafayette reported that 197 students had either dropped out or entered a GED program, representing 9.6 percent of the student population. This single-digit dropout rate masked the rather sobering reality that only 45 percent of the students who began high school as freshmen in 2000 graduated four years later. Despite the fact that a Lafayette student therefore had less than a fifty-fifty chance of graduating in the expected time period, official statistics reported a dropout rate below 10 percent.[9]

- Among those students who were considered "graduates,"
  only six out of ten earned an actual New York State Regents
  Diploma, meaning they had taken and passed the required
  tests in reading, math, and other subjects that all other graduates in the state must take. In fact, a stunning 35 percent of
  the kids who were allowed to participate in Lafayette's graduation ceremony left with what is known as a "local diploma,"
  a school-issued document, not recognized by the state, saying
  nothing more than that the student continued to show up for
  four years.[10]

So only 45 percent of Lafayette's students made it to graduation, and 35 percent of those students graduated with a meaningless certificate of attendance. In other words, only 30 percent of
Lafayette's ninth graders graduated four years later with a regular
diploma. That is a far different reality from the one portrayed by a
9.6 percent dropout rate.

My purpose here is not to pick on the past sins of Lafayette.
Indeed, the New York City school system is now viewed as one
of the nation's leaders in massive secondary school reform, winning
the prestigious 2007 Eli and Edythe Broad Foundation Prize for
Urban Education for demonstrating overall performance improvement in student achievement while reducing academic achievement
gaps between poor and minority students. More specifically, between
2003 and 2006, the New York City School District improved the
white-Hispanic achievement gap by 14 percentage points and 13
percentage points between white and African American students
during the same period.[11] What the long, sad saga of Lafayette
reveals is that nationally the unacceptably low graduation rates,
particularly among young people who live in poverty and students
of color, have been obscured for far too long by inaccurate data,
misleading official graduation statistics, and flawed accountability
systems in states, districts, and schools across the country.

Schools like Shelbyville High School, thirty miles southeast
of Indianapolis, have coasted along for years touting a wildly

inaccurate graduation rate of 98 percent. As *Time* magazine explained, the school arrived at that figure by using a commonly accepted statistical feint of counting any dropout who promised to take the GED test at some point in the future as a graduate. The school, as many in America have done for years, was able to wash its hands of any responsibility for educating the student and count him as a proud graduate.

As much of the country did in the last few years, however, people in Shelbyville started taking a much closer look at the numbers. Of the 315 students who showed up as freshmen for the first day of high school four years earlier, only 215 were expected to graduate. Nearly 30 percent of the class had vanished.[12] Just like that.

This charade has been conducted nationally for decades. Until recently, national high school completion rates were reported by the U.S. Department of Education and other respected agencies as being fairly steady at above 80 percent. Such a figure perpetuated the myth that although a significant number of high school students clearly weren't turning out to be "college material," most kids around the country were doing just fine. The nation, it seemed, was still thinking of the days when a person could afford to leave school early and still support a family with a good manufacturing job. The realization, several years ago, that "good manufacturing jobs" were quickly becoming a thing of the past caused many people to take a closer look at the prospects for high school dropouts.

The national graduation rate went mostly unchallenged for years, and few questioned how schools, districts, and states gathered data and reported on it. Only very recently, in 2003, were reports published by Jay Greene, of the Manhattan Institute for Policy Research, and Christopher Swanson, then with the Urban Institute,[13] and now director of the Editorial Projects in Education Research Center, that raised questions.

The new findings generated by these researchers, which sharply refuted the official government reports that suggested all was well with our high schools, shocked community leaders, parents, the media, labor market economists, and even many educators. Greene and Swanson did not rely on the questionable data and methodologies that serve as the basis for the official reports but rather developed their own methodologies. Their methods—which rely on enrollment figures, by grade, for every high school in the country contained in the Common Core of Data (CCD) collected by the federal government's National Center for Education Statistics—are regarded as sound. Their results, which resonate with the majority of the education policy community and the instincts of practitioners who have long watched students disappearing from their classrooms, found that almost a third of students do not graduate from high school on time with a regular diploma.

Comparing these researchers' estimates to those reported at the state level, one finds the discrepancies are hard to ignore. Although the average difference between state and independent sources is about 11 percent, the gap ranges as high as 25 percent. This can be seen in Figure 4.1.

Tomato, Tomahto

So what causes all these discrepancies? Calculating the graduation rate can be a complicated process. You have to know what is meant by "a graduate," and then keep track of students as they move through and out of the education system. Both of these factors create opportunities—or excuses—to report a misleading graduation rate.

In the case of Shelbyville High School, officials employed a common way for schools to mask their dropout problem: counting as graduates students who enrolled in GED programs at community centers or in prisons. There are several problems with this approach.

If you think of the graduation rate as a way to simply measure the number of students entering adulthood ready for work or college, GED recipients should still not be considered high school graduates.

Figure 4.1 Graduation Rates: Independent (CPI) vs. State-Reported

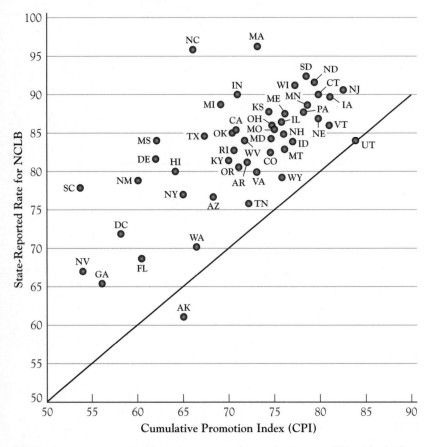

The line represents states' graduation rates according to the accurate CPI method calculated by Chris Swanson at the Editorial Projects in Education (EPE). The dots represent what the states report as their graduation rates. The farther the dot is from the line, the greater the difference between state-reported and independently-reported rates.
SOURCE: Alliance for Excellent Education with data from Editorial Projects in Education Research Center, 2007.

Obtaining a GED is certainly better than dropping out and doing nothing at all, but GED and other alternative certificate recipients should not count for purposes of educational accountability as graduates of the public school system. The requirements for a GED are considerably lower than those for receiving a high school diploma. Counting GEDs as graduates is more troublesome today than it was fifty years ago; in today's economy GED students come up short in the skills and knowledge necessary to excel in the workforce.

Counting GED recipients as graduates becomes even more problematic if the graduation rate is viewed as a basic quality measurement for the education system, or a way to measure high school performance and identify high schools that need improvement. By definition, GED recipients have dropped out of school; the system has in some way failed them, and schools should not receive "credit" as if they had succeeded in educating these students.[14] Counting GED recipients as graduates distorts the public understanding of graduation rates and makes it more difficult to discern the quality of the nation's high schools. Therefore, a graduation or "completion" rate that includes those students who earned a GED should not be communicated as a true graduation rate. The same thing applies to those students who receive something less than a regular diploma, such as those students from Lafayette who "graduated" with a "local diploma."

The Case for Data Systems

A common understanding of what we mean by "graduate," a student who graduates from a high school with a regular diploma, is only one piece of the puzzle. Misrepresentation of the graduation rate has also been widespread, in part because of the inability to track students' whereabouts. Until recently, most states had unsophisticated data systems that did not collect information about individual students over time and were unable to determine the actual outcome for each student. Unfortunately, there are certain populations of students that are hard to keep track of—highly mobile students who drop in and out of school repeatedly, and low-performing students who fall or are "pushed" through the cracks. In some cases, when schools don't know where students are, they are assumed to have gone on to graduate elsewhere. In many other districts and state systems, these students are coded (or categorized) as "students with missing data" or "administrative withdrawal." These students are not counted as graduates, and not counted as dropouts; they simply cease to count at all. The graduation rate can be artificially high when students who are missing or have dropped out are counted as graduates or left out of the picture entirely.

Another common practice is the use of "dropout data" to produce "dropout rates" such as the 9.6 percent reported by Lafayette. Dropout data are often highly unreliable because they depend on those very students who are dropping out to inform the school or district that they are doing so. For this reason, dropout data are not simply considered to be the opposite of graduation data.

Every state should be moving to develop a "longitudinal data system," a high-quality data system that tracks individual student progress from the time a student enters the educational system until he or she leaves. A genuine longitudinal data system can help ensure consistent and accurate accounting for every student. It is

Figure 4.2 A High-Quality Longitudinal Data System

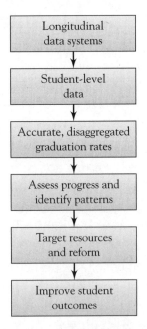

Longitudinal data systems

↓

Student-level data

↓

Accurate, disaggregated graduation rates

↓

Assess progress and identify patterns

↓

Target resources and reform

↓

Improve student outcomes

SOURCE: Who's Counted? Who's Counting? Understanding High School Graduation Rates, 2006.

simple enough: states need longitudinal data systems to provide student-level data. Student-level data are necessary to produce an accurate, disaggregated graduation rate, without which it is impossible to assess the progress being made by the nation's schools and students or target resources to improve outcomes. Careful analysis of accurate high school graduation patterns offer essential insight into the performance of the public education system. Valid and reliable data can both identify problems and drive resources to the areas most in need.

Levers for Change

The combination of a tragically low graduation rate and growing awareness of inaccurate data have moved influential persons and organizations at the local, state, federal, and national levels to launch initiatives to demand reforms in calculating accurate and consistent graduation rates. The Alliance for Excellent Education helped lead the way in raising questions about the validity of graduation rate figures nationwide, and in 2006 released a study summarizing efforts to improve the process called *Who's Counted? Who's Counting? Understanding High School Graduation Rates*.[15]

Stakeholders at every level of government have shown leadership by taking important steps to build capacity to meet those goals. As a result, there are growing state and national efforts for consistently and accurately measuring graduation rates. Most notably, in the summer of 2005 all fifty of the nation's governors, as part of the year-long initiative known as Redesigning the American High School, signed the National Governors Association's Graduation Rate Compact. The compact was a public declaration of the governors' commitment to implement a common, accurate graduation rate and create better systems and methods of collecting, analyzing, and reporting graduation and dropout data. Many other state officials, including boards of education, auditors, and legislators, have joined this campaign to raise awareness, change policies, and improve practices related to collection, calculation, and reporting of graduation rates. There is a significant amount of effort being exerted around these issues, but it remains to be seen if these good intentions will be followed by firm commitments, legislative change, and implementation.

Increasingly, educators, advocates, and policymakers also seem to agree on the need for more accurate education data. States, national organizations, and foundations have invested in building these systems. In June 2007, the Institute for Education Sciences, an arm of the U.S. Department of Education, distributed $62.2 million in three-year grants to thirteen states, in addition to the fourteen states that received grants in 2005, to fund, design, and implement statewide longitudinal data systems.[16]

Despite the momentum these various efforts have spurred, much work remains to be done. Lack of political will, capacity, and funding require a concerted national effort at all levels of government and by concerned citizens across the country to prioritize this issue and make systemic changes to how information is collected, calculated, reported, and used.

The federal government should play a leading role in removing the veil that has allowed too many high schools to hide failure. Schools, districts, and states have a responsibility to accurately measure and report the graduation rate for all students, while significantly progressing toward the goal of having all students graduate from high school prepared for college and work. Although the No Child Left Behind (NCLB) Act offers a powerful lever to force graduation rate transparency, the federal government has largely relinquished this authority.

NCLB requires that Adequate Yearly Progress (AYP) be calculated and reported for all schools. It is undeniable that the graduation rate plays an important role as a measure of high school performance. Some congressional supporters of NCLB recognized that holding schools accountable for just their test scores might create perverse incentives to push out low-performing students; thus high schools should also have to be accountable for meeting graduation goals to make AYP. Unfortunately, there are three significant flaws in NCLB (as written and implemented) that undermine the intention of the law and weaken the role of graduation rates in accountability for student success and as a tool for identifying low-performing high schools and targeting support and interventions:

- NCLB has permitted use of inconsistent and misleading graduation rate calculations that overestimate the true rate.
- NCLB does not require any meaningful increase of graduation rates over time.
- NCLB does not require the disaggregated graduation rates of student subgroups to increase as part of AYP determinations.

The ironic effect of this gross oversight is that by not holding states and schools accountable for the end measure of the K–12 education process, the federal government created an incentive for schools to push out students who will not test well on the annual assessments. This push-out strategy recognizes that without accountability for whether or not a student actually completes the twelfth grade, it is better to weed the low-performing students out early, before they lower the school's overall test performance scores. To reverse this deleterious incentive, the graduation rate for all students and student subgroups must be included in the determination of AYP on an equal footing with test scores and must have similar, annually increasing goals that yield a reasonable trajectory toward achieving the objective of graduating all students prepared for college, work, and life.

There is another consequence of not including accurate graduation rates as part of federal accountability: AYP becomes an inaccurate tool for identifying high schools that need extra support. When high schools such as Lafayette or the approximately eight hundred dropout factories that "made AYP" can fly under the radar with an abysmal graduation rate, the AYP system is not a meaningful lever for school improvement.

Getting a Handle on Our Nation's Graduates

Because of the researchers and practitioners mentioned in this book and many others, we know an awful lot about the schools where the bleeding is the worst. That's the good news: we know where the problems are. Now we need to do something about it.

We know, for example, that about 10 percent of the nation's twenty thousand high schools produce close to half of its dropouts. These are the almost two thousand some high schools, like Lafayette, that the researchers have deemed to be dropout factories, and they should be the starting point of serious efforts to significantly transform the schools themselves. In half the nation's largest one hundred cities, 50 percent or more of the students attend a high school with at least 300 students are in a dropout factory.[17] As we have seen, however, this is a problem that affects all of us, no matter where we live. In fact, there are dropout factories in every state but Utah, the researchers found. Addressing the dropout crisis is crucial, but even this doesn't address the larger reality that many of our "successful" high schools are also outdated and not getting the job done that ensures our remaining a first-rate nation with opportunity for all.

What does the dropout research tell us about these schools? We know, for example, that poverty is a fundamental facet of a low graduation rate. There is a strong connection between a school's poverty rate and its tendency to lose students between ninth and

Figure 4.3 Who's Graduating in the United States?

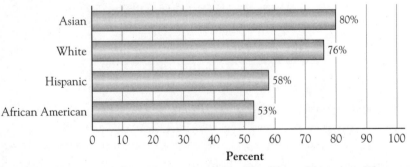

SOURCE: Alliance for Excellent Education, with data from Editorial Projects in Education Research Center, 2007.

twelfth grade. We know that minorities who attend middle-class or affluent schools tend to graduate at similar levels to white students. But we also know that relatively few minorities attend schools of this kind, and that a quality education is the most important factor in helping these students overcome the poverty in which some of them were raised. In fact, we know that nearly half of the nation's African American and Hispanic students attend high schools characterized by high poverty and low graduation.[18] The students who need a quality education the most overwhelmingly attend schools where good education is not happening.

We also know that, as students at Lafayette found when they tried to enroll elsewhere, in numerous cities there are so many underperforming high schools that students have virtually no other choice but to attend a high school with weak promoting power. These students are forced to attend substandard schools because that is all we are offering them. 75 percent of school districts have only one high school, even further limiting students' options for transferring out of a poorly-performing school.

In the low-performing schools themselves, we often see students being subjected to an irrelevant curriculum that lacks rigor. There are often achievement disparities between a large number of students struggling to catch up to the small number of high-performers. Rounding out the list of dire indicators is a large student population with a high student-teacher ratio of adults disconnected from students, and serious issues involving student and teacher safety.

Schools that are considered dropout factories tend to have teacher inequities as well. It is well documented, for example, that poor and minority students are significantly more likely than white, middle-income peers to be taught by inexperienced, uncertified, and ill-prepared teachers.[19]

Conclusion: What We Know

The importance of understanding, recognizing, and addressing the nation's dropout crisis cannot be overstated. The graduation rate is a fundamental indicator of whether or not the nation's public school system is fulfilling its basic mission and an important index of school performance for parents, policymakers, and other concerned members of the community. The first step in understanding the effectiveness of our high schools is to determine how many students are successfully completing the course of study. The second step is to make sure that the diploma they earn has a quality education behind it. But in a world where the high school diploma is both a prerequisite to qualify for additional education and also the minimum credential needed, we must ensure there is proper measurement of how many complete this first step. Accurate graduation rates are also essential for targeting resources and interventions to low-performing schools.

It seems strange that in a society where, with the click of a mouse, a manufacturer can quantify the exact number of products that sit on stockroom shelves across the country and FedEx can identify the exact location of a package, we can still lose track of students in our education system. The fact that we lose so many of them is tragedy enough; we shouldn't be compounding it with inadequate, insufficient, and downright wrong graduation rate data that have been used to guide, or misguide, decades of public education policy.

In terms of dropouts, there needs to be a dramatic sense of urgency, especially in light of the fact that we know that the number of dropout factories identified by researchers has nearly doubled in the last decade. It is time to stop the bleeding, but again we can't stop there. Most of our American middle and high schools are in need of a transfusion of public will and reform. Dealing with our most chronic failures is a good place to start.

In terms of public policy, it is clear that NCLB has largely ignored high schools. This neglect is in line with most other nationwide education reform pushes that have taken place in the last two decades. Only 8 percent of students currently benefiting from the federal Title I funds available for low-performing schools are in high school, yet we have seen problems that long ago reached epidemic proportions.

The lack of federal attention to high schools, exemplified by failing to hold schools accountable on the basis of their ability to move students to graduation and a meaningful diploma, contribute to what has been called the "missing middle." Much more attention must be paid by the federal government to supporting the complete reinvention of these high schools, especially those producing the bulk of the nation's dropouts.

To be sure, this isn't just an NCLB issue, but a national issue of expectations. Making the high school experience truly worthwhile for our students requires federal dedication to pushing all kids over the finish line with a credible diploma. Each diploma should be viewed as the nation's warranty on our children's education, a vote of confidence that our society has prepared them for adult life and the workforce. Providing this quality and opportunity must be uppermost to our society. One reason the warranty on a new refrigerator or computer means something is that the manufacturer has confidence that the appliance will work properly. Surely this nation's government must similarly stand behind the preparation of its students.

5

STRENGTHENING ADOLESCENT LITERACY

A National Priority

When I was governor, the annual celebration of national reading day was always something I looked forward to. Leaving the State Capitol's constant swirl of policy and politics, I would take a quick ride to an elementary school where excited youngsters, teachers, and parents packed an all-purpose room ready to listen to me read a story aloud. The numerous TV cameras, microphones, and reporters further fueled the squirming and fidgeting energy of the seated kindergarten through fifth grade students. Inevitably, I would sit in the rocking chair, pick up the awaiting Dr. Seuss book, and begin slowly reading, taking time to pause after each page and point to the picture. A guaranteed youthful applause-getter was putting on the red-striped Dr. Seuss hat for special effect.

The highly charged enthusiasm of the young children was reason enough to participate. Also, the combination of grade school students, educators, and politicians made this the perfect setting to reinforce the vital message of fostering reading at the earliest age to children and adults alike. For many in political life, this trip to the elementary school is their strongest statement about the importance of reading.

Unfortunately, I did not make enough visits to enough schools. The emotionally rewarding grade school visit was never followed by similar forays to middle schools and high schools. Indeed, the thought never crossed my mind that there would be a problem with reading in later grades. After all, wasn't the important goal to give children in early grades a strong reading foundation that would strengthen as they grew?

Over the past four decades, Congress has directed substantial resources toward improving young children's literacy skills, and the investment has grown significantly in recent years. Through initiatives such as Title I of the Elementary and Secondary Education Act, Reading First, and Head Start, the federal government has spent billions of dollars promoting vital research and improved reading instruction in the home, in preschool settings, and during the first few years of elementary school. As long as millions of young readers continue to struggle, this work should remain a high priority. But focusing on building reading skills in pre-K–3 cannot be the only priority.

America's secondary school students face a literacy crisis every bit as alarming as the one confronting younger children. Millions of secondary students lack the reading and writing skills they need to succeed in college, compete in the workforce, or even understand a daily newspaper. However, even though Congress has demonstrated a real commitment to improve reading instruction in grades K–3, it has made relatively minor investments in the literacy skills of students in grades four through twelve.

When I was reading only to grade school students, I should have been paying more attention to the stark reports from the National Assessment of Educational Progress (NAEP) that more than two thirds of all eighth graders read below grade level, and nearly half of these students are so far behind that they drop off the scale entirely, scoring below what the U.S. Department of Education defines as its most basic level. Students in this group read at the equivalent of two or more grades below their proficient peers. Moreover, though fourth grade reading scores have risen for several years, reflecting the nation's investment in early reading instruction, eighth and twelfth grade scores have remained basically flat since the 1970s.

Students entering high school encounter new demands on their ability to read and comprehend printed words on a textbook page. Their challenge is being able to read three paragraphs and summarize the meaning into a single thought, or extrapolate meanings to solve a problem. As several reading specialists have explained to me, "In the early grades, children 'learn to read.' In high school, they 'read to learn,' and it is a different skill set."

In total, more than six million of America's students in the seventh through twelfth grades are truly "struggling readers" (a term commonly used to denote middle and high school students who read two or more years below grade level). Many of them are likely to drop out—it seems no coincidence that the national dropout rate closely mirrors the percentage of students reading at NAEP's "below-basic" level in eighth grade—and of those who go on to receive their diploma, many will remain unprepared and unlikely to succeed in college or at work. Struggling adolescent readers may be able to sound out the words they see on a page or comprehend simple texts, but most have difficulty understanding substantive reading assignments, following complicated directions, drawing conclusions, or thinking critically about what they read, whatever the subject.

Educators are now beginning to recognize that the teaching of reading and writing cannot end at third grade; they must provide intensive, high-quality literacy instruction throughout the K–12 curriculum. Not only must educators teach decoding skills—the mechanics of reading, such as recognizing and sounding out words—to middle and high school students who still struggle with the very basics of reading, but they must help all students go beyond those basics. They must explicitly teach students reading comprehension strategies, vocabulary, writing, and other forms of communication, or else millions of adolescents will lose whatever momentum they may have gained as a result of improvement in early reading instruction. The good news is that researchers and educators agree on some key steps schools can take to improve adolescent literacy. A major Alliance for

Excellent Education report, *Reading Next: A Vision for Action in Middle and High School Literacy*, outlines what the top researchers in the country agree needs to be done to improve literacy in our nation's high schools.[1]

Elected officials need to catch up to educators in recognizing the need for literacy efforts in all grades, including high school. While in public office, I never thought to call over to our state department of education to ask whether our state had a reading problem among high school students. Until recently, almost no state had a specific strategy that recognized a widespread literacy shortfall in secondary schools. This was echoed by the federal government's assisting K–3 literacy for years with the Reading First program, but devoting almost no dollars to the last nine grades despite more than two-thirds of eighth graders reading below grade level. Unless the nation devotes more attention and resources to literacy in grades four through twelve, it will squander the considerable resources it has spent on grades K–3, and it will leave millions of students without a meaningful opportunity to succeed in high school and beyond.

The Alliance for Excellent Education has played a strong role in helping to move Congress toward increasing investment in adolescent literacy. Created in 2005 with support from President Bush, funding for the Striving Readers program is the first-ever federal investment specifically targeted to literacy improvement of middle and high school students who read below grade level. Through supplemental literacy interventions, cross-disciplinary strategies, and a strong evaluation component, the Striving Readers program seeks to improve the reading skills of struggling readers, while improving the evidence base for identifying literacy strategies that work for older students.

Although the original $24.8 million Striving Readers investment was a sorely needed booster shot for adolescent literacy, Congress must significantly increase investment in this critical area if we are to meet and beat the scope of the adolescent reading problem.

Figure 5.1 Reading First and Striving Readers

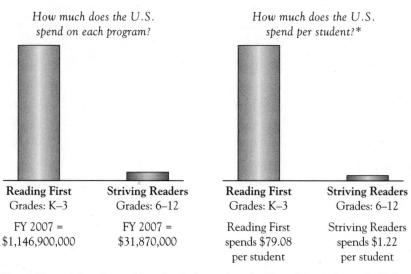

How much does the U.S. spend on each program?		*How much does the U.S. spend per student?**	
Reading First Grades: K–3	**Striving Readers** Grades: 6–12	**Reading First** Grades: K–3	**Striving Readers** Grades: 6–12
FY 2007 = $1,146,900,000	FY 2007 = $31,870,000	Reading First spends $79.08 per student	Striving Readers spends $1.22 per student

NOTE: *Figure is based on public school education in the United States for grades K–3 and 6–12 in 2005–06 (National Center for Education Statistics, 2006).
Source: NCES, 2006.

A Strong Literacy Foundation Is Not Enough

There is a reason education reformers devote so much effort to the early grades: to build a house, you must secure the foundation. But the opposite is true as well: there is little sense in laying a foundation unless there are plans to build something on top of it. Students need a lot of help to raise the roof on learning, even after they learn the foundational skills of reading.

Why isn't a set of third grade literacy skills enough to support the full weight of a middle and high school education? Because sooner or later—typically in the fourth grade—teachers set aside the basic readers and storybooks and start to assign longer, more difficult, and content-rich reading materials, ranging from textbooks, short stories, and biographies to laboratory instructions, technical manuals, and mathematical word problems.

Prior to the fourth grade, children are judged to be competent readers if they can sound out words and follow a simple plot. At the very moment that most schools stop offering reading instruction, however, the demands of literacy change. Middle and high school students have to move beyond merely decoding text to gathering information from it and—in the best and most challenging classrooms—analyzing, interpreting, and responding critically to what they read; writing sophisticated texts of their own; and discussing, debating, and defending their ideas. Just when students need support to reach a higher level of literacy, most schools stop literacy instruction altogether. It is no surprise, then, that data shows a pronounced dropoff in reading achievement at that point, which has long been known as the "fourth grade slump."

To complicate things further, schoolbooks don't just increase in length and amount of information; they also become more varied. In the middle grades, the curriculum divides into the familiar subject areas, with English, math, history, and science composing the academic core, each with its own distinct texts. For students in earlier grades, the main point of reading is to learn to read, whether the text is about nature or trains or a story from history. But when they move into the middle grades the point of reading changes from learning to read to reading to learn; reading becomes the means to learning instead of the end. Students soon discover that what the science teacher writes on the blackboard is nothing like the poems assigned by the English teacher, the math textbook has a very different style from that of the history textbook, and none of them resembles the many other sorts of materials teachers assign, from newspaper stories to reference materials, Web pages, and technical manuals.

Does This Make Sense to You?

The valves are located in the press pit. One valve controls two prefill valves. The valve solenoid is deenergized when initially closing the press. Once the pressure transducer indicates that there is approximately 1,800 PSI pressure in the line, SOL P1-P4 are energized. Oil is then ported to extend the actuators, which shifts the prefill valve spools. Flow from the pumps is now directed to pressurize the main rams. The pressure will initially drop and once again build. The valves remain energized until the pressure reaches the PTP11 setting in Weight Transfer. Flow from the DP pump is then ported to the rod side of the cylinders. The oil that exhausts out of the full piston side of the cylinders returns to tank through the directional valve. The prefill valves shift back to the open position when this occurs. The valves are two-position, three-way, single-solenoid, spring-return, directional-control.

Chances are, unless you've taken advanced coursework in hydraulics, you find this text baffling. You can make out the words just fine, and you understand that some sort of mechanical device is being described, but most of the passage goes over your head.

This is exactly how many high school students feel when asked to read their textbooks in math, history, and other courses. This is why it's so important to give students ongoing and explicit support in reading and writing.

This passage also illustrates the necessity for literacy skills even in traditional blue-collar professions. Read any service manual for the blue-collar trades to see the increasing complexity of today's work skills. Greater literacy skills are required for professions that just a few decades ago required little reading and comprehension.

Difficult texts can make sense, but only if somebody takes the time to go over the specialized vocabulary, explains things step by step, and gives the student the practice and support needed to more fully understand what is being read.

To succeed in high school and beyond, students must become cerebral chameleons, able to adapt to a range of academic contexts, each requiring its own set of literacy skills.

I have had countless middle and high school teachers ask me a perfectly reasonable question: Whose job is it to teach secondary school students the literacy skills they need?

At the elementary school level, the answer is obvious because the child typically has a single teacher for all core courses, and every state requires the teacher to be knowledgeable about reading and writing instruction.

At the middle and high school levels, however, teachers are traditionally defined as specialists in particular academic content areas such as history, math, or science. The responsibility for teaching reading and writing does not directly belong to anyone. Ask the math, science, or history teacher, and she will point to the English Department. But the English teachers shake their heads because they usually regard themselves first and foremost as teachers of literature and only secondarily, if at all, as reading and writing instructors. "By the time they get to me," explained one content area teacher, "I don't expect it is my responsibility to teach them reading skills." This attitude is also a likely result of the fact that most secondary school teachers rarely receive more than a token amount of training in literacy instruction, and they are quite reasonably hesitant to take on responsibility for work they have not been trained to do.

There are other legitimate concerns. Teaching students how to read and write can be quite time-consuming, especially if teachers require students to produce and revise a lot of written work. Given a teaching load of four or five classes with as many as thirty students each, how likely is it that a teacher will assign frequent essays that require additional reading, commenting, and revision?

Further, existing state achievement tests and high-stakes exams for graduation do very little to encourage content area teachers to offer extensive literacy instruction. Today's current assessment systems consist almost exclusively of multiple-choice and short-answer items with an emphasis on recall of factual information, not analytic reading or independent writing. Too many accountability systems tend to create incentives for content area teachers to help students memorize content to be tested rather than encouraging students to read and write like scientists, historians, mathematicians, and other kinds of scholars.[2]

Among researchers, school reformers, and professional associations, the consensus view is that every middle and high school teacher has a role to play in helping students become fully literate—teaching reading comprehension cannot be left to reading specialists alone. That does not, however, mean that all teachers should play precisely the same role. Content area teachers can and should carry out certain types of literacy instruction, but they cannot be expected to do exactly the same work as reading specialists.

Students expected to write and read advanced, high-level texts in all of their academic courses will require this sort of explicit support, particularly when they encounter vocabulary, text formats, stylistic conventions, and other features that are specific to a given subject area. Even those reading at grade level need strategies for understanding what they read in school; but those who have the greatest difficulty require the most help—from all of their teachers. In history class, for instance, students should be taught how to read and write like historians, and in biology class how to write a laboratory report like scientists.

More specifically, teachers in every subject area can help students review the vocabulary in a given text, encourage students to use the dictionary or encyclopedia, and have students summarize the main points of the reading. This kind of reading instruction does not constitute an undue burden on the teacher; nor does it require math, history, and other content area teachers to become reading specialists. In fact, research supports a number of straightforward techniques that all teachers can learn with some targeted professional development.[3] Successful application will also result in the teacher being able to impart more information and improve the student's learning outcomes. For further inquiry into this area, I recommend "Do I Really Have to Teach Reading?" by high school reading specialist and English teacher Cris Tovani.[4]

But when teachers, principals, and school leaders all work together to focus on literacy achievement they get results; students learn and remember more, in all subjects, and they graduate at a higher rate. Indeed, literacy is the cornerstone to better achievement in high schools.

A successful example of a schoolwide approach to literacy is the University Park Campus School (UPCS) in Worcester, Massachusetts. At first glance you might dismiss this innovative charter school as a fluke or one that creams the best students from a poor neighborhood and touts its success as a miracle. Instead, UPCS students come from the most challenging neighborhoods and backgrounds. The only requirement for admission to UPCS is to be a resident of the Main South neighborhood; once students apply, they are chosen by a lottery. It's what happens inside the school, not outside, that predicts and determines the future for students at UPCS.

In 1997, when UPCS opened in the most economically disadvantaged section of Worcester, most of the students were reading below grade level, and many were dropping out in the seventh, eighth, and ninth grades. About 65 percent of these students came from homes where no English was spoken, 70 percent qualified for free or reduced-price lunch, and 60 percent were students of color. Because of these challenges, Worcester public schools partnered with Clark University to create UPCS, a school for the neighborhood's seventh to twelfth graders that would not only help them improve achievement and prevent them from dropping out but also ensure that each student is accepted into college. When UPCS graduated its first class six years later, only one student had dropped out, every student passed the state English and math exams, and every student received a college acceptance letter—many to top-tier universities such as Georgetown, Dartmouth, and Brown, in addition to Clark University.

The key to success at UPCS was a schoolwide approach to literacy; every single teacher helped students master literacy skills in their subject area, and many pitched in before and after school and during the summer, even working with parents and family members to ensure students were improving their reading and writing.

Starting before the school year even begins, all incoming seventh graders must attend UPCS's month-long August Academy, which focuses on intensive literacy development. Students are assessed to understand their needs; those with elementary-level skills are assigned a reading specialist and given an intervention plan, and those with more subtle needs are given extra help or additional classes to help them progress. Yet all teachers are given strategies to use with these students whenever they have them in class so that all the educators are surrounding that student. During the school year, teachers in all classes help students learn not only their subject matter but also the literacy skills required to understand and remember that subject.

But UPCS is not satisfied with improving just literacy, or even the graduation rate. UPCS wants students to do something with their skills and diploma. This is why all students must apply to college. As soon as students enter ninth grade, they are exposed to a rigorous college preparatory curriculum, including a variety of honors and AP classes. Also, UPCS has implemented a writing process model, a guide for students to write effectively across disciplines, so students will have practiced college-level writing before they graduate. During their junior year, students meet with their teachers, guidance counselor, and principal to discuss college options and requirements, and by the end of the meeting, with the help of the faculty, they develop a detailed plan for their college application process.[5]

The Evidence Is Clear on How to Reach Older Students

Like the teachers and leaders in Worcester, practitioners and policymakers must recognize the clear need for literacy to be an integral part of every year in the K–12 continuum. Then they must work together to create the conditions that education leaders and policymakers require to promote the necessary change. Here is a four-part agenda for improving literacy in the middle and high school subject content areas:

1. Some reading comprehension strategies should be taught in every content area. Research and practice have developed fairly simple reading comprehension strategies that every content-area teacher can learn in a fairly short time.

2. In every content area, teachers should provide instruction in the reading and writing skills that are specific to that content area. Even in math and science, much of the work is conducted with the written word. All teachers should know what is distinct about reading and writing in their discipline, and as a matter of basic professional competence they should know how to make those rules, conventions, and practices apparent to students.

3. Schools and districts should invest in reading specialists to address local needs for the teaching of basic reading skills to middle and high school students. Many of the nation's secondary school students require intensive, high-quality interventions that allow them to finally master the basic mechanics of reading that should have been taught in elementary school. Some educators believe struggling readers in middle and high school should be pulled out of their regular curriculum, given intensive support, and then returned to their content-area courses once they can read and comprehend fluently. Other educators argue that basic reading support is an add-on to the regular curriculum, this being preferable because students will not fall further behind in their content-area studies as they catch up on reading skills. Whatever the specific intervention model, the key is to hand the assignment over to teachers who are ready, willing, and trained to carry out such instruction. Though they are part of the process, biology, literature, math, and other content-area teachers cannot be expected to shoulder this role alone.

4. States should revise their standards, assessments, accountability systems, and other policies to encourage more reading and

writing in the content areas. A 2006 ACT study found that no state in the nation included specific reading and writing skills in its standards for academic content areas.[6] But standards are only as good as the resources and incentives that accompany them. Individual districts and schools must be given the flexibility to schedule more time for reading and writing in all content areas. Likewise, content-area teachers must have access to better reading materials in their classrooms and libraries. Once again, the 2006 ACT study found that clear exposure to sophisticated, high-level reading material was a powerful predictor of student success in college-level content courses.[7] Finally, but very important, states should invest in accountability systems that use open-ended writing and analytic reading items in all content-area tests and graduation exams. Such tests can be expensive, but they create an incentive for teachers to offer more and better literacy instruction. There is nothing in NCLB that prohibits states from adopting these more extensive assessments.

Additionally, here are some established research and best practices strongly recommended for federal policymakers:

- Build on the success of Reading First (K–3) by expanding it to the upper grades.
- Give schools the flexibility and resources they need to schedule more time for reading and writing instruction.
- Encourage states to incorporate reading and writing skills into content-area standards.
- Increase federal funding for enhanced assessments to help states use open-ended writing and analytic reading items as part of NCLB accountability systems.
- Increase funding for the federal school libraries program, and target the increase to low-performing high schools to give content-area teachers access to more and better reading materials.

- Support more teacher professional development in adolescent literacy.
- Increase federal support for the National Writing Project.

To succeed in high school, college, and in life, students not only need to master the mechanics of reading but must also develop more advanced reading comprehension, writing, and other communication skills. Some students require help with the basics.

Among the eight million students in grades four through twelve who read significantly below grade level, researchers estimate that perhaps as many as a million struggle with the basic skill of sounding out words on the page.[8] Even students who can decode the words often do so with too little accuracy or the speed that would permit them to grasp the meaning of what they read.[9] Those students need and should get high-quality instruction in phonics and reading fluency, so they can finally master the basic mechanics that they should have been taught in elementary school.

A large percentage of students need assistance with reading comprehension and writing, particularly in academic content areas. In the upper grades, literacy cannot easily be separated from the learning of academic content. Reading and writing are the key means by which students learn, think about, and debate the meaning of the content they study. To require middle and high school students to read and write is not only good instruction, whatever the subject area, but also essential to successful lifetime learning.

Conclusion

As long as millions of American adolescents struggle to read and write, they have little hope of competing in a global economy or becoming the truly engaged citizens the nation needs if it is to thrive. The federal government has a major role to play—as it does in early grades—to help improve adolescent literacy instruction, but this requires the same sort of commitment and resources that have been directed toward the teaching of early reading skills, an investment that has shown results.

During a recent business lunch, the woman with whom I was meeting began peppering me with questions about my organization, and in particular literacy. I quickly learned that it stemmed from her quest to find the answer to a question she had been seeking and deliberating on for several years.

"My twenty-three-year-old cousin dropped out of high school in tenth grade because he couldn't read," she explained, "and it finally became too difficult for him to continue. How did he get that far without anyone noticing that he wasn't able to read?" More important, she was concerned about his future—the job market for an illiterate twenty-something in today's workforce, supporting his wife and child, and his ability to sustain a normal life. She said he is a very talented auto mechanic, but that new cars are becoming so sophisticated that it is not enough to just pop the hood and find his way around the machine. Being able to read complex auto manuals and receive written advanced training is now a prerequisite to compete in the industry that has given him his livelihood.

There are a number of things I could point to in trying to find blame for this young man not being able to read. But the bottom line is that we—as a society—let him pass unnoticed and unassisted through his K–12 experience, and unfortunately he is one of millions. The next time you sit down and skim the menu at your favorite restaurant, think of this young man, ordering whatever the person next to him is having because he can't read the menu, and think of how different his life might have been if literacy had been a vital part of his education at every grade level.

6

CREATING QUALITY HIGH SCHOOLS

What Works?

The Detroit Public Schools (DPS) are not a likely setting for high school success stories. In fact, with the graduation rate hovering in the distressing 25 percent area, this troubled public school system is often used as the poster child for dysfunctional urban school systems in America. Yet from within that same school system emerge examples of success that should cause all of us to understand that we *can* make a difference in the lives of our older students if we set our mind to it and commit to turning things around. These stories of triumph and beating the odds are reminders that as bleak as conditions in our high schools may seem at times, there are pathways for success that are very much within our reach.

Michael Rollins is a perfect example of a student who emerged from DPS with not only a diploma in hand but a future filled with possibilities, including college at the University of Michigan. Rollins, a 2001 graduate of the Academy of Finance at Golightly Career and Technical Center, didn't know much about the world of finance when he first visited the selective program with his mother as a sophomore in high school. "I walked in and everything was neat and orderly and professional," Rollins recalled. "You could see that they had high expectations and that no one was messing around. I wanted to be a part of it."

The two-year program, part of the National Academies Foundation, prepares high school students for careers in financial services and technology. This is not just a job training program.

It involves rigorous, high-level academic course work, along with mandatory paid internships with partner corporations such as Equifax Credit Information Services, Smith Barney, and the Federal Reserve Bank. "You don't sit there wondering why you need to learn things; they help you understand how it will all be used in the real world," Rollins said. Furthermore, teachers in the program participate in "externships" in the finance industry to help bring real-world experiences to the classroom.

Mentors in the classroom and in the finance world work to create meaningful connections with students, showing them what can be theirs if they have a plan and set out to accomplish their goals. "The bar was set high for us, but our teachers showed us that we could meet the expectations," Rollins said. Students aren't just expected to learn math and science and other traditional courses; they learn the kinds of things you need to get a good job—how to write a strong resume, prepare for a job interview, and look people in the eye when shaking hands.

Internships often turn into paid jobs, and it is common for students and their mentors to stay in touch. Rollins, now working for Fidelity Advisors in Ann Arbor (he graduated from the University of Michigan in 2005), still speaks with his mentor every few weeks. "This made all the difference for me," Rollins said, looking back.

As daunting as some of the challenges noted here can seem at times, examples like the Academy of Finance and scores of others around the country prove that with the right kind of services being offered to children, high school is not too late to make a positive academic impression that will last with these young people into their adult years. Many of us have been hearing for so long about the importance of investing early in our students (because if they fall behind too soon they will never catch up) that we forget that the evidence shows this is not entirely true.

University of Chicago economist James Heckman, a Nobel laureate who has made a powerful case in favor of early investment in prekindergarten and the early grades, eventually concluded in 2007 that those investments alone weren't enough to turn the tide for many of today's students. "I now believe that early interventions with children are not so productive if they are not followed up with ongoing investments in children during their elementary and secondary school years. Instead, we need to invest early in children—and not stop".[1]

Not making the most of this last chance we have with our students before they leave secondary school will severely cost our nation. Indeed, our nation's high schools play an essential role in almost every part of our American society, molding young teens and turning them out into the world as young adults. The question remains: What kind of young adults will we help them become?

We know that successful reform can be achieved. As Johns Hopkins University researchers Robert Balfanz and Nettie Legters observed:

> Schools which beat these odds and have high percentages of students who succeed in challenging courses provide multiple layers of support. Strong instructional programs are matched with a schedule that allows for double-dosing in these subjects, and extra help from caring teachers within a personalized interdisciplinary team structure. But this is still not enough for all students to succeed, some require summer school and a few need further focused instruction in the fall to earn promotion to the next grade. Pulling off this level of intensive support requires not only committed adults who refuse to give up on their students, but additional time, resources, training, and materials as well.[2]

Ten Elements of a Successful High School

There is no one-size-fits-all approach to creating excellent schools, but there are a host of factors that I believe are critical in terms of helping all of our nation's high school students become able and active participants in the workforce, as well as in democratic and civic life after high school. Drawing from the work of leading researchers and educators from around the country, my colleagues and I at the Alliance for Excellent Education developed a checklist of ten key elements that high schools should have in place to maximize every student's success. If parents, educators, and community leaders will look first at their own high school, we hope this motivates them to become involved in the overall transformation effort. The necessary elements for an individual school also require supportive federal, state, and local policies.

An Engaging and Rigorous Curriculum

All students must learn the advanced skills that are the key to success in college and in the twenty-first-century workplace. Every student should take demanding classes in the core subjects of English, history, science, and math; no student should ever get a watered-down course of study. Further, students should be given the opportunity to earn industry certification or some college credit while in high school through programs such as Advanced Placement, International Baccalaureate, or those offered through a local college or university.

Elected policymakers now invoke "rigor" in curriculum as a tenet of education reform doctrine, but confirming its presence can be quite challenging. However, there are other subtle indicators besides annual test results.

Ten years ago, I was driving in the afternoon through a rural county. Running late for a meeting two counties away, I realized that I had arrived at a frustrating time, with the daily procession of lumbering school buses taking students to their distant homes. I quickly became trapped behind one with the consistent pattern: ride a half mile at 40 mph, then the rear red lights flash, and the mechanical red stop sign pops out from the driver side, signaling an impending stop to let another student off. Passing a stopped bus is illegal, and passing a moving one on curvy mountain roads is foolhardy.

Stopping every half mile, I began paying attention to the students disembarking, sometimes individually, sometimes in small groups. The students looked normal enough—laughing, talking, relaxed after another day in school. Yet something seemed slightly amiss. Suddenly I realized what I was not seeing: in twenty stops, I had noticed only one book carried off the bus. No one was carrying anything to study for tomorrow, much less the weeks to come.

In any such random, unscientific sampling of approximately forty rural secondary school students, certainly there will be a number of kids who don't see the need to do homework. But there should also be a reasonable sampling of young people applying themselves beyond the regular school hours—though only if others are uniformly communicating this expectation.

When the school bus finally turned up a side road, I roared off, a bit sad and tsk-tsking at the lack of student effort. Actually, I should have been doing some self-criticism. At the time, I was a member of the U.S. Congress. But I never called the county school superintendent or the school's principal to ask why, at a time when the economy and demand for high skills were dramatically changing, no one was requiring the students to study after three o'clock. Apparently neither parents nor the area's business and community leaders (some of them parents themselves) were raising the issue of whether their children needed a more rigorous academic regimen either. Presumably, school administrators, principals, and teachers are most aware of what students will need to succeed. But they weren't making a forceful case.

Perhaps it is too much to expect of the elected members of the school board. Though they govern the county schools, they usually do not have much professional experience in education. Drawn from the community and balancing full-time jobs, families, and political sensibilities, the local school board meets weekly at best. Being the one elected official relentlessly pushing two more hours a day of homework will aggravate a significant number of parents, educators, and newly registered eighteen-year-old voters (the students themselves) and is not the best platform for reelection. The local school superintendent's tenure depends on maintaining the constant support of three of the five board members; this ceaseless high-wire balancing act occurring in almost every school district frustrates advancing rigor or any other area of education reform that requires significant change.

So if the school bus ride home can be one indication of rigor, how do we get more books walking off the bus?

Increasingly, my decade-old school bus survey is underscored by modern data. We already know that a rigorous high school curriculum is a strong predictor of college readiness. Students who take challenging coursework, such as four years of college-preparatory English and three years each of college-preparatory mathematics, science, and social studies, are less likely to need remedial courses later on in college than students who don't take such a rigorous curriculum.[3] The rapid increase in schools offering the College Board's AP courses or the IB program, for example, reflects the increased demand for rigor and challenging courses.

But one of the more disturbing reports in the growing list of indicators that our nation's high schools are not getting the job done came in the winter of 2007 with the release of the Nation's Report Card—the National Assessment of Educational Progress. On the one hand, our high school students seemed to be taking more impressive course loads from coast-to-coast and earning better grades than ever. On the other hand, they seemed to struggle more than ever in the basic NAEP subject areas of reading and math, leading many observers to speculate whether significant grade inflation and watering-down of high school courses was becoming more prevalent.

The sobering NAEP report showed that only about 35 percent of the nation's twelfth graders tested proficient or above in reading; fewer than a quarter were proficient in math. The reading scores were the lowest on record since the test's inception in 1992. At the same time, however, a review of student transcripts nationally showed that high school grade-point averages rose from 2.68 in 1990 to 2.98 in 2005, meaning our high school students on average moved from a B minus to a B, even as their ability to read and do basic math declined.

Figure 6.1 Rigorous Curriculum: 1990-2005 Trends in High School Achievement Data

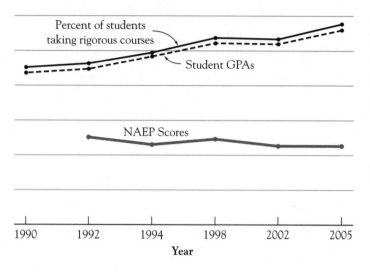

Students are taking more rigorous courses and are receiving good grades in those courses. Yet over the same period of time, NAEP scores, have remained stagnant. Despite taking (and excelling in) "more rigorous" courses, student learning in not increasing. Course content and student learning is not really improving. NAEP, 2007. SOURCE: NCES (2007-467).

Perhaps even more startling than possible grade inflation was that the decline in proficiency came as students appeared, at least on paper, to be taking more rigorous courses. The study found that the percentage of graduating seniors who completed a standard or midlevel course of study rose from 35 to 58 percent in the same time period, while the number of seniors taking the highest-level curriculum doubled to 10 percent. As Sacramento County School Superintendent David W. Gordon noted with the report's release: "For all of our talk of the achievement gap amongst subgroups of students, a larger problem may be an instructional gap or a rigor gap. There's a disconnect between what we want and expect our twelfth-grade students to know and do and what our schools are actually delivering through instruction in the classroom."[4]

It is important to note that there is a big difference between an engaging and rigorous curriculum and one that merely looks that way on paper. Implementation matters, and nowhere is it more important in education than in the classroom. A successful school makes sure that each child is pushed to expand his or her mind, while at the same time linking learning to specific content and skill development. In reporting on the NAEP results, for example, the *Washington Post* compared what was happening in two classrooms fifteen miles apart in Maryland's Prince George's County that were using the same textbook, same course description, and same syllabus. At Bowie High School, students were asked to "compare and contrast the themes of disillusionment, poverty, and frustration in George Orwell's *Animal Farm* and the poems of Langston Hughes."

Meanwhile, over at Suitland High, the assignment for the day was: "What are your immediate goals? How would you feel if no one close to you supported you in reaching your goals?"[5] It doesn't require a lot of imagination to guess which school will produce students who are better equipped to meet the challenges of adulthood in the new world. Engagement and rigor go hand-in-hand, but they must also be accompanied by a host of other complementary factors.

Extra Help for Those Who Need It

With such a significant portion of our high school population unable to read or do math at a proficient level, it is hard to imagine how they could think through and then write the kind of essay that compares Orwell and Hughes. Such shockingly low literacy prevents students from mastering content in most of their subjects, especially in text-heavy courses such as science and history. Clearly, these students require a significant amount of additional help in basic literacy and numeracy, but that extra help too must be rigorous enough not just to help these students catch up but to propel them forward to become the critical thinkers that modern education requires.

Most remedial programs that exist in high schools today focus only on the basics. Low performers are not given ample opportunity to develop the more advanced skills they are undoubtedly going to need to thrive and survive as adults. Seldom are these struggling readers given the chance to comprehend new readings or analyze text for specific purposes. These doses of academic rigor and additional supports, like the right kind of tutoring, can pay dividends. High-quality assistance not only prepares students for the future but makes their own schooling more relevant. It gives them a reason to keep showing up and advancing in their learning.

Successful high-poverty schools regularly assess students' academic progress, identify which students need help, and employ creative scheduling such as afterschool and summer school sessions to give students the instructional time they need.

Research indicates that the right kind of tutoring and interventions can help low-performers achieve at a higher level. For instance, the Southern Regional Education Board's High Schools That Work program helps low-performing ninth graders complete algebra I, geometry, and two years of college preparatory English (including doubling the amount of English and mathematics required in grades nine and ten).[6] Some 58 percent of students in the program who reported getting extra help from teachers had significantly higher achievement.[7]

Every high school should have a system in place to catch kids as soon as they start struggling in reading, math, or any core subject. Every school should also allocate time and resources to furnish the immediate help those kids need if they are to stay on course.

Some districts have found that the best way to bolster such targeted intervention efforts in high school is actually to backtrack and introduce them in earlier grades as well. In Ossining, New York, in northern Westchester County, school officials in the No Child Left Behind Act (NCLB) era noticed that black boys were struggling in the otherwise high-performing district. So they created a special mentoring program that paired these boys with black teachers for one-on-one guidance outside of class, extra homework help, and cultural activities during the school day. The program for black male students began in 2005 with a college-preparatory program for high schoolers. By 2007, the program stretched all the way back to kindergarten.[8]

The Ossining program was controversial in some quarters because it singled out black male students. One critic referred to it as a form of racial profiling. But the point is that the kind of individual attention and meaningful connections between students and adults in the program is what we should be thinking about extending to all our students, if we want and expect them to be able to survive in the future.

Extra help often equates to extra time. Students learn at different paces. Some require more time and attention than others. This can often mean longer learning days, afterschool tutoring, half-day Saturday sessions, or extended school years in the summer. For many students, a legislatively prescribed seven-and-a-half-hour day for not more than 180 class days per year is no longer sufficient. In my first year as governor, I sought to bring more flexibility to the strict 180-day requirement in my state. I expected opposition but was surprised that the first major organization to register opposition was the amusement park industry. "If other states followed your lead," argued their spokesman, "this could disrupt the traditional family summer vacation schedules as well as deny a source of student labor." Nor was he amused at my suggestion that we would have extended fall and spring breaks so the ferris wheels could operate even longer.

Personal Attention for All Students

Every high school should be small enough (or divided into small enough units) to allow teachers and staff to get to know all students as individuals and respond to their specific learning needs. By ninth grade, students should have a detailed plan for graduation.

A Personal Graduation Plan should allow every student to achieve goals and understand the steps needed to reach them. Doing so adds relevance and clarity to the high school experience, helping to identify the specific courses the student must take, opportunities to pursue, and extra help needed in order to succeed in high school and beyond. Every student should receive frequent and ongoing support from at least one academic advisor throughout the high school years. Knowing all students means also knowing where they are at all times. Schools should establish an attendance system that keeps track of students and initiates contact with students and parents whenever an unplanned absence occurs.

Research shows that one of the most important factors behind student success in high school is close connection with at least one adult who demonstrates caring and concern for the student's advancement.[9] As we discussed, the "Silent Epidemic" survey commissioned by the Bill & Melinda Gates Foundation in 2006 found that disengagement among students is often credited to the lack of interest and relevance in their coursework. The survey's authors revealed that a majority of the high school dropouts who responded believed they "fell between the cracks" as the result of simply not being motivated or inspired to work hard.[10]

If students are continuously sent the message that no one cares about them and are allowed to fail, they emotionally distance themselves from school. This detachment results in failure to apply themselves, seek assistance with difficult material, and take appropriate courses, along with high absenteeism. We must recognize this reality and reiterate the necessity for personal connections between adults and students to identify and meet their individual needs.

Providing guidance, information, and support to adolescents is important not only for at-risk students. According to researchers Robert Rossi and Samuel Stringfield, regardless of the communities in which they live "students do not know the required courses they need to take during the middle and high school grades to qualify for college admission in major fields that can lead to a chosen career. Students in these grades may also discount entrance into many more selective colleges because they are unaware of available sources of financial aid. Such lack of knowledge prevents students from seeing the current relevance of working hard in challenging courses to earn admission to more selective colleges or to preferred major fields."[11]

Personal attention can take many forms, among them the extra academic supports I've just noted, but it involves a host of other supports tailored to the individual student as well. Personal attention should be paid to the course load taken by each student, so that she is on track to take the courses needed to graduate and is simultaneously getting the classroom help needed to succeed. Sometimes, personal attention itself can keep a child enrolled in school when he might otherwise be inclined to hit the streets without a diploma.

In 2006, the governor of Georgia pushed through legislation to provide funding for a "graduation coach" in every high school, who works with at-risk youth to keep them academically on track and always moving toward graduation. At Bellevue High School in northern Kentucky, school leaders swung from having one of the highest dropout rates in the region to having zero dropouts by requiring students to meet with school officials several times before they could legally drop out of school. These students and their parents are required to sign a document that lists the negatives of dropping out, including the likelihood of spending time in jail. Principal Mike Wills, a former Marine, explained how he changed the dropout process when he arrived at the school: "We said, 'This is not acceptable. Dropping out is not acceptable, and it is not any longer going to be by the stroke of a pen.'"[12]

Too many students make the decision to leave school without ever talking with a caring adult who understands their specific situation and who can make sure they clearly understand the ramifications of a future life without a completed high school education. This is simply tragic, and indeed it suggests our schools and our society are letting these kids slip through the cracks.

Skilled Teachers

All high school teachers should know the subjects they teach and how to teach all kinds of students, from all kinds of backgrounds. New teachers should get the guidance and mentoring they need to be successful in the classroom. All teachers should have enough time to plan lessons, work with other teachers, carefully review student performance, and continuously improve their teaching.

A growing number of researchers—among them noted academics Ronald Ferguson, Helen Ladd, and William Sanders—have found that teacher characteristics have a greater impact on student achievement gains than any other in-school variable.[13] A study by statistician William Sanders, for example, found that fifth graders who had been taught for the previous three years by very effective teachers gained 50 percentile points more on a state assessment than those taught by ineffective teachers.[14] Studies in New York City have found that more than 90 percent of the variation in reading and mathematics achievement was due to differences in teacher qualifications.[15]

Unfortunately, regardless of how you slice it, effective educators shy away or are pushed from low-performing high schools. Poor students and students of color are more likely to be taught by teachers with less skill, experience, or qualifications, and who are not effective in improving student achievement. Worse, some great teachers who want to work in these settings are deterred by cumbersome hiring policies, poor leadership, and deplorable working conditions that lead to a disturbing trend—turnover. Half of new teachers exit the profession within five years.

For our students to be well educated, we need teachers who themselves were educated at a high level. Studies indicate that improving teacher preparation can boost student achievement. A 1996 analysis of sixty studies on teacher quality found a direct link between improvements in teacher education and student test scores.[16] High-quality professional development for teachers is also an important part of the equation. Professional development is most effective and best promotes student success when it is delivered at the school building and driven by clear goals, useful data, and teacher input.

The clear goal is to focus teaching on the end goal of preparing students for college and work—life beyond high school. All else flows from there. Setting goals starts with strong school leaders who set the tone and culture of a school and who ensure that professional development keeps its eye on the prize: improved student learning toward college and work preparation.[17] Helpful data come not from a single test at the end of the year—however important that assessment may be for accountability purposes—but from ongoing benchmark assessments, aligned to college-readiness standards and administered at regular intervals. The best leaders carve out time for teachers to collaborate, and they gather them regularly to ask, "What are we doing well, and how can we improve so that students learn more?"[18]

From that point on, teacher input is needed because teachers themselves have much of the expertise they need, and they can strategize about ways to improve instruction.[19] Using classroom data on college readiness, teachers discover the need to update their content knowledge in certain areas or home in on a certain teaching strategy. In this way, finding time in the master schedule and leveraging college-readiness data become the means to target and strengthen professional development at the high school level, rather than coming up with money to send teachers to workshops.

A Safe Learning Environment

As we saw with Brooklyn's Lafayette High School in Chapter Four, it comes as no surprise that a high school routinely sending its students to local emergency rooms because of hallway beatings is bound to have a great deal of educational dysfunction as well. Every high school must guarantee the safety of its students, teachers, staff, and visitors; and every school should be kept free of drugs, weapons, and gangs. School leaders should build a climate of trust and respect, which includes encouraging peaceful solution to conflict and responding directly to bullying, verbal abuse, and other threats.

As with psychologist Abraham Maslow's famous hierarchy of human needs, good schools require that students be taught in a setting where they are not likely to be harmed. This means not only preventing crime but also establishing safe, secure, and modern school buildings. If our high school buildings are in a poor state of repair, this sends a clear message to students that their education doesn't matter. Schools that are not safe also tend to be schools where the best teachers, for understandable reasons, want to leave the first chance they get. Students and teachers alike deserve to be able to make it through the school day without fearing for their safety.

Family and Community Involvement

Students thrive when their high school encourages positive learning relationships among families, educators, faith groups, civic organizations, businesses, and other members of the community. Parents should have the opportunity to visit the school building, talk with teachers and staff, voice concerns, share ideas, and serve as volunteers. School leaders should reach out to their neighbors by attending community events and forming partnerships with local organizations to increase effectiveness and tap additional resources. I remember a billboard on a bus shelter that had a sample quiz for parents: "Charles Barkley is a basketball player," and below that, "____ is your child's math teacher." The ad then featured the important tag line: "What you don't know can hurt you." Indeed, we know that good relationships among parents, communities, and schools can go a long way toward strengthening our high schools in a way that enhances student achievement. Parents must play a role in reinforcing at home the lessons that students are learning in school. Teachers and schools must find ways to make it easier for parents to do so. Successful schools encourage parents and teachers to meet regularly to discuss student progress, as well as communicate with each other by telephone and e-mail. Because schools, particularly high schools, are an important piece in the social fabric of their neighborhoods, successful schools not only contribute to what happens in their community but benefit from the resources that their neighborhoods have to offer.

Not all of the challenges students face are within the control of the school. Many students struggle academically because of issues outside the classroom: they lack access to health or mental health care, they need social services to support their family, or they have a substance abuse or relationship problem. Very often, a school with the lowest performance is in a community with the greatest disadvantage, where our best educational efforts alone may be necessary but not sufficient for widespread success. If America is truly going to leave no child behind, students facing such challenges must receive the services they need in order to have a real chance at academic success. Community-based, integrated student services are "interventions" that promote greater student awareness and success "by connecting community resources with both the academic and social service needs of students."[20] Students participating in such services perform better in the classroom and are less likely to drop out of school. The services can offer students interpersonal relationships with mentors and adults, a safe place to learn, and connection to community resources for health care, family needs, service-learning opportunities, and more.[21]

Communities in Schools (CIS), for example, the nation's leading community-based organization, is committed to guiding students to graduation from high school by linking schools and students with the critical resources necessary for success. CIS operates nearly two hundred affiliates in twenty-seven states and the District of Columbia, serving more than thirty-four hundred schools and nearly one million students and their families. Founder William (Bill) Milliken explains his thirty-year commitment and approach to solving the nation's dropout epidemic: "[My] colleagues and I got into education because the kids needed it, not because we had any calling to be teachers or school administrators. [We] worked with young people who had dropped out of school and were now homeless, on drugs, without a future. We quickly discovered that programs don't change kids; relationships do. By forging strong personal relationships with youth, and showing them we valued them and cared about them, we were able to help turn around many young lives. But getting a kid off the streets was only the beginning. What were they supposed to do next, with an eighth grade education at eighteen years old? Like it or not, we were going to have to get involved in the 'education' business."[22]

Linking the Real World to the Classroom

Students are often most inspired in their learning when they make a clear connection to how new knowledge can work for them in the real world. Our schools need to offer lessons that are relevant and tied directly to the skills students need in college and for success in the workforce. High schools should help students see these important connections. Students must develop the work habits, character, and sense of personal responsibility needed to succeed in school, at work, and in society. As part of their class work, students should have opportunities to design independent projects, conduct experiments, solve open-ended problems, and be involved in activities that connect school to the rest of the world. They should acquire knowledge about how to effectively measure whether they have mastered these skills and proficiencies. Use of performance assessments is gaining traction in some states and communities. These assessments measure tasks that require students to evaluate and solve complex problems, conduct research, write extensively, and demonstrate their learning in projects, papers, and exhibitions. These ways of confirming competence have proven successful in motivating students and attaining a high level of learning in redesigned high schools. In fact, research shows that students who experienced "authentic pedagogy or instruction," focused on active learning in a real-world context calling for higher-order thinking, consideration of alternatives, extended writing, and an audience for student work, enjoyed a high level of achievement.[23]

Just as we saw with the example of Detroit's Academy of Finance at Golightly Career and Technical Center, the community must make all of its resources available, including those of the corporate and nonprofit sectors through internships, mentoring, and other community-based opportunities, to show students how their school work has relevance in their future life outside of the classroom.

Strong Leaders

Just as highly skilled teachers are a crucial ingredient in a successful school, leaders who understand the intricacies of both instruction and harnessing the potential of the entire school community are needed to help fundamentally transform our nation's high schools in a way that works for children. Efforts are under way all over the country to find and train this new breed of school leader, but we need far more than what current programs in principal preparation can hope to produce in the short run.

We know that strong leaders, if given the right tools, can make great changes in even tough schools. Leaders such as Craig Benes remind us of what is becoming possible. In his first year alone, Benes, a former marriage and family therapist who was recruited and trained to be a change agent in his struggling school by the nonprofit group New Leaders for New Schools, transformed Talcott School (in the West Town neighborhood of Chicago) from a school that parents were trying to avoid at all costs.

Benes worked as a teacher, a therapist, a college instructor, and counselor for severely disabled kids; and learned how to lead a school community on the job in the New Leaders' "residency" program. The training allowed him to convert Talcott into Chicago's only public museum school (visits to the Art Institute and Field Museum are a regular part of the curriculum) and to beef up the overall quality of teaching and academic offerings for students. He helped bring music and art classes to the school and relaunched a Spanish immersion program.

Three years later, test scores were on the rise, and as one parent noted to a *Chicago Sun-Times* reporter, "It's creating a buzz."[24] Nine teachers at the school earned the prestigious National Board Certification, up from none three years earlier, and parents had their own room for doing volunteer work to help the school. Strong leaders are able to recognize the talents and abilities that exist naturally within the school community and harness them so as to make schools better.

Necessary Resources

Sometimes people don't like to admit it, but running an excellent school costs money. This shouldn't come as a surprise. Having enough adults in contact with children, for example, so that each child gets the kind of personalized attention that I am talking about comes at a price. Constructing and maintaining school buildings so that teachers and students are safe also costs money, especially if the facilities have been neglected for years. Every high school should have the books, computers, laboratory equipment, technology, and other resources needed to be successful. Federal and local dollars should be invested to distribute these needed resources equitably, aiding both systemic and programmatic efficacy. These tools of learning are not extravagant. As I have shown in terms of the impact that a poor education has on a community, all of us must begin to recognize that smart investment in our schools means long-term investment in our communities, and the nation as a whole.

I have previously detailed the return on investment from strategic targeting of funds to education. Here is an example of why this is so important. I recall a ribbon cutting ceremony I attended as governor for the opening of a state-of-the-art juvenile detention facility. Looking back, as I scanned the crowd that day, I calculated that our state was spending more than $8,000 annually to educate the same sixteen-year-old that we would now be spending nearly $23,000 to educate through the juvenile justice system. Strategically spending more for the former would result in spending much less on the latter.

Just as important as obtaining the necessary resources, of course, is making sure they are spent well to benefit students who need a world-class education. Whether at the federal, state or local level, additional dollars should be part of a comprehensive strategy that includes measuring the outcomes. Successful schools align their resources with their academic goals for students as well as what is necessary to bring the needed systemic change.

User-Friendly Data and Information

All community members should have easy access to information that gives a clear, straightforward picture of how well the school is serving students from every income level, ethnic group, and racial background. Key pieces of information include a school's graduation requirements, graduation and dropout rates, and student performance on state and national tests.

As we saw in Chapter Four, meaningful, accurate information about the graduation rate is necessary for communities to understand how well their high school students are advancing. Successful schools often use easy-to-understand, transparent information on student achievement to guide teaching and learning. When teachers understand the specific strengths and weaknesses of their students, they are in a better position to provide the kind of personalized assistance each student needs to catch up and succeed. Parents who are able to understand how well their children are advancing—or not advancing—can evaluate their options before it is too late. If good data are put to use in schools, there are few surprises.

We know what happens when parents, for example, have access to clear and easily understandable data on school performance. Several years ago, after New York City began publishing school report cards showing, among other things, the four-year graduation rate for each high school, parents got a clear picture that told them an awful lot about outcomes, expectations, and the culture of any individual school. Hundreds of parents lined up outside regional enrollment centers looking to transfer their sons and daughters out of schools where the listed graduation rate was as low as 40 percent to schools where at least half the students were graduating. These parents knew the score, and they were doing whatever they could to improve the odds of their children having a bright future. The challenge, obviously, is to get our communities—and, quite frankly, the political leadership—to understand that a 100 percent graduation rate must be the standard. Anything less is inadequate in today's world.

Supporting the Ten Elements

The good news is that much is known about how to address the high school crisis and improve the academic attainment and achievement of secondary school students. This knowledge is reflected in the recommendations of innumerable educators, researchers, and advocates. The time is right for us now to do something about it.

Existing research yields a wealth of information that can serve as a roadmap for political leaders, educators and the leaders of schools and districts in implementing reforms to improve the graduation rate; raise the literacy level; increase the abilities of students in math, science, and other content areas; and give students the skills and knowledge they need to be successful in college and work.

Students need a higher level of academic knowledge than many states currently require. They must also have better communication and problem-solving skills, information technology literacy, and life skills such as self-direction and social responsibility. It is therefore obvious that all students should have a rigorous curriculum, regardless of the path they choose following graduation.

There are common elements for the "odds-beaters," the effective high school models and high schools that have seen significant improvement despite the fact that their student population is high-minority or high-poverty. These successful strategies should be leveraged and supported up and down the education system. When the National High School Center, an independent entity funded by the U.S. Department of Education to help build the capacity of states across the nation to effectively implement the provisions and goals of NCLB, reviewed the practices of high-performing high schools, an overarching framework emerged of common approaches these schools and their districts have taken[25]:

- The schools and districts set explicit academic goals that are aligned with and often exceed state standards.
- Focused professional development activities for teachers support a culture of collaboration.
- Educators embrace broader learning objectives than just their own subject matter and use differentiation strategies to reach students at all levels.
- Teachers interpret student achievement data to make decisions about teaching.
- Schools recognize student and teacher achievement within a context of support.

In that same report, the National High School Center suggested that a number of state-level initiatives affected the ability of these schools and districts to succeed:[26]

- Setting academic standards
- Coordinating states' policy regarding teacher quality, and taking an active role in guiding and supporting professional development for high school teachers
- Administering access to adolescent literacy coaches and supporting technology enhancement
- Guiding educators on how to collect, analyze, and report data so that they are comparable across each state.

In addition, research conducted by Linda Darling-Hammond, a noted educator and researcher (and member of the board of directors of the Alliance for Excellent Education), suggests that four elements are critically important in highly effective urban schools: (1) personalization achieved through teams of teachers working with shared groups of students; (2) well-qualified teachers supported by ongoing peer collaboration and professional development; (3) a common core curriculum organized around performance-based assessment, which engages students with work that resembles what they will do outside of school and which challenges them intellectually; and (4) a variety of supports for struggling students in the context of an intellectually engaging and challenging curriculum.[27]

Recently, MDRC, a nationally respected nonprofit, nonpartisan social policy research organization, studied several comprehensive reform models that are operating in a total of twenty-five hundred high schools across the country. They identified five cross-cutting challenges that high schools face in seeking to influence student outcomes:

- Assisting students who enter high school with poor academic skills
- Improving instructional content and practice
- Creating a personalized and orderly learning environment
- Fostering work-based learning opportunities and preparing students for the world beyond high school
- Stimulating change in overstressed high schools

MDRC concluded that:

Structural changes to improve personalization and instructional improvement are the twin pillars of high school reform. Small learning communities and faculty advisory systems can increase students' feelings of connectedness to their teachers. Especially in interaction with one another, extended class periods, special catch-up courses, high-quality curricula, training on these curricula, and efforts to create professional learning communities can improve student achievement. School-employer partnerships that involve career awareness activities and work internships can help students attain higher earnings after high school. Furthermore, students who enter ninth grade facing substantial academic deficits can make good progress if initiatives single them out for special support. These supports include caring teachers and special courses designed to help entering ninth-graders acquire the content knowledge and learning skills that they missed out on in earlier grades.[28]

Some strategies require comprehensive approaches that involve creating an entire school culture of reform. These approaches range from individual school efforts to models that are replicated and operating nationwide. But as we have seen, common elements are found in each. One national high school redesign organization, the Institute for Student Achievement (ISA) based in New York City, has made great strides in the comprehensive school reform model they have implemented, by applying these representative principles:

(1) a college preparatory instructional program so that students view themselves as future college students; (2) distributed counseling which builds a safety net of support services across the school; (3) dedicated teams of teachers and counselors who provide a consistent four-year school network; (4) continuous professional development; (5) extended school day and year that extends personalized and challenging learning opportunities; (6) encouraging parents to participate in their children's education; and (7) continuous organizational improvement with program accountability and regularly monitoring progress and refining program components.[29]

Other high schools may not require whole-school reform, but must address a specific need or shortcoming. For example, faced with a large number of entering freshmen reading several grades below grade level, a school may adopt a literacy strategy that improves their performance.

The ultimate goal of school transformation is to promote a supportive environment in which students can acquire the knowledge and skills they need; there are many ways to accomplish this. High school students should have access to multiple pathways that engage and interest them, as long as all educational programs are grounded in a rigorous course of study that prepares young people to succeed in college and the workplace. In this way, students cannot help but benefit from the opportunity to choose among multiple high school options, selecting the best fit for their needs and interests.

Portrait of a Successful School

In 2002, the National Association of Secondary School Principals (NASSP), with funding from the Bill & Melinda Gates Foundation, set out to identify as many "breakthrough high schools" as possible from coast to coast. They were looking for high schools that serve high-minority, high-poverty student populations and were sending a sound number of students off to college. They sought schools that were at least 50 percent minority and with at least 50 percent of students poor enough to qualify for a free or reduced-price lunch. For the graduation rate, they were looking for schools that sent at least 90 percent of their students off to some sort of postsecondary education.

They pored over the data and investigated and reinvestigated the claims. From 2004 through 2006, the NASSP eventually identified twenty-five schools to be called breakthrough high schools and worthy of emulation. Each one identified in the project had its own story and path to success, but clear patterns emerged showing that these schools tended to rely on many of the same factors we have just discussed: a personalized environment, rigorous curriculum, collaboration, and effective leadership.[30]

At Washington, D.C.'s Benjamin Banneker Academic High School, for example, parents and students sign a contract making a commitment to student achievement; students are required to take college-prep courses, and community service is mandatory. Incoming freshmen transition to high school by taking a five-week, four-hour-per-day orientation to prepare students for rigorous coursework while also orienting them to school. Advisory groups lend additional support for students. The result of these measures is that the school boasts a 100 percent valid graduation rate and 100 percent college enrollment rate.

Poor attendance and abysmally low reading scores plagued J.E.B. Stuart High School in Falls Church, Virginia, until school officials took action. Administrators at the school, which had the lowest attendance rate in the district, each "adopted" forty students with chronic attendance problems. They sat on top of these kids, making sure they got to school every day. They even resorted to making wake-up phone calls and scheduling parent conferences to discuss the importance of showing up every day. The school schedule was changed from a traditional agrarian September through June calendar to a college-like year-round schedule, with fall, spring, and summer sessions. The school day was extended by a class period and advanced IB courses were added to help raise expectations. In the end, attendance improved, SAT scores for the school jumped more than one hundred points, and enrollment in AP and IB classes increased by 279 percent.

To cite just one other example from the breakthrough schools as to the kind of thinking that can help solve some of our education problems, officials at Crownpoint High School, in Crownpoint, New Mexico, created a "freshman academy" as a school within a school so that freshmen wouldn't have to take classes with upperclassmen. All incoming freshmen were asked to participate in seven-week minicourses in place of traditional elective courses. These minicourses covered wide-ranging topics such as remedial math, career education, abstinence, nutrition, basic technology, and American Indian culture. In addition, each freshman was assigned a staff member who reviewed the student's progress, grades, attendance, and discipline issues at least twice a month throughout the school year. The results: freshman reading and math scores soared, eventually exceeding both state and district averages. With a better start to high school, the dropout rate eventually declined to 0.5 percent.

There are examples of successful programs in large cities and small towns all over the country. The challenge for us as a nation, obviously, is to take what we know works, combine it with a new sense of urgency, and find ways to make sure that all of our young people are given the kind of education they deserve and require for a meaningful adult life in American society.

7

INVESTING IN HIGH SCHOOLS

A New Federal Role

As a former elected official serving at the state and federal levels, I often wrestled with the balance between appropriate federal and state roles in public education. During eighteen years in the U.S. Congress, I had the opportunity to engage in reauthorization of the Elementary and Secondary Education Act (ESEA) every five years and even become involved in the Clinton-era attempt to move states to a standards-based system. Through these experiences, I assumed that although some federal programs came with many strings attached, they were necessary in ensuring that states spent federal monies in a way that promoted national interests. I was also clear that a federal investment in public education was necessary. Every dollar counts when attempting to improve education quality in the United States.

On the other hand, I recall once returning to Washington after having spent a large part of my day in a local school district's central office talking to school administrators about the latest federal action. I came away thinking that the federal government contributed about 8 percent of the K–12 education budget but about 50 percent of the paperwork.

Despite the challenges that may come with federal engagement, there is no denying that national problems require national solutions. The problems with high schools affect every state and territory. To effectively redesign our American middle and high schools to meet the twenty-first century's civil rights, moral, economic, and security needs requires the federal government expanding its existing concern for younger students and supplying the vision and leadership necessary to guide the national transformation of middle and high schools. The Alliance for Excellent Education has called on the federal government to take a strong and appropriate role in secondary school reform, assisting the work in states and communities to make sure all students are given the kind of education they need to survive and thrive in a rapidly changing world.

Historically, the federal government's role in shaping the nation's educational policies and priorities has resulted from periods of emerging recognition of the national importance of education in meeting the needs of society, the economy, and national security. The increasing federal role over the years usually focused on specific major issues linked to schooling, including fighting poverty, encouraging racial equality, and serving the nation's most disadvantaged populations. In our current context and on the basis of past practice, the federal government should already be deeply involved in secondary schools. All of the statistics I have highlighted thus far show clearly that it is in our nation's interest for us to act; indeed, it is to our nation's peril *not* to act. How can the nation retain superpower status when only 70 percent of its students graduate from high school? How can it maintain its economic strength when, of the young people who do graduate, 40 percent don't have the literacy skills that employers say they need? When half of the ninth graders in the typical high-poverty urban school read several grades below grade level, how can the nation's cities even hope to be revitalized?

Without federal leadership, inequities that are unacceptable to American democratic values risk becoming embedded in our way of life. Helping the poor, disadvantaged, and others who have little power or voice in public policy decisions has been one of the major reasons for federal intervention in the nation's education system for more than 150 years. If there was ever a time and reason for the federal government to take on the secondary schools issue, it is now.

The Federal Role in Public Education: Historical Context

Discussion of the need for a system of public education in the United States—programs of instruction offered to children, adolescents, and adults though schools and colleges operated by government—dates back to the very early days of the republic. Indeed, many of the nation's founding fathers believed that some form of universal education was essential to prosperity and survival. In 1785, the Congress of Confederation passed the first of two Northwest Ordinances, reserving one-thirty-sixth of the land given to each western township "for the maintenance of public schools within the said township;" the 1787 Constitutional Convention confirmed that act.

Thomas Jefferson, in particular, advocated a system of taxpayer-supported schools for all children. He argued eloquently for a plan that would have offered a free basic education to every citizen, as well as giving extended tax-supported educational options to talented young people who were otherwise unable to afford advanced schooling. Although Jefferson's plan was not adopted, his belief that an enlightened and educated citizenry was critical to the proper functioning of democracy served as the basis for developing education systems that evolved in the nineteenth century.

In the 1830s and 1840s, there emerged a group of prominent American educators, among them Horace Mann in Massachusetts and Henry Barnard in Connecticut, advocating for increased educational opportunity for all children through the common-school movement—reform efforts that focused on the idea that all young children should be schooled with common educational content. In rhetoric that would be familiar today, the reformers of the early nineteenth century argued that a good education would transform students into virtuous, literate citizens whose contributions to society and the economy would enhance the nation's international competitive position. Further, they opined, a basic education for all children would encourage assimilation of immigrants into American culture, preserve social stability, and reduce crime and poverty. By the end of the nineteenth century, free, publicly funded elementary education that included provisions for making schools accountable to local school boards and state governments had become essentially universal in the United States, and by 1918 all states required children to attend elementary school.

In the early twentieth century, reformers turned their attention to extending educational opportunities to the nation's children beyond the elementary grades. In 1900, only 10 percent of young Americans between the ages of fourteen and seventeen were enrolled in a high school, and the majority of them were from wealthy families. But as the economy moved increasingly away from an agrarian base to an industrial one, and as strict child labor laws were passed, students and their families increasingly saw some high school education as essential to success in a changing society. States agreed, and most changed their laws to require students to remain in school until age sixteen.

As the century progressed, the role of the American high school evolved to meet a variety of expectations, both social and academic. High schools gave adolescents supervision and a place to socialize and sought to supply the tools students needed to meet the challenges of citizenship, further education, and the job market.

America's participation in the higher education system also grew dramatically in the twentieth century. Enrollment in institutions of higher learning increased from 2 percent of eighteen-to-twenty-four-year-olds (157,000) at the beginning of the century to 60 percent of this population (more than fourteen million) by the end of it. The number of two- and four-year colleges and universities grew, during the same hundred years, from less than a thousand to about four thousand, a number that does not include the approximately twenty-three hundred vocational institutions that enroll millions more students but that do not award a bachelor's or associate degree.

State and Local Governmental Authority: An Evolving Influence

Although individual states hold primary authority over America's public K–12 education system, particularly demonstrated by teacher licensing requirements and matters related to health and safety, most have traditionally ceded operational control to a local district and relied on local property taxes to fund them. In 1794, New York was the first state to develop a board of regents to oversee public education. Since then, all states have developed a department of education. In their first hundred or so years of operation, however, the degree of involvement, authority, and oversight responsibility demonstrated by individual states for public education varied widely.

As student enrollment increased in the twentieth century, and to bring order and increased standardization to the public school system, most states took on additional authority, seeking to increase the size and efficiency of schools and districts. By 2000, there were fewer than 15,000 school districts in the United States, down from 117,000 in 1940. Recognizing that the educational values and financial resources of individual communities range widely, some states also began trying to equalize expenditures per student by putting state funds into the system, or using state laws to encourage greater equality in investment. For many states, continued reliance on local property taxes to fund K–12 public education worsened disparities in education. Wealthier regions were able to fund much higher-quality school systems than poorer communities. Whether from legislation, litigation, or a combination, state dollars increasingly exceeded local ones to ensure more equitable education.

After the publication in 1983 of *A Nation at Risk*, states increased their involvement in public education. This growing centralization of authority at the state level was, in large part, the result of a growing consensus among many parents, educators, and policymakers that a concerted reform effort comprising statewide standards and testing was increasingly necessary to address the shortcomings of the existing educational system.

Federal Efforts to Address Poverty and Equity in Education

Despite longstanding recognition of state primacy of control over public education (the U.S. Constitution includes no mention of education, whereas all fifty state constitutions guarantee the right of their citizens to some level of education), the federal government has supported many facets of the development of public education since the birth of our nation. Beginning in the eighteenth century with the Northwest Ordinances, growing through the nineteenth century, and escalating considerably during the twentieth and into the twenty-first centuries, federal legislators have supported, for a variety of reasons, development of America's system of public education for a growing number of students.

The federal role in the educational process is not strictly financial, although it has supplied a growing percentage of K–12 public education funding, particularly over the past sixty years. In 1940, the federal government contributed 2 percent of all education spending; by 2006, that share, nationally, had grown to about 10 percent, coming from the U.S. Department of Education and other federal agencies. Federal spending on K–12 education alone represents slightly less than 8 percent of all K–12 expenditures, although in some large urban districts federal aid covers as much as 30–40 percent of local school costs. In 2005, the U.S. Department of Education's budget represented less than 3 percent of the funds spent by the federal government (Table 7.1).

Over the years, the federal government's role in education has fallen into three major categories supporting activities and principles that it believes to be in the national interest. First is the area of building state and local capacity. Indeed, the original U.S. Department of Education was created in 1867 as part of the executive branch, to collect information on schools and teaching that would help the states establish effective school systems on their own. A history on the current U.S. Department of Education's Website notes that "early emphasis on getting information on

Table 7.1 Changing Sources of Revenue for K–12 Education: Trends in State and Local Funding

Sources of K–12 Education Funds	1940	1999
Local District Contribution (% of total revenue)	68	44
State Contribution (% of total revenue)	30	49
Federal Contribution (% of total revenue)	2	7

FOOTNOTE: This chart describes the sources of funding streams feeding into K–12 public education.
CITATION: National Center for Education Statistics, U.S. Department of Education. *Digest of education statistics: 2006.* Table 158. Washington, DC: Author, 2006.

what works in education to teachers and education policymakers continues . . . to the present day."[1]

We see this continued focus in various examples of federal legislation that offer competitive grants, demonstration or pilot projects, technical assistance, and direct allocations to states and districts in all manner of areas relevant to building the capacity of schools and districts. Perhaps the most significant of these bills, the Elementary and Secondary Education Act of 1965, was created in part to expand the federal government's role in research on effective teaching strategies and bestow on states the resources to considerably expand their departments of education. In 1970, the National Assessment of Educational Progress (NAEP) was authorized, creating a national system of tests designed to track variations and fluctuations in student achievement throughout the country over time. In 1979, the Office of Educational Research and Improvement (OERI) was created to sponsor scholarly research on effective strategies for teaching and learning among diverse populations of students, as well as supporting and disseminating new discoveries in pedagogy, curriculum, administration, and all aspects of schooling.

Another major federal involvement in education since the beginning of the twentieth century has been targeting investments to maintain national security, increase the nation's economic strength, and ensure that the skills of the country's citizens are sufficient to maintain a competitive global advantage. In 1917, Congress passed the Smith-Hughes Act to prepare students for the industrial jobs that were emerging as a result of the manufacturing revolution. The Service members' Readjustment Act of 1944 (much better known as the GI Bill of Rights), which enabled 7.8 million World War II veterans to participate in a higher education or training program, was enacted to avoid what many saw as a looming social and economic crisis that could have led to another recession. Additionally, the Cold War, most particularly the U.S.S.R.'s launch of *Sputnik I*, produced the 1958 National Defense Education Act to support development of students gifted in science, mathematics, and modern foreign languages with the goal of strengthening national security.

Perhaps the most widely recognized federal role in public education, however, is in reducing inequity and serving disadvantaged populations. In the middle and late nineteenth century, the federal government became deeply involved in education with the creation of the Freedmen's Bureau, which focused on improving education opportunities for people freed from slavery, and involvement in administration of schools for Native Americans through the Bureau of Indian Affairs.

In 1957, following the U.S. Supreme Court ruling of *Brown v. Board of Education of Topeka* (1954), the federal government assumed a public role as protector of racial equality and civil rights when President Eisenhower called out the National Guard to escort nine black students into the formerly all-white Central High School in Little Rock, Arkansas. By 1964, the Civil Rights Movement was arguably the most dominant force in American domestic politics. President Johnson, a former school teacher and a consummate politician, recognized the need to move swiftly to enact controversial legislation that was designed to support civil rights and reduce poverty. Within two months of Johnson's assumption of the presidency, Congress passed the Vocational Education Act and the Higher Education Facilities Act of 1963; a few months later, the landmark Civil Rights Act of 1964 helped lay the groundwork for a massive increase in federal aid to education, with a focus on serving the needs of poor and disadvantaged students.

At the time, the largest and most politically popular federal education program was for Impact Aid (designed to assist local school districts that had lost property tax revenue because of the presence of tax-exempt Federal property, such as military bases, or that had experienced increased expenditures owing to enrollment of federally connected children). Impact Aid awarded funds to schools on a loosely regulated basis, and with a formula predicated on total student enrollment instead of just public school enrollment. Johnson and his advisors therefore decided to model the new program along those lines, offering voluntary grants to local schools according to each state's total number of school-aged children with family income under $2,000. The ESEA of 1965 was technically only legislation amending the Impact Aid law (P.L. 81-874) of 1950.

Over time ESEA dramatically changed the impact and involvement of the federal government in education in America. Consisting originally of five sections, or "titles," the legislation funneled unprecedented amounts of federal funding toward instruction and technology in local classrooms, improvement of library resources and multimedia equipment, language acquisition, research on effective teaching strategies, and expansion of state departments of education.

School districts around the country reorganized in an effort to attract as much of this funding as possible, and many states established departments exclusively tasked with applying for and managing the funds. Loopholes were discovered and taken advantage of that allowed relatively wealthy school districts to access the ESEA funds, resulting in concerns that the law's underlying purpose—to help low-income students hurdle the barriers to learning that poverty raised—was being circumvented, and that its impact would be minimized. Block grants, which would have essentially turned administrative and regulatory control over to the states, were proposed as a substitute for the "categorical"—or specifically defined—grants included in ESEA. But congressional action in that direction was abandoned following major resistance by civil rights groups and large-city superintendents, who felt that federal government administration was necessary to ensure that grants were directed to the most disadvantaged students.

Despite the problems accompanying ESEA implementation in the early years, President Johnson continued to see federal resources as essential to addressing the needs of low-income and disadvantaged students. In 1968, following intense lobbying by the administration, Congress added the Bilingual Education Act to ESEA, giving start-up funds for "exemplary pilot or demonstration projects in bilingual and bicultural education in a variety of settings."

Thirty-six years later, another Texan, President George W. Bush, a conservative Republican, used the funding in ESEA to be the carrot and the stick for stricter accountability in the renamed No Child Left Behind (NCLB) Act. Now the federal government was requiring every school to measure and report its progress, and decreeing improvements for schools that did not make the new Adequate Yearly Progress (AYP) benchmark.

The three and a half decades between the two Texan presidents saw the philosophical transition in education policy from "inputs" to "outcomes." The dominant approach in the 1960s and 1970s was that funding for educating low-income students was clearly deficient; therefore the federal effort focused on the amount needed to help shore up the system. State courts mandated more education spending in many ways, often spelling out in great detail exactly how much would be spent for specific activities. By spending the requisite amounts, many assumed that educational outcomes would be improved automatically.

As time passed, people across the political spectrum began objecting that more money "in" did not always result in better students "out." State legislatures bridled at state courts intruding into the traditional legislative function of deciding how much should be spent on education. Additional pressures created by increased education budgets at every level, occasional state budget shortfalls, a fast rising federal deficit, and mounting demands to see tangible results for the money invested led to the growth of the standards and accountability movement. "Standards" meant that someone spelled out what knowledge students should have at various stages in their educational career; "accountability" was measuring how well the students and the educational system were doing in meeting the standards.

More Federal Expansion: Standards, Accountability, and No Child Left Behind

My own political career spanned this input-outcome odyssey. At the height of the input era, I testified in the early 1980s as an expert witness on behalf of citizen plaintiffs arguing that the West Virginia system of funding was inequitable. The early judicial decrees directed more spending; one decision even specified the measurements for rooms in new schools. As with many similar legal actions in other states, the litigation dragged on for twenty years. But the political and educational climate changed over this time. The case that I had testified in as a witness and in which I argued for an input approach in the early 1980s, was not finally resolved until almost two decades later. Ironically, as governor I was responsible for signing the final settlement, which mandated that the funding be tied significantly to demonstrated improvements, or outcomes.

The standards and accountability movement came into full federal bloom during the administration of President Bill Clinton with the passage of Goals 2000 and other attempts to develop means of measuring student progress. But the attempts at federal requirements for accountability that drew considerable resistance, especially from new Republican majorities in Congress during the Clinton era, were eventually adopted as the underlying foundation of the No Child Left Behind Act of 2001. NCLB was driven by a newly elected Republican president working with strong bipartisan support.

The Republican and Democratic leaders who gathered around President Bush for the signing ceremony promised a new era of improving educational equity by requiring that academic achievement of all students be measured and improved over time. A major legislative goal was to mandate that all students would be required to reach proficiency in reading and math by 2014 as measured by their state's standards. States were required to assess their students in math and reading annually in grades three through eight and once during high school. For the first time, whether a school made the federally required Annual Yearly Progress was measured by "disaggregating" the overall student body into designated subgroups: economically disadvantaged students, students from major racial and ethnic groups, students with disabilities, and students with limited English proficiency. Keeping track of overall performance was no longer sufficient; now *each* subgroup had to show progress.

Clearly, the kind of dismal statistics that we've seen regarding our high schools played a role in creating the political climate that led to passage of No Child Left Behind. Although many soon grew disgruntled with the new law's implementation, most policymakers embraced the basic premise of NCLB: to give all children, including poor and minority children, access to a high-quality, standards-based education. Whatever NCLB's shortcomings, applying the law has shone a clear spotlight on the educational achievement gap for large populations of students.

The site for the bill signing belied the legislation's reach. Despite the historic signing ceremony being held in an Ohio high school, the massive law essentially addressed schooling between kindergarten and eighth grade. In the original twenty-eight-page NCLB proposal from President Bush, high school was mentioned only twice. Only one high-school-specific policy was even included at the start, one for more math and science partnerships. Subsequent U.S. Department of Education administrative interpretations of NCLB's legislative language resulted in high schools being omitted from both the supports and the sanctions of the bold new law. The end result is that NCLB policy often neglects, or is even at odds with, the needs of America's fourteen million high school students, including those six million secondary school students who are at risk of dropping out each year.

Here are examples of why the original bill did not effectively reach high schools:

- Only 8 percent of students benefiting from Title I—the main source of federal funds, supplying both the supports and the sanctions undergirding NCLB—are high school students. Because $10 billion of the $13 billion in Title I funding goes to grades K–6, NCLB's consequences—and its limited remedies—do not significantly affect secondary students.

- Although high school is the final stage of a student's K–12 career, NCLB does not measure the extent to which schools graduate their students. Indeed, graduation rate is not a meaningful part of the annual AYP determination that is supposed to identify low-performing schools. Compounding this failure is the fact that the law does not require states, or even school districts, to calculate graduation rates consistently. The cumulative effect of this oversight is equivalent to requiring our children to run a mile race. At every tenth of a mile we hit a stopwatch, methodically measuring each runner's performance, yet we fail to look up when they cross the finish line. Ultimately we cannot even determine who finished.

- Identifying low-performing schools and closing achievement gaps is severely undermined at the high school level because measures of student proficiency are based on inconsistent and low state standards that often assess basic math and reading skills but not the students' level of preparation for college and the workforce. Too often, the state effectively is measuring a student's proficiency in the tenth grade, not what they will need in college or the workplace when they leave the twelfth grade.

- The two main NCLB mandated school improvement actions—tutoring for low-performing students or permitting students to choose whether to move to another school—have little impact at the high school level. Seventy-five percent of high schools are in a single high school district, meaning there is no other choice if the school is deemed failing. Many low-performing high schools are clustered in urban districts with few or no opportunities for students to transfer to higher-performing schools. The tutoring that is supported by NCLB has not proven effective at the high school level; very few high school students take advantage of this option. Many high school students have jobs, take care of siblings, or participate in sports after school.

The Missing Middle

Much of the past federal government response to significant educational reform has been investment in a child's early years such as with the popular Head Start program. Even federal Title I grants, which are part of ESEA, have historically placed significant emphasis on the youngest grades as opposed to middle and high schools. This general practice was based on widely held views that the best bang for the buck involved helping our youngest students succeed, and then allowing their early academic successes to compound naturally as the students advanced through middle school and high school, and later college.

Likewise, because of the strategic necessity and demand for college-oriented programs such as Pell Grants, the GI Bill, and campus-based financial aid, the federal government has long invested heavily in higher education. For fiscal year 2007, for example, the federal government appropriated nearly $18 billion to pre-K–6 programs, and nearly $16 billion for postsecondary education. This higher education figure does not even account for the federal funds spent on student loans, which more than doubles the amount shown in Figure 7.1.

Figure 7.1 Analysis of Major Programs Administered by U.S. Department of Education: Lack of Federal Investment in Secondary Education

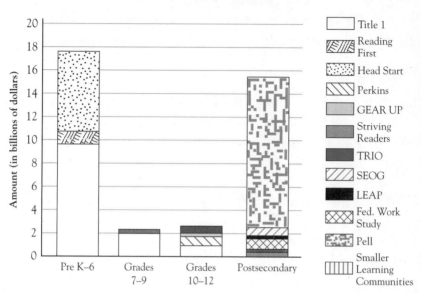

Stuck in the "missing middle" is spending on middle school (just over $2 billion) and high school (just under $3 billion). Again, this low percentage of federal effort is reflected by only 8 percent of Title I federal funds being available for low-performing high schools. Moreover, the only federal education program specifically targeted toward high schools, the $1.2 billion Perkins Act, supports career and technical training rather than programs that directly improve academic performance in reading, math, science, and history.

Although supporting the early years of a child's education and offering financial access to higher education are critical investments that must be continued, the chart's figures demonstrates that federal funding for programs designed to help students in the middle and high school grades has been relatively sparse.

Low-performing secondary students are being left behind because the vital investment to support preschoolers and elementary school students all but vanishes when these students reach middle and high school. In the last thirty years, federal investment in middle and high schools has been minimal at best, especially compared to investments at both ends of the K–16 education continuum. Perhaps not surprisingly, test scores and dropout patterns directly reflect the negative results of this asymmetrical investment pattern.

Test results from the NAEP—the Nation's Report Card—show the returns, positive and negative, on federal investment from the past thirty years. The significant investment made in Head Start and in support of early grade interventions is showing results. Fourth grade NAEP scores have been steadily increasing. But as federal investment lessens in middle and high schools, so do the test results. Eighth grade NAEP reading scores begin leveling off. By twelfth grade, the results are essentially what they were thirty years earlier. These results were recently reinforced by a comprehensive ACT report, *Reading Between the Lines: What the ACT Reveals about College Readiness in Reading*, which finds that reading gains made in the early grades were essentially lost by twelfth grade in the absence of sustained attention.[2]

These results underscore the error that many of us make when we concentrate all our efforts on creating a strong start in a child's early years but then prematurely lose interest as the child ages. I was certainly guilty of this educational policy sin of omission. In Congress, safeguarding Head Start and funding early literacy and preparation programs were among my top priorities. As governor, I resisted strong pressure to delay funding for a newly created comprehensive four-year-old program during an economic downturn. Studies showing the crucial educational impact of the early years in brain development further drove my commitment to supporting quality early childhood programs. My commitment was reinforced by other major longitudinal research that showed continued positive benefits for individuals decades after their early childhood development experience.

I don't question the correctness of any of these actions; what I regret is not looking sufficiently at students' further needs.

Unfortunately, our early childhood orientation has caused us to overlook how we could further maximize those gains. The ultimate expression of this early childhood bias, in my mind, came from a well-meaning funder at an all-day education conference I attended. At the concluding reception, I introduced myself as the president of an organization working to improve high schools. The trim, gray-haired woman looked tolerantly at me and said, "I only give to early childhood efforts; that takes care of it all." I walked away mystified about why she would think that simply furnishing a good early childhood learning experience, critically important as it is, would be sufficient given that NAEP scores show that 71 percent of all eighth graders and close to 90 percent of students of color read below grade level. Who loves his or her children only until fourth grade?

The need to offer the quality early childhood programs essential to a lifetime of worthwhile educational outcomes is well established; but common sense (confirmed by research) dictates that giving children strong early education and then dumping them into seven years of dysfunctional middle and high schools cannot result in achieving anywhere near the optimum outcome.

Recently, I was discussing the value of middle and high school literacy programs with a noted education researcher. What he observed about early literacy also rings true for all early childhood efforts: "Some people look at early literacy as an inoculation. Give it once and it stays forever. But education is more like nutrition. You have to keep giving it consistently."

So Who Sets the Standards?

If you are a parent sending your daughter off to school each morning, do you ever wonder who is deciding what is important for her to learn? As you hope your children will have a better life than yours, do you assume that their education is meeting whatever the new world competition will require? Are you aware that essentially there is no common national standard that is being constantly evaluated and updated so your community's schools are always world-class?

As the nation moves into new awareness and action to contend with the challenges of global competition, many question whether states and local school districts are up to the task of determining what their students should be learning: to function in an increasingly international arena. The usual federal role has been to move into areas where clear shortcomings or needs existed. However, federal forays into mandating the standards each school district should meet have long met fierce resistance.

The Clinton administration pushed for setting voluntary standards in certain subject areas, and was largely rebuffed. NCLB enactment in 2001 resulted in federal expansion of holding schools accountable for meeting standards—but setting the standards was left to the states.

It is this legislative compromise—requiring every student to be "proficient" by the year 2014, but leaving the definition of "proficiency" to each state—that sows the seeds for the next great federal and state evolution in education. Already the nation is seeing greatly differing determinations across states of what is "proficient" that mocks the notion that "no child is left behind."

It is not just this inherent contradiction of the original NCLB that drives the move to some sort of common standards. Our nation's increasing decline in educational international rankings forces the question of whether we are teaching a sufficiently rigorous curriculum. It is not that there is an overall decline in our education system; indeed, it has improved over past decades with a higher percentage of students going on to postsecondary education. But much of the world is now moving up faster.

The business community also drives the discussion about how to determine the standards for education. Even though many business leaders defer to governmental units to decide who sets the standards, they do not shy away from demanding world-class standards that make their workers competitive anywhere. Every business leader wants to know that the company's workers were uniformly prepared wherever they were educated.

Who sets the standards is also a major civil rights issue. Lesser standards in one school district or state often relegate those students to lesser opportunities than higher standards in another jurisdiction.

The almost four hundred years of evolution of education in this country have been built on local control of determining what a child was expected to learn. From covered wagons to circular dial telephones, communications were slow, other regions distant. Local standard setting was a necessity, whether in consumer safety, banking, medicine, or education. But with today's instant access to information and rapid transportation, an increasing national consensus has emerged on various types of standards. The Great Depression brought federal banking regulation. No one seriously argues anymore that a lesser standard of medical care is permissible in Idaho than in California. Products crossing state lines in interstate commerce (and almost all do) are expected to be safeguarded by common standards. In education, as was previously discussed, states assumed a larger role in meeting greater national competition. Now interstate competition has turned international. Arkansas benchmarking its students against New York is now replaced by the need to find a means for the United States to benchmark all its students against the world.

Every governor speaks passionately about his or her state having the highest standards that are internationally benchmarked. Many are engaged in efforts to develop world-class education standards through Achieve, Inc.'s American Diploma Project, Partnership for 21st Century Skills, College Board, or ACT. These are significant commitments, but my observation is that few states have the resources or ability to be constantly involved in this very challenging process. Despite the efforts in many states, the result may be higher individual state standards, though not necessarily uniform ones, that we can be assured will always top the world.

The general political aversion to a federally imposed set of standards has deep historical roots. The concern is not unreasonable. Many urge developing a process that results in developing "national" standards—created and agreed to by the states—as opposed to federal standards imposed from Washington. Whatever the process, ensuring that every child regardless of zip code has access to education measured by world-class standards will be the next test of educational federalism.

Conclusion

In sum, the federal government has historically sought to give critical support for educational improvement. In most instances, the federal role has tried to reflect the needs and interests of the entire nation while simultaneously challenging citizens to look beyond existing norms and encouraging a national desire to achieve excellence. Building on its historic role in public education, Congress and the administration now must extend their support and vision to help solve the crisis in America's high schools.

We need to focus more of our resources and attention on reinventing the American high school experience, but this should not in any way be viewed as a call for less spending on early and post-secondary education. In fact, I am convinced that greater attention to the needs of America's middle and high school students will protect and enhance our existing investments in education.

Building the knowledge and skills needed for life during the school years is analogous to building a house. Most people would not consider it sufficient to hire a contractor to lay a foundation; they would also want to see walls and a roof included in the contract. Americans deserve to have prekindergarten and elementary schools that give their children a strong learning foundation. Equally important is a comprehensive educational process of quality instruction in middle and high schools that safeguards the earlier gains by ensuring that students expand their understanding and develop higher-level skills in every classroom and grade.

Certainly, transforming secondary schools from bastions of outdated and limited expectations into high-performing centers of teaching and learning for all cannot be accomplished by federal action alone. Indeed, a national partnership that includes local, state, and federal governments leveraging and accelerating change with the help of educators, administrators, the business and labor communities, philanthropy, civic organizations, parents, students, and other concerned citizens is necessary to address a crisis of this magnitude. No single entity, working in isolation, can hope for total success.

But a rapidly changing world requires that action be taken now. There is no doubt that Congress and the federal administration have an important leadership role to play, one that is appropriate to the crisis and in line with the federal government's historic tradition, in the education arena, of intervening to ensure national security, reduce poverty, increase equity, and advance research to inform effective practice.

8

ACHIEVING THE VISION

As at other epic times in our nation's history, the federal government must play a vital role in transforming our high schools. A quartet of imperatives—moral, equitable, national security, and economic—necessitate active federal involvement.

From America's pioneers building one-room schoolhouses to today's virtual classroom, the federal role in education has evolved to meet obvious needs and shortcomings. Today's challenges once again require federal leadership to demonstrate that it can support national goals such as economic competitiveness and equity by playing a strong role in revitalizing high schools for the twenty-first century.

There is a major difference between past spurs for federal action and what drives today's need. The traditional federal response has been fairly narrow to meet what was seen as a relatively specific need, such as a GI Bill for millions of returning veterans, Title I funds for low-income students, and math and science scholarships for engineering shortages. But as the twenty-first-century imperatives for action have become inextricably entwined, so has the need for comprehensive—not piecemeal—federal policy.

Nowhere is this better illustrated than in what motivated federal action in education more than fifty years ago. This book opened by discussing the impact of the Soviet Union's first satellite launch and the immediate U.S. response, in 1957. In the same year there was another major event—this one within U.S. borders—equally jarring as the launch of *Sputnik*. Although each dramatic event, taken individually, prompted a tectonic shift in the federal role in education, no one saw any connection between them.

What could compete in impact with such a dramatic challenge to U.S. national security as the first-ever Soviet satellite? Two weeks before *Sputnik* lifted off, the president of the United States ordered federal troops to protect nine black teenagers as they took their place as students at the all-white Central High School in Little Rock, Arkansas. For the first time, the federal government was enforcing the right for all schoolchildren to receive the same educational opportunities. The two events seemed entirely separate. Little Rock was a domestic situation enforced by the U.S. Supreme Court decision ending "separate, but equal" education. *Sputnik* was perceived as a foreign threat to national security.

In the midtwentieth century, the civil rights and national security challenges generated separate federal responses. In the early twenty-first century, these supposedly internal and external events are joined—and demanding a dramatic and comprehensive response.

Today's *Sputnik* is as much about global military competition as it is a massive international economic competition. For *Sputnik*, the United States essentially responded by directing people already in the knowledge pipeline to critical subject areas. College scholarships and research opportunities in math, science, and engineering were made available. Even the massive commitment to putting a man on the moon in 1969 did not necessitate expanding K–12 quality education opportunities to a much greater number of students.

Today's world competition demands steadily rising skill levels; if 60 percent of current jobs require postsecondary education, then all our students must receive a quality education. No longer can the United States handle a *Sputnik* moment by relying on a limited portion of its more fortunate students to meet the need; our national and economic security needs everyone able to respond.

For today's federal leaders, the imperatives of Little Rock and *Sputnik* have converged. The urgency that drove significant federal action fifty years ago is required today, only this time with the clear understanding that growing international economic achievement gaps will not be resolved without eliminating the educational achievement gaps found in race and economic status. Fortunately, the federal government finds experienced partners in transforming our nation's high schools. Business leaders, educators, parents, researchers, and students have increasingly been pointing out the crisis in which many of them live. Philanthropists and their investments have encouraged development and implementation of middle and high school reforms that range from addressing a specific aspect of student achievement to complete overhauls of buildings, teachers, and curricula with the goal of changing the entire teaching and learning experience. These investments have created the necessary experiences and research on which policymakers can make informed decisions.

Likewise, public officials at the state and local levels have begun to take action to improve their middle and high schools. But just as individual states could not have responded meaningfully to *Sputnik*, so the federal government must actively become engaged in high school reform.

Federal Rules of Engagement

The problems of America's middle and high schools are complex. They are also daunting in their magnitude and scope. The tough truth is that changing the status quo is a difficult process—but more important, it is possible.

As in other epic times in our nation's history, the federal government must play a vital role in transforming our high schools. Although four major imperatives—security, moral, equity, and economic—justify active federal involvement, there are some underlying premises that should guide federal policymakers as they craft a reform strategy.

The first premise is the familiar physician's maxim: *do no harm*. Well-intentioned federal legislation that sounds reasonable in a congressional committee room in Washington may result in unintended difficulties for those carrying it out hundreds of miles from

Capitol Hill. One aspirational paragraph in federal legislation can generate dozens of single-spaced pages of administrative regulations that cause thousands of hours of local effort to be spent on compliance.

When I returned to state office after almost twenty years in the U.S. Congress, I learned that the ultimate governmental irony is actually implementing locally what I had voted for at the federal level. Six months into my governorship, a major health care problem arose involving Medicaid. Calling a roomful of health officials together, I thundered, "How did we get into this mess?" One savvy department head smiled and replied, "You voted for it three years ago."

A second premise is that *additional funding—and, yes, it is needed—should not be invested without accompanying education reforms.* Injecting more federal dollars to make an already dysfunctional system more expensive is not a worthwhile objective. Further propping up the current system with its dismal outcomes is unacceptable. Federal policy and dollars must drive systemic change grounded in evidence-based research and practice.

A third premise is to *ensure that the federal role enables all students, regardless of where they live, to receive a quality education.* Given existing inequities in the quality of public education received by students in America, the traditional federal role that has sought to make up for shortcomings between states and school districts must be bolstered and expanded. The competition is no longer between Boston and Birmingham high school students; both are vying with their Beijing and Berlin counterparts. Americans deserve to have schools that provide their children with a strong start in the basic skills, but they expect and should get the quality of instruction and supports that enable students to leave high school capable of addressing the challenges the world of postsecondary education, work, and citizenship will offer.

As a fourth premise, *federal policy is most effective if undertaken in partnership with other major stakeholders,* especially state and local authorities. I learned a long time ago that a federal command-and-control model rarely works. Washington is too far away, and it cannot anticipate every situation faced by local officials, much less by the principal walking the hallway or the teacher in the classroom. The best federal approach is establishing flexibility that sets important policy goals while leaving state and local officials as much leeway as possible in reaching them.

The fifth premise is that *federal policy is at its best when it takes what has proven successful for thousands across the country and puts it to work for millions*. Good federal policy has respect for those actually creating and implementing effective high school reform models and seeks to make their work applicable to many other school systems. Successful interventions such as adolescent literacy programs, personalized educational structures, and data-driven educational practices all began at the state and local levels. Regardless of what federal policy is enacted, the state and local educators will be implementing it. Where the federal government operates most effectively in education is in furthering the ability to replicate for all children what has proven to be successful in specific areas.

Most importantly for federal policymakers is that numerous examples of positive high school reform justify increased federal commitment of effort and dollars to replicate successful models. These examples also demonstrate that all students, regardless of home environment, ethnic origin, disability, economic status, or previous academic performance, can learn and achieve in high school.

Make no mistake: the work and teaching challenges are incredibly difficult. But a concerted strategy employing evidence-backed methods and implemented by committed educators can turn around the most at-risk student population.

Whether we are tackling the transformation of an entire dysfunctional high school or focusing on one definite need, the tools have been developed for making a difference. What federal policy can do is furnish the incentive and means to distribute them for wide use.

A Framework for Federal Involvement

There are a number of actions the federal government can take that are both economically and politically viable to help fix America's broken and obsolete secondary schools and ensure that all of the nation's high school students graduate prepared for college, the contemporary workforce, and success in life.

In developing a federal policy framework, there are three guiding principles on which to base all aspects of high school reform:

- All students and educators must be held to high expectations to ensure that every student graduates ready for college and the modern workplace.
- The system must be designed to address the individual needs of students and schools, ensuring that vulnerable students in particular get the supports they need to succeed.
- Educators and policymakers must be given the necessary data and research to make informed decisions to improve policy and practice.

Through incorporation of both a philosophy of how to approach developing federal education policy and a set of guiding principles to measure each action, there are major areas where federal involvement will support comprehensive secondary school reform. These actions are broadly stated; more detailed legislation is required. Though they are actions where the federal government can assist, state and local officials can also benefit by seeking to implement them.

Establishing Meaningful High School Accountability

At the high school level, the federal accountability system does not adequately measure student preparedness for college or work, nor whether a high school is even graduating its students. The current system focuses too narrowly on test scores as the only measure of school quality, and too often these tests reflect only a student's proficiency in the tenth grade. Federal policy should ensure accountability for what really matters: graduating students who are prepared for success in college and work.

Just as students require assistance that meets their individual needs, so do failing high schools. When a school is found deficient, federal policy should combine with state and local efforts to identify problems and develop the strategies that build, not diminish, the capabilities in low-performing high schools. Evaluating high schools without accurately measuring the graduation rate is a meaningless exercise. Measuring a high school's performance, especially a low-performing one, should also be directly tied to the school's improvement.

By supplying reliable and timely data to educators and policymakers and establishing processes that allow them to act in response to what the data tell them, accountability can drive changes in behavior, policy, and resource allocation that lead to improved student achievement. For this strategy to be successful, accountability must exist throughout the education pipeline and affect stakeholders at every level of the system. Effective accountability requires clear goals and performance expectations, meaningful indicators that accurately measure performance against those goals, and an adequately resourced system to support improvement.

Funding Secondary School Improvement

Title I of the Elementary and Secondary Education Act (also known as No Child Left Behind) provides the main federal investment in addressing high-poverty, and often low-performing, schools. However, when the funds are distributed at the school district level, this investment usually fails to reach most eligible secondary schools, leaving the vast majority of these high-poverty and low-performing schools without the additional supports necessary for successful school improvement. Title I also fails to build much-needed capacity at the state and local levels for a systemic approach to improving low-performing secondary schools. The answer is not diverting limited Title I funds from the early grades where 75 percent of such funding is currently spent; indeed, the strongest gains in student performance are being seen on the fourth grade National Assessment of Educational Progress (NAEP) scores reflecting the value of this investment.

Instead, the federal government must recognize the need to make a corresponding investment targeted to turning around low-performing high schools. These improvement systems should be locally developed and based on interventions with solid evidence of success in meeting the needs of students. This targeted funding should finance both individual assistance for students and school-wide interventions, while also building the capacity needed at the state and local levels to make secondary school improvement possible. To ensure that investments are efficient and effective, federal policies must seek partnership with state and local officials to drive this investment to where it is needed most.

Promoting Innovation, Research, and Data

The world's structure and way of operating changed rapidly at the end of the twentieth century and the beginning of the twenty-first. American innovation played a critical role in the transformation, but few anticipated the revolutionary changes that would accompany introduction of digital technology that allows essentially instantaneous global communication. To be truly competitive, our nation's high schools must also enter the twenty-first century by updating their methods of operation and instruction. It is fortunate that at the same time the global economy is demanding higher skill levels for workers, advanced technologies and increased innovation are expanding possibilities for educators to make breakthroughs in reaching more students. To effectively reach these students, all levels of education, including the higher education system and communities, must embrace and support development of innovative models to educate our nation's secondary school students to higher standards. Such innovative models should be rigorously evaluated to determine best-practices and methods for replication by other schools.

High-quality longitudinal data systems that keep track of student, teacher, and school performance are also critical to improving secondary schools across the nation. Being able to follow students as they transition from school to school or even district to district, and quickly mapping their needs, is paramount to maintaining their educational progress through the secondary school system. At a relatively small level of investment, the federal government can accelerate assistance to states to build the infrastructure needed for data to be collected, reported to the public, and used meaningfully by policymakers and educators to improve education. The return on investment is great, as good data could be used to reach informed education decisions—both long-term and short-term—ranging from the classroom to the congressional committee room.

The United States also needs to increase its knowledge base through expanded investment in research. Decades of federal investments have yielded little information on where the money was going, what it was being used for, and whether or not those expenditures were making a difference in student achievement. Resources need to be allocated and used efficiently and effectively to ensure that investments are made in research-based practices that improve student achievement. The directive is twofold: there is a need to federally invest in high school improvement, and there must be a shift to make better use of current funds by targeting funding to align with our policy goals, where data show a need and where evidence demonstrates promising practices.

Alignment and Rigor: Creating Voluntary National Standards Aligned to College and Work Readiness

Perhaps the greatest systemic flaw in the original No Child Left Behind Act is that despite the mandated testing, measuring, sanctions, and holding schools accountable, it is up to each state to determine the standard of "proficiency" for their students. Children in every state are being held to differing standards, some much more rigorous than others. Is this really what we want in a global society? The military does not train soldiers according to which state houses its boot camp. No multinational business expects employees from different states to be measured by contrasting standards.

Against this backdrop of fifty standards of education, one-third of students do not graduate from high school at all, and another third graduate without the skills and knowledge to succeed in college or the workforce. There is a strong need for the federal government to foster incentives for common education standards so that all students and parents, no matter where they live, can be confident that their educational process is preparing them to meet the same challenges as students anywhere in the United States. This will not be an easy process. Given longstanding resistance to federal standards being imposed on local school districts, the states themselves could collaborate to develop world-class standards. Once jointly created, each state could then decide whether to adopt them. The federal government could assist by funding development of these shared education standards to ensure that all students are held to the same high expectations of readiness for postsecondary education and the modern workplace. For the states that agree to participate, the federal government could also pay for high-quality assessments to regularly measure student progress toward these standards. This supportive federal role could help remove the significant financial burden currently carried by states to develop their own assessments, while supporting creation of high-quality assessments overall. In addition, the federal government could offer states incentives and supports for adopting such standards and aligning them with their key systems, such as their curricula, graduation requirements, and professional development opportunities.

The federal government could also assist states that wish to compare their education outcomes with the rest of the world. Every three years, the Organisation for Economic Co-operation and Development (OECD) examines the performance of fifteen-year-olds in key subject areas as well as a range of educational outcomes. This Program for Internal Student Assessment (PISA) exam, which draws on representative samples of between forty-five hundred and ten thousand students, has seen participation from more than sixty OECD and partner countries, representing almost 90 percent of the world's economy. Though participating in the nationwide sample, the United States is the only federal nation whose individual components, the states, do not also participate. Every other nation's states, cantons, länder, or provinces can measure their performance against other nations. To assist our states to be more fully prepared for international competition, the federal government in the United States could provide funding to any state that wanted to have its students take the PISA examination.

Developing and Distributing Skilled Teachers and Principals

It is no secret that having all high school teachers be highly qualified in the subjects they teach and prepared to work with students of every skill level and social background is critical. Or that a high-achieving school needs good leaders who supervise personnel effectively, manage finances capably, and help define an academic vision of excellence. Yet too many schools across the country, especially those serving low-income and minority students, are characterized by teachers ill-equipped to teach their subjects and principals without the skills needed to lead these complex organizations effectively.

The federal government attempted in NCLB to improve classroom instruction by requiring a "highly qualified teacher." However, much more must be done to improve teaching in our secondary schools. Similarly, more attention must be given to the training and distribution of effective school leaders who can serve as role models for teachers and students alike. Placement of good teachers and principals is critical to improving learning, particularly in low-income schools. However, it is also critical to give teachers and principals the supports they need to succeed—especially with the most disadvantaged students. Induction, mentoring, professional development, and common planning time are among the hallmarks of good high schools. Too often the lowest-performing schools lack the highest-performing teachers. Many factors play into why they are not evenly distributed throughout our nation's schools. The federal government must assist state and local authorities to address these factors, with improvements in equitable distribution of funds, targeting of funding for quality professional development, and recruitment and retention efforts through better pay and induction programs.

Increasing College Access

Every high school student should graduate with the academic and financial ability to have access to postsecondary education. Increasingly, research has shown that the skills and knowledge to succeed in postsecondary education and the workforce are the same. Further, nearly all decent-paying jobs require some postsecondary education, a requirement that will only increase over time.

Reflecting this growing convergence of the requirements for success in either college or the workforce, the federal government should offer incentives to states to make a college preparatory curriculum the baseline for all students and ensure that such a curriculum is aligned to the state's university system admission standards. Despite the U.S. Congress currently appropriating nearly $40 billion annually to K–12 and higher education, there is no requirement that these separate education entities coordinate their policies at the state level for maximum effectiveness. The federal government should require all states to form P–16 (grades prekindergarten to sixteen) councils where the heads of the early childhood, K–12, higher education, community, and technical education systems; the governor and other appropriate state officials; and business leaders meet regularly to guarantee that the standards for high school learning are in synch with the expectations of higher education and employers.

To improve students' preparation for college, the federal government should also support efforts to personalize the learning environment in high schools and ensure that students and families have the tools and information necessary to plan for high school graduation and success in college or other postsecondary education or training. Part of this must be financial planning for college. To help lower financial barriers that keep students from going to and completing college, the federal government must increase financial aid, make student loans more affordable, and support policies that lower college costs. Pell grants and other need-based aid must be increased significantly to catch up with rising college costs. Whatever additional federal cost is incurred will be repaid many times over by increased income tax revenues, higher productivity, and the other economic gains that come with a flourishing knowledge-based economy.

Engaging Local Communities

Every high school needs a safe and supportive community—inside and outside of the classroom—to ensure that students can focus on achievement. Every high school should encourage positive relationships among educators, families, and other members of the community. The school environment is critical to student success, but it is not the only factor important to the academic and social success of secondary school students. Families and communities also play a key role in shaping the environment critical to student success. High schools should engage their community stakeholders by encouraging positive relationships among educators, families, businesses, faith-based community groups, nonprofit organizations, and other members of the community. Parents should have many chances to visit the school building, talk with teachers and staff, voice concerns, share ideas, serve as volunteers, and suggest ways to improve the school. School leaders should attend community events, form partnerships with local organizations, and reach out to their neighbors.

The federal government can help to foster these linkages by supporting development of community-based partnerships and programs that support student enrichment opportunities that assist meeting students' academic goals and college and career objectives. Additionally, federal agencies addressing the nonacademic needs of students could work together and encourage coordination of grants and services at all levels. Federal policy could also leverage opportunities and reduce barriers for student learning to occur within the local community.

Providing Supports and Options to Students

For students to reach their full potential and graduate prepared for college, work, and life, every high school student must have access to an engaging, rigorous, options-based curriculum and the interventions necessary to succeed in that curriculum. Students should be able to take demanding classes in core subjects such as English, history, science, and math and have the option of accessing opportunities such as Advanced Placement courses, International Baccalaureate programs, or the opportunity to study for part of the day at a local college or university. To prepare students for these options and ensure that they continue to thrive while accessing them, every high school should have a system in place to identify students as soon as they start to struggle in reading, math, or any core subject.

The federal government could encourage school districts to develop other means of personalizing the education experience. One means is for schools to develop a method of having every student paired with at least one adult in the building to maintain regular contact and communication. With school guidance counselors often responsible for 500 students and teachers sometimes teaching

120 students a day, the at-risk student can quickly get lost unless someone is directly responsible for keeping in close contact with him or her. This leads naturally to identifying what specific interventions or supports are necessary to assist a student in achieving maximum potential. Indeed, the school should reserve time and resources for the intensive, focused help some students need to get back up to grade level quickly. The federal government can help to establish a framework that enables all high schools to make these student options and interventions available.

Expanding Support for Adolescent Literacy

According to the federal NAEP examination, almost 70 percent of eighth grade students read below grade level. The below-grade-level rates for African American and Latino high school students are even higher. The lack of adequate reading skills among older students contributes greatly to their failure to master the knowledge they need to succeed after graduation, or to their simply dropping out of school entirely. Unfortunately, the predominant federal investment in reading skills—the Reading First program—ends at third grade, which is exactly the point at which expectations for student literacy increase.

Given the magnitude of the literacy challenge, the federal government must support efforts to integrate literacy skills and learning in secondary schools. The Striving Readers initiative for middle and high schools is a significant step in this direction, but its funding level and scope must be increased to meet the needs of the vast number of adolescents who are struggling to read and write.

The criteria, principles, and areas for action outlined in this chapter can be met, but only if the federal government complements the activities of other levels of government by taking on a new, expanded role to ensure that high schools are preparing their students for the challenges and opportunities of the evolving global economy. There are encouraging signs that federal officials are expanding their interest in the critical area of secondary school improvement; it is the responsibility of federal officials to offer and support a long-term vision for the nation that leads to a new reality, one in which America produces significantly more high-skilled workers ready for the global economy and in which a high school diploma becomes as common as a sixth grade education is now. Clearly a high-quality high school education is vital for the individual student if he or she is to have a meaningful life; as important, a well-educated populace is critical for the security of our nation in the increasing competition of an information-driven economy.

Building the Public Will to Achieve the Vision

Sputnik may have been a dramatic challenge to the United States, but the jarring statistics discussed throughout this book should be no less clear a call for federal action. Just as Sputnik launched a new era of federal involvement in education, so must our rapidly changing economy and demographics also demand a national response.

Many argue that with the federal government contributing only about 8 percent of the total K–12 expenditure, any financial contribution merely tinkers at the margins. Conservatives object to additional federal mandates without accompanying dollars to carry them out.

While holding elected office, I frequently wrestled with the argument of "unfunded" mandates. During one heated congressional debate on the House floor over renewing clean water legislation in the mid-1990s, I paused momentarily, tempted by the siren song of limiting federal standards until the federal government could supply all the dollars to cities and states for implementation. After all, why should the federal government tell state and local governments what to do without supplying all the necessary dollars to implement the stiffer requirements? "Hmmm," I thought. "This sounds reasonable."

Then I remembered the 39th Street sewer that emptied into the Kanawha River where I grew up. As a youngster waterskiing in the 1960s, I noticed the water was always warmer in one particular area and, spending an hour immersed in the brown river always necessitated a shower. One day I asked an engineer why the area around the large pipe emptying into the river at 39th Street was noticeably warmer than upriver. Bemusedly, he explained that this was one of the main sewage disposal areas. "So how is the sewage treated?" I asked. "By putting a right angle turn in the pipe," he replied.

Not until 1972, when the federal Clean Water Act set national standards for pollution discharge, did the thousands of gaping 39th Street pipes around the country actually begin treating the foul goop they were spewing out. The complaint was the same: the federal government should not impose mandates it is not paying for.

Almost twenty-five years later on the House floor, I recalled the 39th Street sewer. With each glass of water that is poured, the public assumes (and rightly expects) that it meets the necessary health standards—not merely what the federal government is able to fund. Often, only the federal government is able to make the tough political call that everyone will have to improve. State and local governments often meet resistance—as was the case in raising environmental water standards—that hard action in this state will put us at a competitive disadvantage for business with more lax states.

The same arguments are playing out in education issues as in environmental ones. When I was governor, facing the newly enacted NCLB in 2001, I muttered about unfunded mandates and questioned whether the state should have to comply until a higher level of federal funding accompanied the new standards.

When a large number of schools failed to meet Adequate Yearly Progress (AYP), the complaints—including mine—only increased. For a while, I considered joining litigation to challenge the federal government's ability to require without reimbursing.

I was wrong. Though Congress and the Administration should have continued the promised increases in funding to support the act, the increased measurement and accountability was moving us to a higher standard of education. As with the glass of water, we can argue over how much is absolutely necessary to protect us, but we must accept that there is indeed a standard that everyone should meet.

Unlike the case of water standards, however, the federal government still leaves it up to individual states to define the appropriate standard, or level of "proficiency," that each student should achieve. Although some bold leaders are moving to improve state, district, and high school initiatives to meet higher standards, there still is no national guarantee that every child can expect to receive—and be measured by—the education truly needed to perform well in college or the modern workplace.

The Advocacy Imperative

Most citizens assume that important educational policy decisions are made within the academic world by professional educators at the state, school, and district levels. Yet ultimately almost every key systemic decision on education will be made by an elected official. This may be a local school board member voting on her school district's annual budget setting fiscal priorities for education or a U.S. representative on a congressional committee enacting sweeping legislation. The learned findings of ten Harvard Ph.D.s with decades of expertise in education can be trumped by one official elected to a two-year term of office. This political reality requires important strategic actions for parents, educators, organizations, businesses, and others who want to improve the quality of public education in America.

The Clean Water Act discussed earlier did not simply happen because people like me water-skied through raw sewage. Over long years, the work of many thousands of individual citizens, working singularly and collectively, pushed policymakers to understand that access to clean drinking water for every American is a fundamental need. As we now confront the deplorable state of many of our high schools, it is time for each of us to recognize and accept our role in convincing policymakers that a quality and equitable education should be the birthright of every American child.

Sometimes a dramatic Sputnik-like event is sufficient to move the legislative process quickly. More often, major legislation results from a combination of forces. Passage of the Clean Water Act was the result of dramatic events (such as rivers catching fire) steadily building health concerns, and concerted efforts to organize expressions of public will. The public came to understand the danger both to them as individuals as well as to the overall national ecosystem. The challenge in bringing high school reform to fruition is moving the public to demand the federal action necessary for high school reform that will then create improved educational outcomes for every student and a greatly enhanced socioeconomic outlook for our country.

Bounceback

The final votes occur in the nation's Capitol, but moving the federal government to significant action will happen only outside the Washington beltway. During my eighteen years serving in the U.S. Congress, I met with thousands of constituents and representatives of many types of organizations. Most of these folks had some sort of direct tie to the state I represented. An overwhelming number of meeting requests flood every congressional office; many are declined. Years after I left Congress, as the new leader of the Alliance for Excellent Education, I realized that as a congressman I would have turned down a meeting with my own organization despite its laudable mission. Why? Because the Alliance was just another Washington, DC–based national organization without a clear constituency or relevance to my home state.

Little happens in Washington unless public demand is "bouncing back" from the congressional district or state. Groups such as the Alliance—and their causes—become relevant only when a congressperson travels home to the district to find ten people lined up, saying, "Our local high school has a 35 percent dropout rate, and according to the Alliance for Excellent Education, we are losing millions of dollars in opportunities." Much more federal legislation is passed because of local experience than from international reports. High school reform will be enacted only as more people see the direct impact of inadequate education in their communities and constantly communicate their desire for action to their elected representatives.

How people—and their elected representatives—view the need for high school reform differs with the congressional district. Parents and community residents who live next to a high school dropout factory live the painful experience. Residents of affluent suburban areas often do not directly see or feel the impact of failing high schools. They don't drive by the aging structures; their children don't experience a lackluster curriculum. Statistics about the dire social result of a high dropout rate do not resonate ten miles away, where the high school is sending 90 percent of its students to college.

What will motivate the elected representatives from these two diverse areas to act is that classic prod of democracy; the electorate's understanding that one group's problem is everyone's problem. The students in the failing high school may be ten miles or ten states away, but their plight affects us all. Whether or not we have personally encountered a failing high school, we are increasingly affected by its outcomes. The employer desperate to find ten skilled workers, the realtor constantly looking for the next upscale home buyer, the taxpayer grumbling over increased social welfare spending, a police officer contending with rising crime, a car salesperson trying to sell new models instead of ten-year-old clunkers, a mayor trying to attract well-paying jobs to her city all directly live with the results of dysfunctional high schools.

Understanding how education affects each of our lives is essential to clearing the basic political measurement I call the

25–75 hurdle. Only 25 percent of the American public has direct involvement with the public school system. The other 75 percent are too young, senior citizens, baby boomers with their children grown, or a small percentage of parents with children in private schools. The success of bounceback depends on having full participation by the 25 percent as well as a large number of the 75 percent to communicate the need for action to elected officeholders. Once again, education, like any other major part of our lives—defense, transportation, environmental protection, national security, public safety—ultimately is determined by political decisions.

Whether part of the 25 or the 75, every citizen can find motivation for political involvement. The moral imperative is the first call to action. Every child should grow up in this country with access to the high-quality education that enables him or her to succeed in life. This nation's political psyche has never accepted the concept of widespread entitlement of a social welfare state. But if entitlement is not available to assist disadvantaged individuals to climb up the social and economic ladder, then quality education must be the alternative. Closely aligned with a general moral imperative are equity and civil rights. Fifty years ago, the federal government enforced the right of children of color to attend the same public schools as white children; now a quieter—but equally important—battle rages over the quality of education they are receiving in the schools they attend.

Following equity is an economic imperative, both for the student and society. The solid link between an individual's education attainment and the ability to participate economically is well documented. The opportunities and quality of life that a person experiences are largely determined by level of education. For society's self-interest, we need the skills, buying power, and entrepreneurial spirit that this generation of educated young people can bring. Economic strength also promotes social well-being. High school dropouts are barely renters; well-educated persons have mortgages and the home ownership that creates strong communities.

A final imperative is our nation's national security. Whether contending with increasingly complex explosive devices in Iraq or fending off computer terrorists who would cripple the U.S. economic and communications systems, our nation's defense depends upon highly educated personnel.

Getting Involved

Changing high schools will happen only through political activity. The final decisions about education are made by more than fifteen thousand local school districts, fifty state boards of education, 7,382 state legislators, fifty governors, 535 voting members of the United States Congress, and one president of the United States. Anyone endorsing at least one of the four imperatives I previously listed now has to accept another: the imperative for change in our high schools. Change comes about only because of political action.

Wherever concerned persons want to start—school boards, state agencies or legislature, or with their congressional representative—it will require direct action that gains elected policymakers' attention. Politics and placid ponds both require someone to make a ripple to change their look.

There are numerous political pebbles—writing opinion editorials for your local newspapers, visiting schools, or joining membership organizations focused on change—that a parent, community leader, or concerned citizen can use to push for education reform. These are the traditional tried-and-true exercises of democracy. Tiring, often frustrating, seemingly pointless, but undertaken with commitment, energy, and determination, these practices produce results—this time for millions of struggling adolescents. I have provided a comprehensive list of activities in Resource F to help you understand the range of options available to you as an empowered and engaged citizen.

The understandable entry point for most educational grassroots advocacy is at the school district or state level. But given the vital role the federal government must assume, citizen engagement that also affects national policy is desperately needed. The location of the nation's Capitol forces congressional representatives to spend much of their time in Washington, D.C., removed from the states and communities where they live and represent. Also, given the large role states and localities have in making public education decisions, federal policymakers require frequent reminders about their special role in supporting quality and equitable education.

Advocates do not need to travel to Washington to make their case; being heard in each community is what makes bounceback effective. Indeed, walking with a U.S. Senator or Congresswoman through a local high school hallway is the most effective way to reach the halls of Congress. Writing the letters, making the telephone calls, sending the e-mails, arranging the meetings all are crucial. The federal government will address high schools only when advocates make a concerted effort to project their strong concerns for students in their communities to their federal policymakers.

Conclusion: Where Do We Go from Here?

What an amazing and tumultuous time for our nation and its education system: an economy rapidly shifting to meet new technologies, global competition constantly threatening U.S. economic preeminence, waves of immigrants changing the social fabric, and an outmoded education system weakening under new demands for higher-quality universal education.

This is not a hopeful vision of the future, but a recounting of the situation our nation was in as it prepared to enter the twentieth century. Facing these great social and economic pressures, much like today, the United States rose to the challenge and, in the late nineteenth century, embarked on a redesign of its education system by ushering in sweeping reform and launching a new era of American economic achievement—that educational structure still dominates the present century.

Much of our current education tradition was cutting-edge in the era of the Spanish-American War, the horse-drawn carriage, gas lights, and the telegraph. The education system that adapted to meet the demands of a fast-growing manufacturing-based economy functioned well when only 10 percent of students finished with a high school degree. The objective was that most children (at least if they were white) required a uniform basic education, but few needed to proceed past high school.

Even in the early twentieth century, public education was considered one way America ensured equal opportunity to its citizens: enroll in public schools, participate in the academic and civic life at those schools, and emerge with a chance to make something of yourself in the adult world.

America's economic needs evolved, and the educational system also grew somewhat. High school became more important, and a larger percentage of students went onto college. Despite many major events, including two world wars, what continued to mark America's greatness was the unspoken promise that public education could provide the means to a well-paying job and a meaningful life.

Yet in today's world of high dropout rates, mediocre international performance rankings, and rising workplace and college expectations, our middle and high schools, largely designed for a completely different era, are not living up to the long-established social compact.

It was only a few years ago, really, that we Americans started to see the signs that many of our middle and high schools were no longer meeting the nation's needs. Policymakers understood that education itself was stumbling, but they largely opted to tackle the problem by significantly investing in the front end of the education system, hoping that better preparation in the early grades would provide continuing dividends to students as they worked their way through the upper grades. But despite academic gains in the early grades, in time research and experience have demonstrated the effects of sending students to outdated high schools.

The academic progress stops and the return on investments made in the early years are largely diminished.

The dark clouds have been forming for years, and inertia is no longer an acceptable secondary school policy. Every year without fundamental change in our middle and high schools translates into doors slammed shut for millions more of our youngest citizens who can't compete.

The economic future, national security, social stability, and democratic values of the nation are greatly dependent on secondary schools. Middle and high schools must play a pivotal role in educating all of their students for the needs and expectations of college and the modern workforce. They must produce graduates who have the critical attributes that will allow individuals to succeed today, tomorrow, and fifty years from now if the country is to remain strong and prosperous.

Policymakers joined with educators must plan for the educational needs of the future rather than merely address the demands of the present. Many of the nation's middle and high schools, designed in the nineteenth century, must be systemically redesigned to respond to the needs of the twenty-first century. Minor tweaks of the past are no longer sufficient. As Johns Hopkins dropout experts Robert Balfanz and Nettie Letgers put it, failing to recognize the high schools that produce America's dropouts as a priority in our overall education reform efforts is "tantamount to treating a chronic illness with a manicure—pleasant, but ultimately pointless."[1]

The current condition begs federal action; viewing what could be our future compels it. Working in close partnership with local and state governments, federal assistance will create revamped high schools characterized by a rigorous curriculum, individualized help for students, and caring and skilled adults taking responsibility for every child. Teachers, principals, and administrators—who generally flock to education because they want to make a difference for future generations—will be given the tools, training, and support to effectively make those goals a reality. Transformed dropout factories will offer our middle and high schoolers the skills they need to become successful, economically self-sufficient adults.

An all-out push to reinvent the American high school experience would also reactivate our own democratic values, reconnecting a disenfranchised public with the public education system that helped make our country great. Quality high schools for all support the opportunity and common experiences that unite an increasingly diverse population. An excellent education can, and must, resume its standing as a great equalizer of opportunity.

Businesses will have the quality workforce they need to remain competitive in a demanding global environment. Our nation will have the kind of educated workers that maintain and enhance the collective quality of life (while simultaneously making a handsome contribution to the local, state, and federal tax base). A skilled, innovative, and healthy workforce will expand the nation's economy, and perpetuate its global leadership.

This book describes many statistical, economic, and sociological reasons for an active federal role in high school reform. But the best reason I have found is in a small, wallet-sized photograph proudly displayed on the dashboard of a taxicab in a midsize American city I recently visited.

Jumping into this cab at the airport, I glanced at a picture of a smiling girl who appeared to be in her teens. The driver was a beaming father as he described his daughter. She was entering the ninth grade, and "she is determined" he said, "to be an epi . . . epi . . ." and we both said simultaneously, "epidemiologist."

"She knows she has to study hard," he continued, "and she is taking hard courses like science and chemistry and math."

I reflected quietly on her odds, with one-third of her class likely not to graduate and another third not finishing with the skills they would need for college or the modern workplace.

Then I thought of our world, and what this young person could mean in a few years. Perhaps she would be part of the team that identifies the next avian flu. Would she find a cancer hot spot in a

community? Or she might be safeguarding large urban water systems that serve millions.

She, above all else, is an example of why we must act to transform
our high schools. As a nation, we certainly are going to need her.

And right now, she desperately needs us.

IN NEED OF IMPROVEMENT: NCLB AND HIGH SCHOOLS

On January 8, 2002, President Bush signed the No Child Left Behind Act of 2001 (NCLB) into law at a ceremony at Hamilton High School in Ohio. During that event, the president said that, as a result of NCLB, "all students will have a better chance to learn, to excel, and to live out their dreams."

NCLB was passed with bipartisan support in Congress because consensus had been reached that the nation needed to close the achievement gaps that existed between students of differing racial, ethnic, and economic backgrounds, and that schools should be held accountable for the success of all students. But despite the location chosen for the signing of the bill into law—a public high school—flaws in the design and implementation of NCLB related to funding, measurements, and improvement

Why the Crisis in America's High Schools Matters to Individuals and Society

- Only 70 percent of all entering freshmen and barely half of students of color finish high school with a regular diploma four years later. Every school day, nearly 7,000 American high school students become dropouts.

- Only 30 percent of students entering high school read at grade level, so it is not surprising that only a third are prepared for college and work by the time they finish high school.

strategies largely neglect secondary schools and students, thwarting the goal of ensuring that America's students graduate prepared for the twenty-first century.

NCLB is the current version of a landmark law passed by Congress over forty years ago. The Elementary and Secondary Education Act of 1965 (ESEA) was signed into law at the height of the civil rights movement as a central component of President Johnson's War on Poverty. ESEA recognized the role of education in securing social, political, and economic equality across race and class and was designed to supplement educational opportunity for poor children. NCLB continues this focus on equity and retains its role as an important civil rights law by requiring the academic achievement of all students to be measured and to improve over time.

- Among developed nations, the United States ranks 17th in its high school graduation rate. American fifteen-year-olds rank 15th in reading scores; 23rd in math scores; and 30th in problem solving skills.

- An estimated 85 percent of current jobs and almost 90 percent of the fastest-growing and best-paying jobs now require some postsecondary education.

- Dropouts from the Class of 2006 cost the nation more than $309 billion in lost wages, taxes, and productivity over their lifetimes.

- High school dropouts often have trouble finding stable, well-paying jobs. Individuals with less education are generally less healthy, die earlier, and are more likely to become parents when very young. Dropouts are also more at risk of becoming embroiled in the criminal justice system, or of needing social welfare assistance from government and other sources.

Although there are debates and legitimate concerns about some of the law's methods and requirements, consensus has emerged on one of its major flaws: NCLB focuses on improving outcomes for students in grades K–8. While many of the provisions of NCLB do apply to all public schools, including high schools, the law was designed primarily with the earlier grades in mind. The law does not take into account either the nation's evolving needs for a better educated populace or the considerable differences between elementary schools and secondary schools. Thus, NCLB emerged with provisions that often neglect, or that are even at odds with, the needs of America's millions of secondary students, particularly the six million students who are most at risk of dropping out of school each year. As a result, the educational and equity promises of NCLB fail to extend to America's older students. These are some examples of this mismatch:

- NCLB is the primary federal instrument for supplementing elementary education funding in areas of concentrated poverty, but many low-income secondary students are left behind. Only 8 percent of students benefiting from NCLB's Title I*—the law's signature program allocating funding to states and districts with the highest numbers of low-income students—are high school students. The other systemic funding stream in NCLB designed to address inequities in low-performing schools, Reading First, serves only students in grades K–3.

- Funding aside, the goal of identifying low-performing schools and closing achievement gaps is severely undermined at the high school level. Measures of student proficiency are based on inconsistent and low state standards and often measure basic math and reading skills, not the students' levels of preparation for college and the workforce. The law does not require graduation rates to be calculated consistently, nor does it require schools to improve the graduation rates of student subgroups.

- Despite the intent to leverage improved teaching, learning, and outcomes, NCLB's school improvement provisions are

*For purposes of this brief, Title I refers specifically to Title I, Part A grants to local education agencies.

not designed to drive high school improvement. NCLB mandates that low-performing schools must take certain actions when they don't meet annual progress goals, but because high schools often don't receive the Title I funds that trigger (and support) this requirement, the requirement lacks teeth at the high school level. Furthermore, the federally mandated improvement actions—including school choice and tutoring—are not effective at the high school level.

In short, the provisions of NCLB that are currently central to closing achievement gaps and leveraging effective high school reform are largely incompatible with what is known about improving high school policy and practice.

NCLB Overview

With each reauthorization of the ESEA, Title I and other programs of the law have evolved to serve a number of additional political and educational purposes. Today, the legislation and its funding streams are leveraged beyond their initial purposes of supplementing education funding in disadvantaged communities; they are also used as devices for requiring reform and improvement at the state, district, and school level.

In 1994, two pieces of federal education legislation—Goals 2000 and the Improving America's Schools Act (the ESEA reauthorization)—became law, cementing a federal role in the standards-based reform movement. These bills required all states to develop content and performance standards in reading (or English language arts) and math and to develop and implement assessments aligned with those standards once in each of the following grade spans: from grades three through five, six through nine, and ten through twelve. States were also required to establish annual benchmarks for improvement referred to as Adequate Yearly Progress (AYP). District leaders would use those scores on the state assessment to decide if schools had made AYP and provide technical assistance to those that needed improvement.

In the No Child Left Behind Act of 2001, Congress built on the goals, frameworks, and requirements of the earlier laws to leverage increased "accountability" for schools and districts to demonstrate results, particularly for poor and minority children, by disaggregating (or breaking down) results for each of the following subgroups of students: economically disadvantaged students, students from major racial and ethnic groups, students with disabilities, and students with limited English proficiency. Since the passage of NCLB, the notion of educational accountability has taken center stage as a critical (and potentially powerful) tool for increasing student success and closing achievement gaps. The basic premise of the NCLB accountability system is that it will set goals, identify schools struggling to meet those goals, and require these low-performing schools to implement improvement strategies.

Some of NCLB's design flaws are problematic for all grades. Currently, states decide what students should learn, how to determine if they have learned it, and how to report schools' progress in meeting those goals. Meanwhile, the federal government established an arbitrary deadline of the year 2014 for states to meet their goals, devised a detailed formula to determine annual progress, and prescribed one-size-fits-all educational strategies that should be used in the schools that do not meet those annual benchmarks. The result is a system of inconsistent goals, unreliable standards, and tests that vary across the states—along with a "school improvement" system micromanaged by the federal government.

Snapshot of NCLB's Core Requirements

- All students must be proficient in reading and math by 2014, as defined and measured by state standards and assessments.
- States must assess students in math and reading once annually in grades 3–8 and at least once during their high school years.

- Every public school is evaluated to see if it has made Adequate Yearly Progress (AYP), based largely on the percentage of students scoring "proficient" or above on state assessments, overall and for each of the following subgroups of students: economically disadvantaged students, students from major racial and ethnic groups, students with disabilities, and students with limited English proficiency.

- Schools that do not make AYP for two years in a row are identified as "needing improvement." School and district AYP information is communicated to parents and to the public through annual school report cards.

- Those schools that receive federal Title I funding and are identified as "needing improvement" must develop a school improvement plan and, for each additional year that they don't make AYP, must undertake specific actions. These schools are required to spend federal funding to implement federally mandated strategies—public school choice, supplemental education services (SES), corrective action, and restructuring.

At best, these strategies and specific provisions of NCLB do not make sense when implemented at the high school level and represent a missed opportunity to leverage meaningful school improvement. At worst, the law and its implementation create mixed and sometimes perverse incentives and act as barriers to meaningful high school improvement.

NCLB: Setting Goals and Measuring Progress in America's Schools

NCLB set a national goal that all students would be proficient in reading and math by 2014 and that disaggregated data would be used to inform school improvement actions that would close the achievement gap. For high schools, the annual benchmark of

AYP is determined primarily by (1) performance on a state test that is administered sometime between grades ten and twelve, and (2) the graduation rate. There are several inherent flaws in both the proficiency and graduation rates provisions of the law.

Proficiency

The universal goal of "100 percent of students proficient by 2014" is problematic for two reasons: there is neither a universal definition of proficiency nor a common way of measuring it. Instead, each state develops its own standards, sets it own definition of

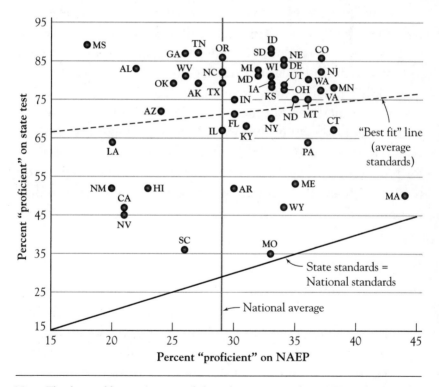

NOTE: The diagonal line represents eighth graders' scores on the NAEP assessment. The dots represent eighth graders' scores on their state's assessment. The further the dot is from the line, the greater the difference between that state's standards and assessments and NAEP.

SOURCE: Liu (2006).[1]

proficiency, and develops its own assessments. Despite infusions of significant funds and the expenditure of considerable political capital over the years to improve state standards and assessments, most expert analysts report that they are not aligned to college and workplace demands and are wildly inconsistent across states.[2] This is demonstrated in the graphic on the preceding page.

While the problem of low and inconsistent standards plagues the education system at every grade level, it is exacerbated at the end of the K–12 education pipeline. In today's increasingly competitive global economy, graduating from high school with a college- and work-ready diploma is a critical step towards securing a good job and a promising future. But if proficiency does not mean college and work preparedness, then proficiency is the wrong goal for high school students, particularly when (as is the case in most states) the test used for NCLB purposes is administered in tenth grade and measures tenth grade (or lower) reading and math skills.[3] Even within a single state, proficiency can mean different things at different times. As evidence, consider that twenty of the twenty-six states that use a high school exit test as their NCLB measure require a lower passing score for graduation than for proficiency under NCLB.[4] Therefore, students can pass the test—and graduate—without attaining what the state considers proficiency.

Graduation Rates

In drafting NCLB, Congress recognized that holding schools accountable for their test scores could create perverse incentives to "push out" low-performing students; that is, the easiest way to increase test scores and meet progress goals could be to encourage or force low-performing students out of the school before they take the test. To ensure that AYP "shall not be met or exceeded based solely on increased dropouts,"[5] as noted in the Congressional Committee Report accompanying the law, the legislation was intended to require high schools to also meet state-set graduation goals to make AYP. Unfortunately, there are significant flaws in the calculation, reporting, and role of graduation rates as implemented by the U.S. Department of Education (the Department) and the states. These flaws undermine the intention of the law, render graduation rate accountability virtually nonexistent, and dilute the usefulness of AYP as a tool for identifying low-performing schools.*

The first result: graduation rate calculations that fail to account for large numbers of students who left school without a regular diploma. As with the definition of proficiency, high school accountability is weakened by inconsistent and unsatisfactory state-determined definitions of graduation rates. On the surface, NCLB's definition and requirements related to graduation rates seem rigorous enough to produce meaningful and comparable rates that would be useful to parents, educators, the public, and policymakers. Unfortunately, states proposed and the Department approved a range of methods—there are at least five different types of graduation rate calculations in use by states across the country—some of which are quite misleading. More than five years after the law was enacted, states are still using a variety of flawed methods and, in some cases, different methods for different subgroups of students, depending on the availability of data in that state. State-reported graduation rates differ from those rates reported by respected independent sources by an average of 11 percentage points and as high as 30 percentage points.[6] Not only does this obscure the graduation rate crisis, particularly for low-income and minority students, but it also makes it impossible to compare graduation rates across schools, districts, and states. These misleading graduation rates also undermine the AYP system, by discounting its ability to accurately identify low-performing high schools.

---

*Visit http://www.all4ed.org/publications/wcwc/index.html to learn more about the graduation rate in your state.

Second, NCLB does not set an ultimate graduation rate goal; therefore, states are not required to set—and schools are not required to meet—meaningful progress benchmarks (annual measurable objectives) toward that graduation rate goal. While a few states have elected to set meaningful ultimate graduate rate goals, most have not. Only New Mexico, Ohio, and Tennessee have set graduation rate goals of 100 percent by 2013–14.[7] Interestingly, thirty-three states set the same graduation goal for the impending year and for 2013–14. As a result, in many states, schools do not have to increase their graduation rates to make AYP. Only a handful of states have set graduation rates benchmarks that increase over time, but most actually allow schools and districts not achieving those targets to still make AYP if they meet a far less meaningful minimum requirement. (In most states, that minimum requirement is just 0.1 percent, or less.[8])

Third, only aggregate (not subgroup) graduation rates are used in the determination of AYP—so graduation gaps and the low graduation rates of poor and minority students, students with limited English proficiency, and students with disabilities are not factored into AYP determinations. While NCLB requires states to report disaggregated graduation rates, most states received waivers

---

The Undermining of Graduation Rates

Graduation rates are an undoubtedly important measure for identifying low-performing high schools and targeting support and interventions. Yet three key flaws in current policy undermine this goal:

- Inconsistent and misleading graduation rate calculations that underestimate the problem.

- No meaningful requirement to increase graduation rates over time.

- No requirement to include (or improve) the graduation rates of student subgroups as part of AYP determinations.

on this requirement because they did not have the capacity to collect the data. In a controversial decision, the Department decided that graduation rates did not have to be disaggregated by minority subgroups for accountability purposes, except for the "safe harbor" provision (an alternative formula for meeting AYP for low-performing schools). This means that high schools can make AYP despite a consistent, or even a growing, graduation gap. As the well respected Civil Rights Project has noted, "In essence, by approving these permissive plans while holding firm on test-driven accountability, the Department has effectively allowed the incentives to push out low-achieving minority students to continue unchecked."[9]

AYP: NCLB's Blunt Approach to Identifying Low-Performing High Schools

As a result of the above described problems with proficiency measures and graduation rate calculations, AYP for high schools is fundamentally flawed. The administration of only one test for the purposes of NCLB accountability during the high school years, combined with the lack of meaningful graduation rate accountability, allows schools to hold back or "push out" low-performing students or to focus on improving the scores of a relatively small number of students to improve specific subgroup achievement, instead of working to systematically improve the academic performance of all students.

The problems with AYP for high schools are exacerbated by its application. NCLB's current "pass or fail" system (a school either makes AYP or fails AYP) is quite simplistic and makes no effort to distinguish—in labeling, prioritization, or in prescribed interventions—between schools that are failing almost all students (and thus that need schoolwide reform) and schools that need to focus on raising the achievement of one subgroup of students or on improving results in one subject area. Educators regularly report that AYP tells them what they already knew: "The bad schools don't make AYP and the good schools do." Not only is this a crude approach to identifying and prioritizing schools, but it also does not reflect research and best practices that base school-improvement actions on finer-grain analyses using multiple measures of school performance.

NCLB's rigid provisions requiring certain interventions in certain years (described below) do not take into account the specific needs of schools that are not making AYP. Some schools may need intensive intervention (or even closure) immediately, rather than going through the five- to seven-year process of ineffective interim "fixes" that the law currently mandates. Others need to give their specific school-improvement measure, which is proving successful, more time to become fully effective. In low-performing schools, in particular, NCLB's requirements exacerbate the "churn" of school reform by requiring different actions every two years.

NCLB's Interventions for Low-Performing Schools Don't Work for High Schools

Under current law, Title I-receiving schools that fail to make AYP for two years in a row are identified as "needing improvement." These schools are required to spend federal funding on a series of federally prescribed interventions that change every two years: first, public school choice which allows students to transfer to another school; then supplemental education services (SES) such as tutoring; then corrective action, which might include replacing the school staff or appointing an outside advisor; and finally, after another year, school restructuring, which might include reopening the school as a charter school or turning the operation of the school over to the state.

Best practice and research demonstrate that, while there is no silver bullet for improving high schools, successful efforts share common strategies. These include increasing personalization, raising the rigor of coursework, and improving the basic literacy and numeracy skills of low-performing students. High school interventions should be based on these known factors and informed by rich data that identify each school's and district's specific weaknesses and strengths, rather than implementing the one-size-fits-all solutions found in the current law.

Furthermore, NCLB universally prescribes interventions for low-performing schools based on *how long* they have not met AYP, rather than on how poorly or well students are performing and regardless of individual school performance and need. Neither public school choice nor SES is driven by school performance data, capacity, or needs, nor do those options fundamentally improve teaching and learning within the school.

Even if there were evidence for prescribing these specific interventions, the reliance on intradistrict public school choice and SES as remedies for chronically low-performing high schools is a flawed strategy. Seventy-five percent of America's school districts have only one high school,[10] and many failing schools are concentrated in urban areas where the vast majority of schools are performing poorly. Thus, high school students often have few, if any, successful schools to which they can transfer. In fact, a recent analysis found that only between 0.2 and 0.4 percent of high school students participated in school choice.[11] And while afterschool tutoring by outside providers may help the very small percentage of students who participate, this strategy cannot effect change in schools where the majority of students need extra help. Furthermore, many older students have afterschool commitments, such as jobs, activities, or caring for siblings, making them unlikely to choose SES. A recent analysis found that fewer than 5 percent of eligible high school students participated in supplemental educational services.[12]

Title I Is a Faulty Trigger for High School Improvement

Even if the problems with the goals, measures, and interventions required by NCLB

"The fact that most of th[e] high-poverty, high-minority high schools do not receive Title I funding, *the* federal program designed to offset *the* impact of poverty, is outrageous."

Balfanz and Legters
Education Week, July 12, 2006

were addressed, low-performing high schools would still be left out and their students left behind. All public schools submit to the NCLB mandates triggered by the acceptance of Title I funds at the state level, including testing, reporting, and being labeled "in need of improvement." However, only those *schools that actually receive* Title I funds are required to implement improvement actions.

This funding stream may serve as a meaningful lever for change in the earlier grades, but it is an ineffective hook on which to hang high school accountability. Because of the way funds are allocated by the various states and districts, which are often likely to direct additional resources toward meeting the needs of younger students in the hope of correcting problems early in students' educational careers, the vast majority of resources provided by Title I of NCLB go to elementary schools. While this funding is intended to assist *all* low-income students, only 8 percent of those students receiving Title I services are high school students (and only 17 percent are middle school students).[13] This imbalance is caused by under-reporting of poverty levels at the high school level, district-level decisions about the allocation of funds, and overall underfunding of Title I. As a result, most secondary schools receive little support for improvement and are exempt from undertaking significant reforms.

NCLB Leaves Adolescent Literacy Deficits Unaddressed

Congress has long recognized the importance of literacy skills in determining students' success in school and has spent billions of dollars over the years promoting vital research and improved reading instruction in the home, in preschool settings, and during the first few years of elementary school. NCLB recognizes the importance of literacy skills by including a systemic intervention in every state through the Reading First program—a $1 billion early literacy program targeted to students in grades K–3.

America's adolescents face a literacy crisis every bit as alarming as the one confronting younger children. Millions of middle and high school students lack the reading and writing skills they need to succeed in college, compete in the workforce, or even understand their daily newspaper.

Although Congress has demonstrated a real commitment to improving reading instruction in grades K–3, it has made relatively little investment (mainly through the small Striving Readers program) in the literacy skills of students in grades 4–12.

It is in the higher grades that expectations and demands for student literacy increase dramatically, yet educators have fewer tools or resources available to support efforts to improve students' ability to read and write at high levels of comprehension and fluency. Partly because of this de facto national policy of ending specific reading instruction after third grade, almost 70 percent of eighth-grade students read below grade level. This lack of the most basic learning skill contributes greatly to students' failure to master the knowledge and skills they need to succeed in their classes and after graduation and results in many of them simply giving up and dropping out of school.

How much does the U.S. spend on each program?

Reading First	**Striving Readers**
Grades: K–3	Grades: 6–12
FY 2007 = $1,146,900,000	FY 2007 = $31,870,000

How much does the U.S. spend per student? *

Reading First	**Striving Readers**
Grades: K–3	Grades: 6–12
Reading First spends $79.08 per student	Striving Readers spends $1.22 per student

NOTE: * Figure is based on public school education in the United States for grades K–3 and 6–12 in 2003–04 (National Center for Education Statistics, 2004).

The current meager federal investment in adolescent literacy through the Striving Readers program provides only $1.22 per student, compared to the $79.08 provided by Reading First, as demonstrated in the graphic on the preceding page. The lack of federal attention is reflected at the state level, where very few states have significant literacy programs in place and fully functioning for the secondary grades. In other words, the extensive reading efforts in early childhood and early grades have been presumed to have created a sufficient foundation by fourth grade that will successfully carry students through the rest of their educational lives. But research and data clearly show that establishing a strong foundation, while vitally important, does not guarantee later education success.

Conclusion

In 2001, when the president's proposal for a significant expansion of ESEA was introduced and later debated, amended, and ratified by Congress, very little attention was being paid by policymakers, the national education community, or the public to the nation's high schools. In fact, President Bush's original twenty-eight-page proposal for ESEA reauthorization only mentioned the term "high school" twice.

As the law comes up for reauthorization in the 110th Congress, much more is known about the crisis in America's high schools and the need for an appropriate federal role as part of a national solution.

In fact, discussions about the future of NCLB often include calls for "expanding" or "extending" NCLB to high schools. While these calls underscore the point that secondary schools are not properly addressed through the provisions and policies of NCLB as it currently exists, they are nevertheless both inaccurate and misleading. As described in this brief, NCLB does currently apply to high schools—albeit in neglectful or even detrimental ways. Proposals that merely extend testing requirements to high school are shortsighted, as are those that suggest simply reserving portions of current funding streams for high schools. **Instead, there must be a comprehensive appraisal of how the entire accountability and improvement system leveraged under the law currently applies to high schools; then a systemic solution that reflects all that is known about improving high schools from research and best practice must be crafted.**

Despite its shortcomings, NCLB directed a spotlight onto the achievement gap and focused the nation on providing all children, especially those at risk of dropping out, with a high-quality, standards-based education. When Congress reauthorizes the law, it will have a unique opportunity to build on the ideals of "no child left behind" and pass legislation that will lead the nation toward "every child a graduate."

References

Alliance for Excellent Education. (2007). *Understanding high school graduation rates*. Washington, DC: Author.

American Federation of Teachers. (2006). *Smart testing: Let's get it right. How assessment-savvy have states become since NCLB?* Washington, DC: Author.

Balfanz, R., and Legters, N. (2006, July 12). Closing 'dropout factories': The graduation rate crisis we know, and what can be done about it. *Education Week, 26*(42).

Center on Education Policy. (2006). *High school exit exams: Standards differ from the No Child Left Behind Act*. Washington, DC: Author.

———. (2007). *No Child Left Behind at five: A review of changes to state accountability plans*. Washington, DC: Author.

Editorial Projects in Education. (2007, June 12). Diplomas count: An essential guide to graduation policy and rates. *Education Week, 26*(40).

Finn, C., and Petrilli, M. (2006). *The state of state standards*. Washington, DC: Thomas B. Fordham Foundation.

National Center for Education Evaluation and Regional Assistance. (2006). *National assessment of Title I interim report*. Washington, DC: U.S. Department of Education, Institute of Education Sciences.

Orfield, G., Losen, D., Wald, J., and Swanson, C. (2004). *Losing our future: How minority youth are being left behind by the graduation rate crisis*. Cambridge, MA: The Civil Rights Project at Harvard University. Contributors: Advocates for Children of New York, the Civil Society Institute.

U.S. Congress. Conference Committee. (2001). *No Child Left Behind Act: Conference report to accompany H.R.1.* 107th Congress, 1st session. Committee Print 107–334. Washington, DC: U.S. Government Printing Office.

U.S. Department of Education, Office of Planning, Evaluation and Policy Development, Policy and Program Studies Service. (2007). *State and local implementation of the* No Child Left Behind Act, *Volume I—Title I school choice, supplemental educational services, and student achievement.* Washington, D.C: Author.

1. Alliance for Excellent Education with assistance from Goodwin Liu. 2007. 8th Grade Reading, 2007. Washington, DC: Author. VT and DC are excluded from this graph as the data is not disaggregated by grade level. 2006 data is used for the following seven states: HI, NE, NC, NJ, OR, TN, and WI as 2007 data is not available by grade level. Chart is based on the best data available at the time of publication.

2. ACT, 2007; Partnership for 21st Century Skills, 2006; ACT, 2006; AFT, 2006; Finn and Petrilli, 2006; ADP, 2004.

3. Center on Education Policy, 2007.

4. Center on Education Policy, 2006.

5. U.S. Congress, Conference Committee, 2001.

6. Alliance for Excellent Education, 2007.

7. *Education Week*, 2007.

8. Ibid.

9. Orfield et al., 2004.

10. U.S. Department of Education, 2006.

11. U.S. Department of Education, 2007.

12. Ibid.

13. Ibid.

HIDDEN BENEFITS:
THE IMPACT OF HIGH SCHOOL
GRADUATION ON HOUSEHOLD
WEALTH

Several recent reports have highlighted the earnings gap between high school graduates and dropouts; however, earnings tell only part of the story. Families rely on income from salary for regular expenses, but real economic security requires accumulated wealth (Conley, 1999; Shapiro, 2004; Hertz, 2006). Household wealth, also known as "assets," is broadly defined as the accumulation of investments that appreciate over time. This wealth may take various forms, including cash investments (savings, equities, 401(k) accounts, and individual retirement accounts), material possessions that hold monetary value (homes, cars, small businesses), and investments in nontangible property such as degrees.

Education can be the key to higher earnings, but it is even more importantly linked to the accumulation of assets. Research by Elena Gouskova and Frank Stafford of the University of Michigan Institute for Social Research shows that, on average, households headed by a high school graduate accumulate *ten times* more wealth than households headed by a high school dropout (Gouskova & Stafford, 2005). In other words, for every $500 of wealth households headed by a high school dropout have, their peers with diplomas have accumulated approximately $5,000. Based on this finding, the Alliance for Excellent Education has determined that the **citizens of the United States would have**

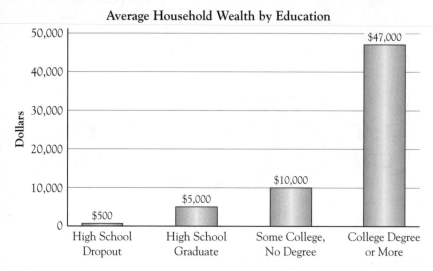

Average Household Wealth by Education

SOURCE: Gouskova and Stafford, 2005.

over **$74 billion** more in accumulated wealth if all heads of households had graduated from high school.

The Importance of Wealth

Wealth is critical to the economic well-being of individuals and families for a host of reasons. Indeed, wealth is the best gauge of a household's financial security and prospects (Conley, 1999). Yet, according to a recent report by the Ford Foundation, while "fewer than 13 percent of American households live below the official poverty line . . . more than a quarter live paycheck to paycheck with negligible or nonexistent net worth" (Ford Foundation, 2007).

Perhaps the most important benefit of wealth is the cushion that accumulated assets provide for families that face sudden unemployment, disabling medical situations, or any kind of financial emergencies (Kochhar, 2004; Doron &

> **Assets matter. Assets mean economic security. Assets mean mobility. Assets mean opportunity.**
>
> Corporation for Enterprise
> Development, 2002

Fisher, 2002). Regular income helps families pay for day-to-day living expenses; assets allow them to survive financial hardships. But "25.5 percent of all American households had insufficient net worth to sustain living *at the federal poverty level* for three months if their income were to be disrupted" (Corporation for Enterprise Development, 2002).

The ownership of assets that can be converted to cash can make the difference between a family's continuing economic viability and bankruptcy, homelessness, or other lasting financial calamity. For instance, families can convert assets to cash to cover living expenses. They can also borrow against assets (e.g., a retirement account) at much better commercial loan rates and with greater ease than those without similar assets.

Accumulated wealth has other long-term benefits. For example, assets can be invested in higher education, which leads to ever increasing levels of income and wealth (Kochhar, 2004; Doron & Fisher, 2002). Families with greater wealth are also more likely to have the resources, time, and educational background to support their children's education, such as fostering the development of reading skills, participating in school activities, and encouraging their children to make ambitious academic choices (Sawhill, 2006; Orr, 2003; Hertz, 2006). The National Conference of State Legislatures notes that "research . . . suggests positive effects on the children of participants [in asset-building programs], such as improved living conditions, educational opportunities, and positive modeling of savings behavior" (2005).

Wealth also confers other advantages that make further wealth generation more likely. Buying a house in a desirable neighborhood, starting a business, paying for higher education, or funding a comfortable retirement are all ways that families increase their long-term financial security and improve the financial prospects for themselves and their children (Mishel, Bernstein, & Allegretto, 2006).

The capacity to improve financial prospects for one's children and grandchildren is the most enduring benefit that wealth offers. Young people who have resources for college costs, professional training, housing, or starting businesses have significant advantages over their peers. They are better able to absorb the opportunity costs of education or internships that strain personal finances but have powerful impacts on later earning power, and they have less debt as they begin their careers and start their own families. Indeed, it is in great part because wealth can be inherited that it has greater impact on individual prosperity than income (Conley, 1999).

Most economists view wealth as a much more important determinant of economic status than earnings because of the long-term advantage it provides in almost every aspect of life (Doron & Fisher, 2002; Oliver & Shapiro, 1995). Both wealth and poverty tend to perpetuate themselves; the effects of wealth are so significant that it can take as long as five generations for the effects conferred by wealth to disappear (Sawhill, 2006).

As individuals and families benefit from greater wealth, so do the communities in which they live. Research indicates that communities benefit from increased homeownership, greater levels of entrepreneurship, and higher levels of educational attainment that come with asset accumulation. Communities also benefit through greater neighborhood stability, increased civic involvement and voting participation, and reduced need for public assistance (Center for Social Development, 2002).

The Wealth Gap vs. the Earnings Gap

Assets are very unevenly distributed in the United States, and the disparities not only reflect historical inequities, including segregated education systems, but also help to perpetuate the inequalities that still exist (Conley, 1999; Shapiro, 2004). And wealth inequality, between whites and minorities as well as between those with high and low incomes, is increasing. According to recent data from the Federal Reserve Board compiled by Citizens for Tax Justice, the share of assets owned by the wealthiest Americans (the top 1 percent) increased by 3.3 percent between 1989 and

2004, while the share of the poorest 50 percent declined from 3 percent to 2.5 percent (Citizens for Tax Justice, 2006). Putting it another way, 20 percent of Americans hold 84 percent of the nation's wealth; the least affluent 40 percent hold only 1 percent of the country's assets (Ford Foundation, 2007).

Hispanics and African Americans lag much farther behind whites in wealth than they do in earnings. On average, the earnings of minorities are approximately 55 percent of those of whites, while the average net worth of minorities is under 30 percent of that for whites (Kochhar, 2004). Although there have been some fluctuations, the wealth gap remains significant. The groups on the lowest rungs of the economic ladder are the most vulnerable to economic dislocation—and the least able to provide that "leg up" for their children.

Debt plays an important role in limiting these groups' financial security. More than 60 percent of black and 54 percent of Hispanic households have either no financial assets or are in significant debt (Corporation for Enterprise Development, 2002). In fact, about one quarter of low-income families have significant household debt (including credit cards, car loans, and other loans apart from home mortgages), compared to 13 percent for whites, and these families must devote as much as 40 percent of their income to paying off this debt (Mishel, Bernstein, & Allegretto, 2006). Thus, rather than accumulating and transferring enduring assets to their children and grandchildren, poor families struggle to provide for their daily welfare and are ill-equipped to support the educational and economic advancement of their families.

Increasing High School Graduation Rates to Increase the Nation's Collective Wealth

Building the capacity to accumulate wealth for groups that have lagged behind is a key strategy for breaking the cycle of poverty and fostering a solid middle class in the United States, but this is a goal that cannot be met without education (Shapiro, 2004).

Policymakers have long supported asset-building programs like the Homestead Act of 1862 that gave land to 1.5 million families and the G.I. Bill that allowed millions of World War II veterans to earn college degrees and buy houses. For the past decade, there has been a growing focus by governments, philanthropists, banks, and community organizations on supporting poverty reduction by creating opportunities for expanded asset ownership, particularly through additional options for homeownership and access to subsidized savings programs. One current policy focus is on the idea of creating savings accounts for all children that would be funded at higher levels for children from poorer families (Ford Foundation, 2007).

Given the connection between education and asset accumulation, another strategy for narrowing the wealth gap would be to increase the educational attainment of those at the low end of the wealth spectrum. To estimate the size of the impact, the Alliance for Excellent Education analyzed existing data to ask: What would be the impact on this country's collective wealth if every head of household graduated from high school?

The Alliance used 2005 U.S. Census Bureau numbers for households by educational attainment in each state and then multiplied the households by their median financial wealth (Gouskova & Stafford, 2005) to derive the total financial wealth of each education level by state. Additional household financial wealth gained by high school graduation was calculated by multiplying the number of households headed by an individual with less than a high school degree by the median financial wealth of those households headed by an individual with a high school diploma. The current estimate of the financial wealth of households with less than a high school diploma was subtracted by this number to derive the additional household financial wealth that would be gained by each state (and the nation) if every household were headed by someone with at least a high school diploma.

There would be, according to these calculations, an additional $74 billion in collective wealth in the United States if every household were headed by an individual with at least a high school diploma. The results for each state and the nation are shown in the table at the end of this Issue Brief. It should be noted that this is a conservative estimate, as the calculation does not include the value of housing. Although homeownership may offer the greatest asset-accumulation opportunity for most Americans, the decision was made to exclude the value of homes, because mortgage holders may also have considerable debt associated with the home and since the value of homes may fluctuate in unpredictable ways; developing a firm estimate of the value of this particular asset is complex and outside of the scope of the Alliance's analysis. That said, since a home is the most valuable asset most families have—and graduates are more likely to be able to afford that investment—the $74 billion figure is likely to significantly understate the potential loss to non-graduates.

Even the conservative estimate of $74 billion, however, represents much more than extra money in the pockets of low-income individuals. This figure represents the additional financial security and opportunities that are lost—by individuals, families, communities, and states—because of an education system that is failing the approximately 1.2 million students who drop out of high school each year.

For more information about the state of America's high schools and to find out what individuals and organizations can do to support effective reform at the local, state, and federal levels, visit the Alliance for Excellent Education's website at www.all4ed.org.

This issue brief was made possible with the generous support of MetLife Foundation.

Increase in Wealth if All Heads of Households Were High School Graduates[1]

State	Number of Households Headed by High School Dropouts	Household Wealth Accumulated by High School Dropouts	Number of Households Headed by High School Graduates	Household Wealth Accumulated by High School Graduates	Potential Additional Household Wealth if All Heads of Households Were High School Graduates
Alabama	351,620	$175,810,000	544,616	$2,723,080,000	$1,582,290,000
Alaska	20,489	$10,244,500	63,185	$315,925,000	$92,200,500
Arizona	317,026	$158,513,000	520,782	$2,603,910,000	$1,426,617,000
Arkansas	204,273	$102,136,500	367,480	$1,837,400,000	$919,228,500
California	2,051,413	$1,025,706,500	2,430,339	$12,151,695,000	$9,231,358,500
Colorado	184,583	$92,291,500	417,417	$2,087,085,000	$830,623,500
Connecticut	158,485	$79,242,500	370,180	$1,850,900,000	$713,182,500
Delaware	44,929	$22,464,500	96,493	$482,465,000	$202,180,500
District of Columbia	37,208	$18,604,000	48,297	$241,485,000	$167,436,000
Florida	999,805	$499,902,500	2,013,765	$10,068,825,000	$4,499,122,500
Georgia	550,222	$275,111,000	929,718	$4,648,590,000	$2,475,999,000
Hawaii	42,599	$21,299,500	117,584	$587,920,000	$191,695,500
Idaho	67,927	$33,963,500	145,914	$729,570,000	$305,671,500
Illinois	632,699	$316,349,500	1,254,359	$6,271,795,000	$2,847,145,500
Indiana	348,924	$174,462,000	872,897	$4,364,485,000	$1,570,158,000

Iowa	125,286	$62,643,000	418,456	$2,092,280,000	$563,787,000
Kansas	116,357	$58,178,500	309,981	$1,549,905,000	$523,606,500
Kentucky	351,273	$175,636,500	542,644	$2,713,220,000	$1,580,728,500
Louisiana	329,976	$164,988,000	550,431	$2,752,155,000	$1,484,892,000
Maine	58,869	$29,434,500	189,943	$949,715,000	$264,910,500
Maryland	246,974	$123,487,000	514,207	$2,571,035,000	$1,111,383,000
Massachusetts	286,424	$143,212,000	632,429	$3,162,145,000	$1,288,908,000
Michigan	496,318	$248,159,000	1,145,179	$5,725,895,000	$2,233,431,000
Minnesota	184,242	$92,121,000	538,137	$2,690,685,000	$829,089,000
Mississippi	235,487	$117,743,500	334,285	$1,671,425,000	$1,059,691,500
Missouri	334,894	$167,447,000	732,401	$3,662,005,000	$1,507,023,000
Montana	33,870	$16,935,000	112,997	$564,985,000	$152,415,000
Nebraska	71,201	$35,600,500	202,559	$1,012,795,000	$320,404,500
Nevada	138,477	$69,238,500	252,470	$1,262,350,000	$623,146,500
New Hampshire	48,078	$24,039,000	144,389	$721,945,000	$216,351,000
New Jersey	420,011	$210,005,500	878,971	$4,394,855,000	$1,890,049,500
New Mexico	123,753	$61,876,500	194,879	$974,395,000	$556,888,500
New York	1,081,614	$540,807,000	1,963,174	$9,815,870,000	$4,867,263,000
North Carolina	579,243	$289,621,500	953,756	$4,768,780,000	$2,606,593,500
North Dakota	33,555	$16,777,500	76,828	$384,140,000	$150,997,500
Ohio	616,295	$308,147,500	1,574,436	$7,872,180,000	$2,773,327,500
Oklahoma	210,859	$105,429,500	418,627	$2,093,135,000	$948,865,500

(continued)

Increase in Wealth if All Heads of Households Were High School Graduates[1] (*continued*)

Oregon	167,164	$83,582,000	348,141	$1,740,705,000	$752,238,000
Pennsylvania	643,215	$321,607,500	1,787,923	$8,939,615,000	$2,894,467,500
Rhode Island	66,409	$33,204,500	113,231	$566,155,000	$298,840,500
South Carolina	299,878	$149,939,000	489,043	$2,445,215,000	$1,349,451,000
South Dakota	35,992	$17,996,000	99,233	$496,165,000	$161,964,000
Tennessee	443,798	$221,899,000	779,513	$3,897,565,000	$1,997,091,000
Texas	1,563,621	$781,810,500	1,964,935	$9,824,675,000	$7,036,294,500
Utah	72,659	$36,329,500	192,510	$962,550,000	$326,965,500
Vermont	25,742	$12,871,000	75,180	$375,900,000	$115,839,000
Virginia	413,061	$206,530,500	723,873	$3,619,365,000	$1,858,774,500
Washington	243,442	$121,721,000	583,352	$2,916,760,000	$1,095,489,000
West Virginia	141,072	$70,536,000	291,817	$1,459,085,000	$634,824,000
Wisconsin	248,936	$124,468,000	730,851	$3,654,255,000	$1,120,212,000
Wyoming	18,568	$9,284,000	64,002	$320,010,000	$83,556,000
United States	16,518,815	$8,259,407,500	31,117,809	$155,589,045,000	$74,334,667,500

[1] The Alliance for Excellent Education used 2005 U.S. Census Bureau's numbers for households by educational attainment and multiplied them by their median financial wealth (Gouskova & Stafford, 2005) to derive the total household wealth accumulated by education level by state. The difference in the median financial wealth between nongraduates and those with a high school diploma ($4,500) was multiplied by the number of heads of household who did not graduate from high school for the potential additional wealth if all heads of household were high school graduates.

References

Citizens for Tax Justice (2006, May 12). *New data show growing wealth inequality: Federal reserve report shows need to preserve estate tax.* [Press release]. Washington, DC: Author.

Conley, D. (1999). *Being black, living in the red: Race, wealth, and social policy in America.* Berkeley, CA: University of California Press.

Corporation for Enterprise Development (2002). *State asset development report card: Benchmarking asset development in fighting poverty.* Washington, DC: Author.

Doron, S., & Fisher, E. (2002). *Black wealth/white wealth: An issue for the South.* Research Triangle Park, NC: Southern Growth Policies Board.

Ford Foundation. (2007). *Saving's grace: The power of building financial assets.* New York: Author.

Gouskova, E., & Stafford, F. (2005). *Trends in household wealth dynamics, 2001–2003.* Ann Arbor, MI: Institute for Social Research, University of Michigan.

Hertz, T. (2006). *Understanding mobility in America.* Washington, DC: Center for American Progress.

Kochhar, R. (2006). *The wealth of Hispanic households: 1996–2002.* Washington, DC: Pew Hispanic Center.

Mishel, L., Bernstein, J., & Allegretto, S. (2006). *The state of working America 2006/2007.* Washington, DC: The Economic Policy Institute.

National Conference of State Legislatures. (2005). *Individual development accounts: How legislators can use IDAs as a tool to increase homeownership and promote asset development.* Washington, DC: Author.

Oliver, M., & Shapiro, T. (1995). *Black wealth, white wealth: A new perspective on racial inequality.* New York: Routledge.

Orr, A. (2003). *Black-white differences in achievement: The importance of wealth.* Sociology of Education, 76, 281–304.

Sawhill, I. (2006). *Opportunity in America: The role of education.* Washington, DC: Brookings Institution.

Shapiro, T. (2004). *The hidden cost of being African American: How wealth perpetuates inequality.* New York: Oxford University Press.

U.S. Department of Commerce, Bureau of the Census (2006). *Educational attainment in the United States: 2005, Table 8.* Washington, DC: U.S. Department of Commerce.

THE HIGH COST OF HIGH SCHOOL DROPOUTS: WHAT THE NATION PAYS FOR INADEQUATE HIGH SCHOOLS

Every school day, seven thousand students become dropouts. Annually, that adds up to about 1.2 million students who will not graduate from high school with their peers as scheduled. Lacking a high school diploma, these individuals will be far more likely to spend their lives periodically unemployed, on government assistance, or cycling in and out of the prison system.

Most high school dropouts see the result of their decision to leave school most clearly in the slimness of their wallets. The average annual income for a high school dropout in 2005 was $17,299, compared to $26,933 for a high school graduate, a difference of $9,671 (U.S. Bureau of the Census, 2006). The impact on the country's economy is less visible, but it is nevertheless staggering.

If the nation's secondary schools improved enough that they were able to graduate all of their students, rather than the 68 to 70 percent of students that are currently graduated annually (Editorial Projects in Education, 2006), the payoff would be significant. **For instance, if the students who dropped out of the class of 2006 had graduated, the nation's economy would have benefited from an additional $309 billion in income over their lifetimes.**

Everyone benefits from increased graduation rates. The graduates themselves, on average, will earn higher wages and enjoy more

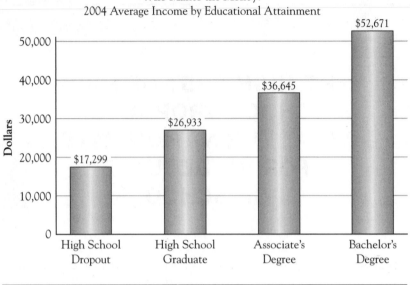

Who Makes the Money?
2004 Average Income by Educational Attainment

SOURCE: U.S. Bureau of the Census (2006).

comfortable and secure lifestyles. At the same time, the nation benefits from their increased purchasing power, collects higher tax receipts, and sees higher levels of worker productivity.

Students Who Learn More Earn More

Research by Cecilia Rouse, professor of economics and public affairs at Princeton University, shows that each dropout, over his or her lifetime, costs the nation approximately $260,000 (Rouse, 2005). Unless high schools are able to graduate their students at higher rates, more than 12 million students will drop out during the course of the next decade. The result will be a loss to the nation of *$3 trillion.*

The calculations in the table at the end of this Issue Brief show the monetary benefits each state could accrue over the lifetimes of just one year's dropouts if those students could be converted to graduates. The numbers vary from state to state, of course: Vermont (at the low end) would see its economy increase by

$416 million, Colorado (near the middle) would add $4.2 billion to its economy, and California's economy (at the high end) would accrue an additional $40 billion over the lifetime of each graduating class. These figures are conservative, and do not take into account the added economic growth generated from each new dollar put into the economy.

Who Doesn't Graduate?

- Only about 58 percent of Hispanic students and 53 percent of black students will graduate on time with a regular diploma, compared to 80 percent of Asian students and 76 percent of white students (EPE, 2006).

- Among all races and ethnicities, females graduate at a higher rate than their male peers—74 percent versus 66 percent (EPE, 2007).

- Graduation rates are significantly lower in districts with higher percentages of students who are eligible for free or reduced-price lunches (a measure of poverty) (Swanson, 2004).

- High school students living in low-income families drop out of school at six times the rate of their peers from high-income families (U.S. Department of Education, NCES 2004).

- The lowest-achieving 25 percent of students are twenty times more likely to drop out of high school than students in the highest achievement quartile (Carnevale, 2001).

More Graduates Benefit Society

Obviously, dropouts are a drain on the economies of each state and the nation. Lower local, state, and national tax revenues are perhaps the most obvious consequence of higher dropout rates; even when dropouts are employed, they earn significantly lower wages than graduates. State and local economies suffer further when they have less-educated populaces, as they find it more difficult to attract new business investment. Simultaneously, these entities must spend more on social programs when their populations have lower educational levels.

The nation's economy and competitive standing also suffers when there are high dropout rates. Among developed countries, the United States ranks eighteenth in high school graduation rates and fifteenth in college graduation rates (Organisation for Economic Co-Operation and Development, 2007). Dropouts represent a tremendous waste of human potential and productivity, and reduce the nation's ability to compete in an increasingly global economy.

High school graduates, on the other hand, provide both economic and social benefits to society. In addition to earning higher wages,

---

How Much Does a High School Dropout Cost?

Researchers have started to examine various annual and lifetime costs associated with high school dropouts.

- The United States could save between $7.9 and $10.8 billion annually by improving educational attainment among all recipients of Temporary Assistance to Needy Families, food stamps, and housing assistance (Garfinkel et al., 2005).

- A high school dropout contributes about $60,000 less in taxes over a lifetime (Rouse, 2005).

- If the male graduation rate were increased by only 5 percent, the nation would see an annual savings of $4.9 billion in crime-related costs (Alliance for Excellent Education, 2006b).

- America could save more than $17 billion in Medicaid and expenditures for health care for the uninsured by graduating all students (Alliance for Excellent Education, 2006a).

which results in attendant benefits to local, state, and national economic conditions, high school graduates live longer (Muennig, 2005), are less likely to be teen parents (Haveman et al., 2001), and are more likely to raise healthier, better-educated children. In fact, children of parents who graduate from high school are themselves far more likely to graduate from high school than are children of parents without a high school degree (Wolfe & Haveman, 2002). High school graduates are also less likely to commit crimes (Raphael, 2004), rely on government health care (Muennig, 2005), or use other public services such as food stamps or housing assistance (Garfinkel et al., 2005). Additionally, high school graduates engage in civic activity, including voting and volunteering in their communities, at higher levels (Junn, 2005).

Reducing Dropouts by Improving High Schools

To increase the number of students who graduate from high school, the nation's secondary schools must be dramatically improved. Although the investments made in the early grades are beginning to pay off, with higher student reading scores and a reduction in the achievement gap between white and minority students (U.S. Department of Education, 2005), too many of America's high schools are still serving their students poorly.

In a recent survey of high school dropouts, respondents indicated that they felt alienated at school and that no one even noticed if they failed to show up for class. High school dropouts also complained that school did not reflect real-world challenges. More than half of respondents said that the major reason for dropping out of high school was that they felt their classes were uninteresting and irrelevant (Bridgeland & di Iulio, 2006). Others leave because they are not doing well academically; only about 30 percent of high school students read proficiently, which generally means that as the material in their textbooks becomes increasingly challenging, they drop increasingly further behind.

Whatever the causes, the nation can no longer afford to have a third of its students leaving school without a diploma. Our high schools must be improved to give all students the excellent education that will prepare them for college or work, and to be productive members of society.

For more information about the state of America's high schools, and to find out what individuals and organizations can do to support effective reform at the local, state, and federal levels, visit the Alliance for Excellent Education's website at www.all4ed.org.

The Alliance for Excellent Education is grateful to MetLife Foundation for providing the generous to originally support develop this brief in Januray 2007. The findings and conclusions presented are those of the Alliance and do not necessarily represent the views of the funder.

Estimated Additional Lifetime Income If High School Dropouts Graduated With Their Class in 2006–2007[1]

States	9th Graders (2003–2004)	Estimated Graduation Rate (2006–2007)	Estimated Number of Dropouts for the class of 2007	Total Lifetime Additional Income if Dropouts Graduated
Alabama	62,718	59.0%	25,714	$6,685,738,800
Alaska	11,803	65.1%	4,119	$1,071,004,220
Arizona	87,576	68.4%	27,674	$7,195,244,160
Arkansas	37,301	72.2%	10,370	$2,696,116,280
California	528,564	70.7%	154,869	$40,266,005,520
Colorado	63,312	74.6%	16,081	$4,181,124,480
Connecticut	48,643	79.8%	9,826	$2,554,730,360
Delaware	11,009	62.0%	4,183	$1,087,689,200
District of Columbia	5,656	58.2%	2,364	$614,694,080
Florida	253,565	60.5%	100,158	$26,041,125,500
Georgia	135,091	56.1%	59,305	$15,419,286,740
Hawaii	16,459	64.1%	5,909	$1,536,283,060
Idaho	20,771	77.0%	4,777	$1,242,105,800
Illinois	174,343	75.7%	42,365	$11,014,990,740
Indiana	85,025	70.9%	24,742	$6,432,991,500

(continued)

Estimated Additional Lifetime Income If High School Dropouts Graduated With Their Class in 2006–2007[1] (continued)

Iowa	40,486	81.1%	$1,989,482,040
Kansas	38,684	74.4%	$2,574,807,040
Kentucky	54,730	70.0%	$4,268,940,000
Louisiana	58,514	61.4%	$5,872,465,040
Maine	16,891	76.2%	$1,045,215,080
Maryland	78,690	74.7%	$5,176,228,200
Massachusetts	83,759	73.2%	$5,836,327,120
Michigan	153,567	69.1%	$12,337,572,780
Minnesota	69,744	78.7%	$3,862,422,720
Mississippi	39,536	62.1%	$3,895,877,440
Missouri	77,175	75.0%	$5,016,375,000
Montana	12,915	76.2%	$799,180,200
Nebraska	24,374	79.8%	$1,280,122,480
Nevada	34,779	54.0%	$4,159,568,400
New Hampshire	18,286	76.0%	$1,141,046,400
New Jersey	108,480	82.5%	$4,935,840,000
New Mexico	29,840	60.1%	$3,095,601,600
New York	257,475	65.0%	$23,430,225,000
North Carolina	122,508	66.1%	$10,797,855,120
North Dakota	8,952	79.4%	$479,469,120

Ohio	160,873	74.7%	40,701	$10,582,225,940
Oklahoma	49,529	70.4%	14,661	$3,811,751,840
Oregon	46,213	71.1%	13,356	$3,472,444,820
Pennsylvania	162,097	78.2%	35,337	$9,187,657,960
Rhode Island	14,188	70.6%	4,171	$1,084,530,720
South Carolina	69,415	53.8%	32,070	$8,338,129,800
South Dakota	10,375	78.5%	2,231	$579,962,500
Tennessee	79,195	72.2%	22,016	$5,724,214,600
Texas	377,912	67.3%	123,577	$32,130,078,240
Utah	36,028	83.8%	5,837	$1,517,499,360
Vermont	8,422	81.0%	1,600	$416,046,800
Virginia	107,033	73.1%	28,792	$7,485,888,020
Washington	88,869	66.5%	29,771	$7,740,489,900
West Virginia	23,723	71.7%	6,714	$1,745,538,340
Wisconsin	77,798	77.3%	17,660	$4,591,637,960
Wyoming	7,346	75.8%	1,778	$462,210,320
United States	4,190,237	69.9%	1,265,016	$328,904,058,340

[1] The Alliance for Excellent Education determined the average additional lifetime income if one class of dropouts were to graduate by multiplying the number of dropouts as determined using enrollment data for the ninth-grade 2002–03 school year (National Center for Education Statistics, Common Core of Data: 2002) and the high school graduation rate in 2006 (Editorial Projects in Education, 2006) by the $260,000 estimated lifetime earnings difference between a high school dropout and a high school graduate (Rouse, 2005).

References

Alliance for Excellent Education. (2006a). *Healthier and wealthier: Decreasing health care costs by increasing educational attainment*. Washington, DC: Author.

Alliance for Excellent Education. (2006b). *Saving futures, saving dollars: The impact of education on crime reduction and earnings*. Washington, DC: Author.

Bridgeland, J., & di Iulio, J. (2006). *The silent epidemic: Perspectives of high school dropouts*. Washington, DC: Civic Enterprises.

Carnevale, A. P. (2001). *Help wanted . . . College required*. Washington, DC: Educational Testing Service, Office for Public Leadership.

Editorial Projects in Education. (2006, June 22). Diplomas count: An essential guide to graduation policy and rates. *Education Week, 25*(41S).

Garfinkel, I., Kelly, B., & Waldfogel, J. (2005). "Public assistance programs: How much could be saved with improved education?" Paper prepared for the symposium on the Social Costs of Inadequate Education, Teachers College Columbia University, October 2005.

Haveman, R., Wolfe, B., & Wilson, K. (2001). "Childhood events and circumstances influencing high school completion." *Demography, 28*(1).

Junn, J. (2005). "The political costs of unequal education." Paper prepared for the symposium on the Social Costs of Inadequate Education, Teachers College Columbia University, October 2005.

Muennig, P. (2005). "Health returns to education interventions." Paper prepared for the symposium on the Social Costs of Inadequate Education, Teachers College Columbia University, October 2005.

National Center for Education Statistics, Common Core of Data: 2002. Washington, DC: Institute of Education Sciences, U.S. Department of Education. Retrieved from http://nces.ed.gov/ccd/bat/ on November 15, 2006.

Organisation for Economic Co-Operation and Development. (2006). *Education at a glance*. Paris: Author.

Raphael, S. (2004). *The socioeconomic status of black males: The increasing importance of incarceration*. Goldman School of Public Policy, University of California, Berkeley.

Rouse, C. E. (2005). "Labor market consequences of an inadequate education." Paper prepared for the symposium on the Social Costs of Inadequate Education, Teachers College Columbia University, October 2005.

Swanson, C. (2004). *Who graduates? Who doesn't? A statistical portrait of public high school graduation, class of 2001*. Washington, DC: The Urban Institute, Education Policy Center.

U.S. Bureau of the Census. (2005). *Educational attainment in the United States: 2005*. Table 8. Washington, DC: U.S. Government Printing Office. Retrieved from http://www.census.gov/population/socdemo/education/cps2005/tab08-1.xls on November 15, 2006.

U.S. Department of Education, National Center for Education Statistics. (2004). *The condition of education 2004*. Washington, DC: U.S. Government Printing Office, Indicator 16, p. 61.

U.S. Department of Education, National Center for Education Statistics. (2005). *The nation's report card: Reading 2005*. Washington, DC: U.S. Government Printing Office.

Wolfe, B. L., & Haveman, R. H. (2002). "Social and non-market benefits from education in an advanced economy." Paper prepared for Conference Series 47, Education in the 21st Century: Meeting the Challenges of a Changing World, Federal Reserve Bank of Boston, June 2002.

PAYING DOUBLE: INADEQUATE HIGH SCHOOLS AND COMMUNITY COLLEGE REMEDIATION

Americans are beginning to recognize that many of the nation's high schools are in crisis, as policymakers, business leaders, and celebrities call attention to the country's low graduation rates. But the dropout problem, although severe, is only one indicator of the trouble plaguing the country's secondary schools.

Because too many students are not learning the basic skills needed to succeed in college or work while they are in high school, the nation loses more than $3.7 billion a year. This figure includes $1.4 billion to provide remedial education to students who have recently completed high school. In addition, this figure factors in the almost $2.3 billion that the economy loses because remedial reading students are more likely to drop out of college without a degree, thereby reducing their earning potential.

Of those who enter high school, only about 70 percent will graduate—one of the lowest rates among industrialized nations (Greene & Winters, 2006). As important, however, is the fact that, of those who do receive a diploma, only half are academically prepared for postsecondary education (Greene & Winters, 2005). A recent study of high school juniors and seniors taking the ACT college entrance exam confirms this; half of the students were ready for college-level reading assignments in core subjects like math, history, science, and English (ACT, 2006).

1201 Connecticut Avenue, NW - Suite 901 - Washington, DC 20036

Phone 202 828-0828 - Fax 202 828-0821 - www.all4ed.org

Despite these daunting statistics, the vast majority of America's high school students are optimistic about their prospects for the future, which they anticipate includes both higher education and rewarding careers. In fact, according to a recent national survey, an overwhelming 81 percent of high school students expect to attend college (High School Survey of Student Engagement, 2005). This is a wise goal, since 80 percent of the fastest-growing jobs in the United States require at least some postsecondary education, according to the U.S. Department of Labor (Hecker, 2005).

Playing Catch-Up: Getting the Knowledge and Skills Needed for College

When the increased demand for postsecondary education is coupled with the poor preparation many students receive in high school, it is perhaps not surprising that colleges and universities are being forced to offer, and often require, remedial courses to large numbers of students. These classes have the sole objective of teaching precollegiate subject matter.

Across the nation, 42 percent of community college freshmen and 20 percent of freshmen in four-year institutions enroll in at least one remedial course (NCES, 2004b). That is almost one-third of all freshmen. Community colleges already bear the greatest share of the remediation burden, and trends indicate that their responsibilities in this arena are likely to grow. For instance, eleven states have passed laws preventing or discouraging public four-year institutions from offering remedial courses to their students, thus concentrating unprepared students in community colleges (Jenkins & Boswell, 2002).

Analyses of students' preparation for college-level work show the weakness of core skills, such as basic study habits and the ability to understand and manage complicated material. The lack of preparation is also apparent in multiple subject areas; of college freshmen taking remedial courses, 35 percent were enrolled in math, 23 percent in writing, and 20 percent in reading (NCES, 2004b).

It is important to note that many students take remedial coursework for reasons having little to do with the failings of the nation's high schools. Community colleges have become a significant resource that offers opportunities to retrain laid-off workers, reeducate older students, and teach English to recent immigrants. Some of these enrollees are likely classified as "freshmen" and may be taking courses that are considered "remedial."

However, about half of all community college students are under the age of twenty-five (NCES, 2004c), and almost one-third of freshmen who take remedial courses are nineteen years old or younger (Phipps, 1998). Recent high school graduates are more likely to take remedial courses because higher percentages of them are pursuing bachelor's degrees, which require specified levels of preparation, than are older students. Additionally, younger students are more likely to be enrolled full-time than older students, and many community colleges do not require part-time students to enroll in remedial courses (Jenkins & Boswell, 2002).

Thus, the vast majority of students who take remedial courses in college do so to gain the skills and knowledge they should have gotten in high school and which are necessary for them to succeed in "regular" college classes. Most view the time, effort, and resources dedicated to remedial classes to be an additional investment in their academic futures.

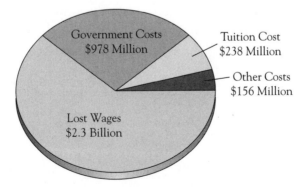

The Cost of Remediation

A number of components contribute to the high price that colleges, students and their families, and taxpayers pay to get students "up to speed" for postsecondary education. Colleges must pay faculty to teach the remedial courses; provide the classroom space; and supply a variety of support services, including counseling, administrative support, parking, facilities maintenance, etc. Often, because of trade-offs required by limited space and resources, schools must reduce the numbers of nonremedial courses offered to students, courses which would provide greater benefits to the community and its economy.

Through tuition, students and their families directly pay only about one-fifth of the overall cost of remediation. That relatively small portion totals approximately $283 million in community college tuition alone, but it is not the only cost. Another factor is students' time, which could be more productively spent taking college-level courses that would advance their goals and increase their earning potential. And because many colleges offer no credit for remedial courses, students are expending energy on study that, while necessary, delays the quest for a degree.

Taxpayers provide about a billion dollars a year to cover the direct and indirect instructional costs of remedial courses, through the subsidies which community colleges receive from state and local governments. These tax dollars are in addition to the taxes

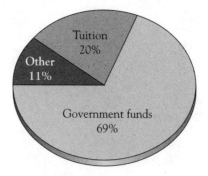

allocated to support communities' secondary schools. Thus, taxpayers are essentially paying twice for the coursework and skill development students are expected to receive in high school.

Economically, Remediation is a Poor Substitute for Preparation

Individual states, and the nation as a whole, are not only paying to academically remediate thousands of young adults, but they are also facing future financial loss because students who need remediation are more likely to leave college without a degree, becoming more likely to earn less than if they had gotten a college diploma. Research shows that the *leading predictor* that a student will drop out of college is the need for remedial reading. While 58 percent of students who take no remedial education courses earn a bachelor's degree within eight years, only 17 percent of students who enroll in a remedial reading course receive a B.A. or B.S. within the same time period (NCES, 2004a).

Students who enroll in a remedial reading course are 41 percent more likely to drop out of college (NCES, *The Condition of Education*, 2004).

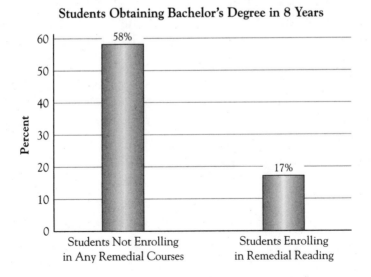

Students Obtaining Bachelor's Degree in 8 Years

The wages of individuals with some college average about $20,171 less each year than those of college graduates. Therefore, when students enter but do not complete college, not only do they lose future income, but governments take in less tax revenue, and state and national economies are deprived of the additional earnings that would make them stronger and more robust.

Losing Now and Losing Later

The nation would realize an additional $3.7 billion annually in combined reduced expenditures and increased earnings if:

- More students who graduate from high school were prepared for college, and thus did not require remediation; and
- The students who drop out of college because they were not prepared for college-level reading demands were to continue and earn a bachelor's degree at the same rate as nonremedial students.

The chart on the last page of this Issue Brief shows the breakdown of this national figure by state.

However, the real price of college remediation is likely much higher than this conservative estimate, which does not include the costs of remediation for students attending public or private four-year colleges, or for older community college students. Nor does it count other, noncommunity-college-related remediation expenditures. There are additional costs, such as the cost for employers who either provide training programs to teach basic skills to employees or must purchase technology which substitutes for the lack of basic skills among employees, as well as the costs of programs offered and paid for by nonprofits and government agencies that include training in adult literacy, technology, and other academic and occupational skills.

Reducing the Need for Remediation by Improving High Schools

America's high schools are not preparing many of their students for the demands of both college and the modern workforce. Weak curricula, vague standards, and lack of alignment between high school content and the expectations of colleges and employers result in the need for remediation. In order to graduate students prepared for success, high schools must align the content of their coursework with the skills and knowledge students need in today's increasingly competitive and demanding world. If students are effectively taught what they need to know in high school, the need for remediation in college will drop dramatically.

A rigorous high school curriculum is a strong predictor of college readiness (Adelman, 2006). Students who take challenging coursework, such as four years of college-preparatory English and three years each of college-preparatory mathematics, science, and social studies, are less likely to need remedial courses than students who don't take such a rigorous curriculum (Abraham & Creech, 2002).

Statewide performance standards for college admission would enable educators to assess student progress toward readiness for college. Such standards would also convey clear expectations to students, parents, and high schools regarding student performance. States with these standards in place, such as West Virginia and Florida, have seen a long-term decline in the proportion of students who need remediation (although the number of students needing remediation initially rose due to the higher standard; Abraham & Creech, 2002).

Reforming the nation's high schools will not be an easy process, and the kind of comprehensive school reform needed to ensure that all students have the opportunity to succeed and graduate prepared for the future is not simple. But in an increasingly global economy, American secondary schools and their students must achieve at increasingly higher levels to allow the country to maintain its competitive advantage. Ensuring that all secondary students are prepared to succeed in college and work is a giant step in the right direction for this country and will benefit individuals and society for decades to come.

For more information about the state of America's high schools and to find out what individuals and organizations can do to support effective reform at the local, state, and federal levels, visit the Alliance for Excellent Education's website at www.all4ed.org.

This issue brief was made possible with the generous support of MetLife Foundation.

Annual Savings and Earnings Benefits from a Reduced Need for Community College Remediation[1]

State	Annual Remediation Savings	Additional Annual Earnings	Total Benefit to State Economy
Alabama	$23,985,384	$29,063,995	$53,049,379
Alaska	$182,126	$489,822	$671,948
Arizona	$32,949,507	$70,778,193	$103,727,700
Arkansas	$8,151,404	$14,897,902	$23,049,306
California	$135,307,841	$552,597,892	$687,905,733
Colorado	$21,208,099	$30,906,311	$52,114,410
Connecticut	$12,593,382	$16,401,363	$28,994,745
Delaware	$3,042,392	$4,637,957	$7,680,349
District of Columbia	$782,861	$806,772	$1,589,634
Florida	$70,920,812	$122,832,024	$193,752,835
Georgia	$27,716,795	$47,754,362	$75,471,157
Hawaii	$4,298,600	$9,355,236	$13,653,836
Idaho	$2,295,457	$4,195,290	$6,490,747
Illinois	$80,904,713	$129,292,923	$210,197,636
Indiana	$17,917,376	$22,366,592	$40,283,968
Iowa	$26,015,510	$27,063,035	$53,078,545
Kansas	$15,470,969	$27,368,260	$42,839,229
Kentucky	$24,728,740	$27,543,353	$52,272,093
Louisiana	$10,031,411	$17,465,447	$27,496,858
Maine	$3,991,127	$3,667,451	$7,658,579
Maryland	$37,973,289	$42,012,478	$79,985,767
Massachusetts	$26,026,101	$31,081,404	$57,107,505
Michigan	$50,519,097	$75,963,362	$126,482,459
Minnesota	$48,902,190	$40,241,442	$89,143,633
Mississippi	$12,452,546	$24,519,981	$36,972,527
Missouri	$21,579,586	$31,447,674	$53,027,260
Montana	$2,025,704	$2,702,063	$4,727,767
Nebraska	$8,947,788	$13,831,625	$22,779,413
Nevada	$8,564,638	$17,275,732	$25,840,371
New Hampshire	$7,971,978	$5,170,913	$13,142,891
New Jersey	$44,825,218	$50,782,121	$95,607,339

(continued)

Annual Savings and Earnings Benefits from a Reduced Need for Community College Remediation[1] (continued)

New Mexico	$9,788,171	$22,027,006	$31,815,177
New York	$98,614,826	$93,473,405	$192,088,230
North Carolina	$27,632,861	$69,779,176	$97,412,036
North Dakota	$2,917,150	$3,271,207	$6,188,358
Ohio	$69,286,395	$62,795,190	$132,081,585
Oklahoma	$16,039,658	$23,477,830	$39,517,488
Oregon	$30,209,541	$34,107,335	$64,316,875
Pennsylvania	$81,846,059	$43,113,116	$124,959,175
Rhode Island	$1,918,568	$5,822,669	$7,741,237
South Carolina	$26,383,966	$27,884,767	$54,268,732
South Dakota	$1,969,637	$1,992,552	$3,962,189
Tennessee	$19,648,932	$27,196,457	$46,845,389
Texas	$88,507,734	$193,898,993	$282,406,727
Utah	$6,807,382	$10,878,802	$17,686,184
Vermont	$2,747,050	$1,821,115	$4,568,165
Virginia	$36,615,053	$55,307,858	$91,922,911
Washington	$55,887,556	$69,503,194	$125,390,750
West Virginia	$1,363,464	$2,451,304	$3,814,768
Wisconsin	$43,227,424	$42,942,409	$86,169,833
Wyoming	$3,564,487	$6,550,822	$10,115,309
United States	$1,417,258,558	$2,292,808,179	$3,710,066,738

[1]Annual remediation savings were estimated by multiplying the cost of one course by the number of students under twenty-five years of age who take at least one remedial course. The College Board estimates that student tuition covers one-fifth of the cost of education. Therefore, to calculate the full cost of a community college course, annual tuition was multiplied by five. The resulting number was then divided by ten, which is the average number of courses a student takes over two semesters. To estimate the number of students under twenty-five years of age who enroll in at least one remedial course, the percent of students under twenty-five years of age (52 percent) was multiplied by the percent (42.5 percent) of public, two-year students who report enrolling in at least one remedial course (NCES, 2004c). District of Columbia data are based on the University of the District of Columbia, which has open enrollment.

To calculate additional annual earnings, the salary difference between students who attend "some college" and students who earn a bachelor's degree was multiplied by the number of students who would have graduated if they didn't need remedial reading (potential new graduates). Using 2004 NCES data, the number of potential new college graduates was calculated by multiplying the remedial student count (above) by the percentage (20 percent) of community college freshmen enrolled in remedial reading and by 41 percent, the difference in bachelor's degree attainment between those who enroll in remedial reading (17 percent) and those who do not (58 percent). This new graduate count was then multiplied by the average earnings difference between "some college" and "bachelor's degree," as listed in 2005 Census data.

References

Abraham, A., & Creech, J. (2002). *Reducing remedial education: What progress are states making?* Atlanta, GA: Southern Regional Education Board.

ACT. (2006). *Reading between the lines: What the ACT reveals about college readiness in reading.* Iowa City, IA: Author.

Adelman, C. (2006). *The toolbox revisited: Paths to degree completion from high school through college.* Washington, DC: U.S. Department of Education.

Greene, J., & Winters, M. (2005). *Public high school graduation and college-readiness rates: 1991–2002.* New York: Manhattan Institute.

Greene, J., & Winters, M. (2006). *Leaving boys behind: Public high school graduation rates.* New York: Manhattan Institute.

Hecker, D. (2005). Occupational employment projections to 2014. *Monthly Labor Review, 128*(11), 75.

High School Survey of Student Engagement [HSSSE]. (2005). *HSSSE 2004 overview.* Bloomington, IN: Indiana University, HSSSE.

Jenkins, D., & Boswell, K. (2002). *State policies on community college remedial education: Findings from a national survey.* Denver, CO: Education Commission of the States.

National Center for Education Statistics [NCES]. (2004a). *The condition of education 2004, indicator 18: Remediation and degree completion.* Washington, DC: U.S. Department of Education.

National Center for Education Statistics. (2004b). *The condition of education 2004, indicator 31: Remedial coursetaking.* Washington, DC: U.S. Department of Education.

National Center for Education Statistics. (2004c). *National postsecondary student aid study.* Data Analysis Systems (DAS-T) online computation, run on April 10, 2006. Analysis by the Alliance for Excellent Education.

Phillipe, K., & Sullivan, L. G. (2005). *National profile of community colleges: Trends and statistics.* Washington, DC: American Association of Community Colleges.

Phipps, R. (1998). *College remediation: What it is, what it costs, what's at stake.* Washington, DC: Institute for Higher Education Policy.

SAVING FUTURES, SAVING DOLLARS: THE IMPACT OF EDUCATION ON CRIME REDUCTION AND EARNINGS

America's standard of living and international competitiveness will be strengthened if its high schools are improved. Research indicates that about 75 percent of America's state prison inmates, almost 59 percent of federal inmates, and 69 percent of jail inmates did not complete high school. Additionally, the number of prison inmates without a high school diploma has increased over time (Harlow, 2003). Reforming the nation's high schools could potentially increase the number of graduates and, as a result, significantly reduce the nation's crime-related costs and add billions of dollars to the economy through the additional wages they would earn. Increasing the graduation rate and college matriculation of male students by only 5 percent could lead to combined savings and revenue of almost $8 billion each year.

To achieve those savings and that additional revenue, the nation's schools—especially its high schools—must change for the better. Only about 70 percent of students—approximately 65 percent of males and 73 percent of females—currently graduate from America's high schools on time (Editorial Projects in Education [EPE], 2006).

Crime Reduction Through Better Education

Lower educational attainment levels increase the likelihood that individuals, particularly males, will be arrested and/or incarcerated. For instance, a study that looked at state prisoners' education levels in 1997 showed that "male inmates were about twice as likely as their counterparts in the general population to not have completed high school or its equivalent," and four times as many males in the general population had attended some college or other postsecondary classes than those in prison (Harlow, 2003).

Theories abound as to why people with more education commit less crime. To list a few:

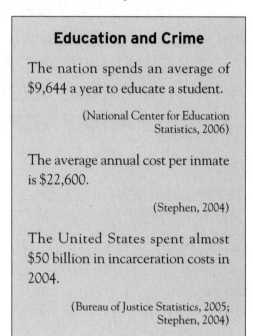

Education and Crime

The nation spends an average of $9,644 a year to educate a student.

(National Center for Education Statistics, 2006)

The average annual cost per inmate is $22,600.

(Stephen, 2004)

The United States spent almost $50 billion in incarceration costs in 2004.

(Bureau of Justice Statistics, 2005; Stephen, 2004)

- People who have high school diplomas or better earn higher wages through legitimate work, thus reducing the individual's perceived need to commit a crime and/or raising the potential cost of crime to that person (i.e., getting caught and being incarcerated) to unacceptable levels.

- The stigma of a criminal conviction may be greater for professional workers, who tend to have higher levels of education, than for those in lower-paying, lower-skilled jobs.

- More time spent in the classroom may play a role in instilling values that are opposed to criminal actions.

- Criminal behavior that begins during youth can continue into adulthood. By keeping adolescents in the classroom and off the streets, later criminal activity may be avoided (Lochner & Moretti, 2004).

Whatever the underlying causes, education clearly has a strong impact on crime prevention and the personal safety of Americans.

Obviously, dropping out of school does not automatically result in a life of crime; the vast majority of individuals who leave high school without diplomas are, and remain, law-abiding citizens. High school dropouts, however, are far more *likely* than other people to be arrested or incarcerated. Estimates vary somewhat; the Coalition for Juvenile Justice finds that "dropouts are three and a half times more likely than high school graduates to be arrested" (2001), while a more recent survey of dropouts concludes that they are "more than eight times as likely to be in jail or prison" (Bridgeland, DiIulio & Morison, 2006). However the numbers are calculated, the larger message remains the same: individuals with lower levels of education are more likely to commit crimes and be jailed than their better educated peers.

Crime Doesn't Pay; Diplomas Do

The financial cost of crime to communities, states, and the nation cannot be overstated. It includes expenses related to medical care for victims, loss of victims' income, reduced tax revenue as a result of lost wages, and rising police payrolls and court operating budgets. Most expensive of all is the cost of incarcerating convicted criminals.

Using methods outlined by economists Lance Lochner of the University of Western Ontario and Enrico Moretti of the University of California, Berkeley (2004), the Alliance for Excellent Education conservatively estimates that if the male graduation rate were increased by just 5 percent, *annual crime-related savings* to the nation would be approximately $5 billion dollars. The benefits would vary from state to state: South Dakota (at the low end) would save

$1.6 million, Oklahoma (near the middle) would save $63 million, and California (at the high end) would save almost $753 million.

Beyond the savings related directly to crime reduction, almost $2.8 billion in *additional annual earnings* would enter the economy if more students graduated from high school. Using 2004 U.S. Census Current Population Survey data, the Alliance calculates that if an additional 5 percent of male students not only graduated, but also went on to college in the same percentages as current male high school graduates, their average earnings would increase significantly. The benefits, again, would vary from state to state: Wyoming (at the low end) would see an increase of $5 million, Massachusetts (near the middle) would add $55 million to its economy, and California's economy (at the high end) would accrue an additional $352 million. These numbers reflect only additional wages earned, without considering the added economic growth produced by each new dollar in the economy or the additional tax revenues that would be produced.

Education and Crime

A ten percent increase in the male graduation rate would reduce murder and assault arrest rates by about 20 percent, motor vehicle theft by 13 percent, and arson by 8 percent.

(Moretti, 2005)

Of black males who graduated from high school and went on to attend some college, only 5 percent were incarcerated in 2000.

(Raphael, 2004)

Of white males who graduated from high school and went on to attend some college, only 1 percent were incarcerated in 2000.

(Raphael, 2004)

State prison inmates without a high school diploma and those with a GED were more likely to be repeat offenders than those with a diploma.

(Harlow, 2003)

State-by-state estimates of the annual economic benefits generated from crime-related savings and additional annual earnings can be seen in the chart on the last page of this Issue Brief.

High School Improvement Is Key to Graduating More Students

To increase the number of students who graduate, the nation's schools—particularly its high schools—must dramatically improve. Low graduation rates are particularly severe in urban areas and in schools serving large numbers of poor and minority students. The Editorial Projects in Education Research Center estimates that of the approximately four million students who entered ninth grade four years ago, 1.2 million did not graduate with a regular diploma this year. Only about 52 percent of African American and 56 percent of Hispanic students graduate on time, compared to 76 percent of their white peers (EPE, 2006).

> Over a third of jail inmates said the main reason they quit school was because of academic problems, behavior problems, or lost interest.
>
> (Harlow, 2003)

Transforming high schools with the goal of having every student graduate ready for college or a good job is not easy. There is no silver bullet, but researchers and educators are developing and implementing innovative programs and interventions to help students—even those who enter ninth grade performing far below grade level—graduate successfully. Much is known about what students need to achieve at high levels academically, and some schools and districts are applying this knowledge with excellent results.

Policies must be put into place at the national, state, and local levels that will support effective reforms and innovative practices. Interventions that bring struggling students up to grade level and experiences that bring real-world relevance into classrooms are critical, as are school environments that support excellence in teaching and learning.

Improving high schools will lead to increased graduation rates, which will result in lowered crime and incarceration rates and increased economic activity. Individuals, communities, states, and the nation will be the beneficiaries.

For more information about the state of America's high schools and to find out what individuals and organizations can do to support effective reform at the local, state, and federal levels, visit the Alliance for Excellent Education's website at www.all4ed.org.

This issue brief was made possible with the generous support of MetLife Foundation.

The Impact of a Five Percent Increase in Male High School Graduation Rates on Crime Reduction and Earnings[1]

State	Annual Crime-Related Savings	Additional Annual Earnings	Total Benefit to State Economy
Alabama	$82,114,178	$42,695,448	$124,809,626
Alaska	$10,385,910	$8,229,446	$18,615,356
Arizona	$130,548,518	$53,146,250	$183,694,768
Arkansas	$52,527,329	$24,825,605	$77,352,934
California	$752,933,848	$352,182,007	$1,105,115,855
Colorado	$49,051,830	$42,954,144	$92,005,974
Connecticut	$31,624,059	$31,692,936	$63,316,995
Delaware	$9,923,632	$7,271,214	$17,194,846
District of Columbia	$66,503,310	$3,237,663	$69,740,973
Florida	$332,386,028	$174,243,833	$506,629,861
Georgia	$185,633,644	$90,744,324	$276,377,968
Hawaii	$6,835,886	$11,203,133	$18,039,020
Idaho	$7,374,662	$13,817,814	$21,192,476
Illinois	$263,078,679	$115,756,032	$378,834,711
Indiana	$95,731,795	$56,133,136	$151,864,932
Iowa	$17,544,077	$26,798,824	$44,342,901
Kansas	$36,327,968	$26,397,581	$62,725,549
Kentucky	$50,190,235	$37,221,909	$87,412,144
Louisiana	$164,467,403	$39,778,515	$204,245,917
Maine	$3,046,026	$11,679,610	$14,725,636
Maryland	$160,557,762	$50,869,458	$211,427,220
Massachusetts	$59,187,389	$55,535,231	$114,722,620
Michigan	$175,304,759	$105,034,655	$280,339,414
Minnesota	$30,608,540	$47,171,157	$77,779,698
Mississippi	$66,976,174	$26,274,832	$93,251,006
Missouri	$95,613,931	$51,781,495	$147,395,426
Montana	$10,637,756	$8,967,258	$19,605,015
Nebraska	$16,519,921	$16,469,451	$32,989,371
Nevada	$55,973,838	$22,464,341	$78,438,180
New Hampshire	$3,397,405	$12,032,017	$15,429,423
New Jersey	$120,008,948	$69,283,091	$189,292,039

(continued)

The Impact of a Five Percent Increase in Male High School Graduation Rates on Crime Reduction and Earnings[1] *(continued)*

New Mexico	$37,905,377	$19,840,422	$57,745,799
New York	$286,896,473	$170,426,743	$457,323,216
North Carolina	$151,947,826	$80,880,868	$232,828,694
North Dakota	$2,480,026	$6,408,013	$8,888,039
Ohio	$126,369,800	$106,527,438	$232,897,238
Oklahoma	$63,248,994	$33,164,601	$96,413,595
Oregon	$21,053,644	$30,029,888	$51,083,532
Pennsylvania	$182,071,834	$106,127,515	$288,199,349
Rhode Island	$5,946,578	$9,485,971	$15,432,549
South Carolina	$105,184,170	$45,366,883	$150,551,053
South Dakota	$1,636,287	$7,048,154	$8,684,441
Tennessee	$132,841,628	$50,196,980	$183,038,608
Texas	$428,340,492	$263,016,258	$691,356,750
Utah	$15,180,026	$24,155,106	$39,335,132
Vermont	$3,518,159	$5,783,710	$9,301,869
Virginia	$109,091,336	$70,200,407	$179,291,743
Washington	$50,235,943	$60,499,296	$110,735,239
West Virginia	$19,811,155	$15,995,614	$35,806,769
Wisconsin	$47,775,714	$53,395,707	$101,171,421
Wyoming	$4,467,005	$5,081,534	$9,548,539
United States	$4,939,017,909	$2,799,523,519	$7,738,541,428

[1] Crime-related savings were calculated using methods outlined by economists Lance Lochner and Enrico Moretti (2004), which estimate the costs (e.g., incarceration, property loss, and costs to victims) of crimes such as murder, rape, robbery, assault, burglary, larceny, and motor vehicle theft and the percent change in those crimes based on a 1 percent increase in the male graduation rate. For this Alliance analysis, 2003 Uniform Crime Report data on the number of crimes in each state were multiplied by the percent change for each crime due to a 5 percent increase in the male graduation rate. Increased earnings were calculated using 2004 U.S. Census Current Population Survey data, which finds that, on average, male, year-round, full-time workers of all races who are high school dropouts earn $11,173 less than high school graduates, $19,174 less than those that attend some college, and $53,850 less than those with a bachelor's degree or higher. According to the National Center for Education Statistics' 2003 Condition of Education report, of male students finishing high school, 26.3 percent earn only a high school diploma, 46.8 percent attend some college, and 26.9 percent earn a bachelor's degree or higher. These educational attainment percentages were then multiplied by the number of additional male high school graduates, assuming a 5 percent increase in the male high school graduation rate. Finally, the number of additional students attaining these levels of education was multiplied by the earnings difference between a high school dropout and each respective level of educational attainment.

References

Bridgeland, J., DiIulio, J., & Morison, K. (2006). *The silent epidemic: Perspectives of high school dropouts*. Washington, DC: Civic Enterprises.

Bureau of Justice Statistics (1995). *Prisoners in 1994*. Washington, DC: U.S. Department of Justice, Bureau of Justice Statistics.

Bureau of Justice Statistics (2005). *Prison Statistics*. Washington, DC: U.S. Department of Justice, Bureau of Justice Statistics. Retrieved from http://www.ojp.usdoj.gov/bjs/prisons.htm on July 13, 2006.

Coalition for Juvenile Justice. (2001). *Abandoned in the back row: New lessons in education and delinquency prevention*. Washington, DC: Author.

Editorial Projects in Education [EPE]. (2006). Diplomas count: An essential guide to graduation policy and rates. *Education Week, 25*(41S), 6.

Harlow, C. (2003). *Education and correctional populations*. Bureau of Justice Statistics Special Report. Washington, DC: U.S. Department of Justice.

Lochner, L., & Moretti, E. (2004). The effect of education on crime: Evidence from prison inmates, arrests and self-reports. *American Economic Review, 94*(1), 155–189.

Moretti, E. (October 2005). *Does education reduce participation in criminal activities?* Research presented at the 2005 Symposium on the Social Costs of Inadequate Education. Teachers College, Columbia University, New York.

National Center for Education Statistics [NCES]. (2003). *The condition of education 2003, indicator 22: Postsecondary attainment of 1988 8th-graders*. Washington, DC: U.S. Department of Education. Retrieved from http://nces.ed.gov/programs/coe/2003/pdf/22_2003.pdf on July 13, 2006.

National Center for Education Statistics. (2006). *The condition of education 2006*. Washington, DC: U.S. Department of Education.

Raphael, S. (2004). *The socioeconomic status of black males: The increasing importance of incarceration*. Berkeley: Goldman School of Public Policy, University of California.

Stephen, J. (2004). *State prison expenditures, 2001*. Bureau of Justice Statistics Special Report. Washington, DC: U.S. Department of Justice.

U.S. Census Bureau. (2005). *Current population survey, table 9: Earnings in 2003 by educational attainment of workers 18 years and over, by age, sex, race alone, and Hispanic origin*. Washington, DC: Author. Retrieved from http://www.census.gov/population/socdemo/education/cps2004/tab09-2.pdf on July 13, 2006.

U.S. Department of Justice. (1990). *Crime in the United States*. Washington, DC: Author. Retrieved from http://www.ojp.usdoj.gov/bjs/ on January 24, 2006.

U.S. Department of Justice. (2003). *Crime in the United States*. Washington, DC: Author. Retrieved from http://www.fbi.gov/ucr/03cius.htm on January 24, 2006.

Elements of a Successful High School: Advocacy Action Matrix

For the most effective use of the Advocacy Action Matrix, refer also to the Ten Elements of a Successful High School brochure at www.all4ed.org.

Target Audience	Local	State	National
Action Level			
Students	Tell your teachers, counselors, relatives, and friends that you want and expect to go to college. Make sure that your counselor has enrolled you in a course of study that prepares you for college. Develop a plan for graduation, college, and career with the help of your counselor, parents, guardian, or mentor.	Make a video of students giving testimonials about their high school experiences.	Make a video of students giving testimonials about their high school experiences.
	Take pictures, make a video, keep a diary, or make a list of the problems students in your high school face. Post this information on a website for classmates and others who may be interested.	Call or write to your Congress members and ask them to review the video and share it with their colleagues.	Call or write to your Congress members and ask them to review the video and share it with their colleagues.
	Talk to your parents or other family members about the problems in your high school. Ask your parents or guardian to join and seek change through a parent education organization or other local organization dedicated to education reform.	Organize your friends and classmates to launch a letter writing campaign requesting that your governor, chief state school officer, and state representatives and senators reform high schools for the better.	Organize your friends and classmates to launch a letter writing campaign requesting that the president and Congress reform high schools for the better.
		Organize a group of students to take a trip to your state's capitol to schedule meetings with state legislators.	Organize a group of students to take a trip to Washington, D.C., to schedule meetings with congressional representatives and senators.

(continued)

Target Audience	Local	State	National
Action Level			
	Write a letter to the school newspaper or local newspaper editor to share your views about how to make high schools better.		
	Launch a civic engagement activity with your classmates, seeking to share your views with the mayor, city council members, business leaders, and school administrators in your city. Ask local business leaders to sponsor a high school community forum, video showing, or student advocacy trip to the state capitol or Washington, D.C.		
Parents	Talk with your teenager regularly to assess the quality of education he or she is getting. Make sure your teenager attends classes regularly and on time.	Invite your elected officials to visit your child's high school to engage administrators, teachers, and students in conversation about how high schools should be improved.	Invite your elected officials to visit your child's high school to engage administrators, teachers, and students in conversation about how high schools should be improved.

Visit your state's school report card website to learn more about your high school's graduation, drop-out, literacy, and school safety rates and visit www.schoolmatters.com to compare your school to others in your area.

If you want your teenager to graduate on time prepared for college, talk to his or her teacher and counselor to ensure that your teenager is enrolled in a college preparatory curriculum and is on track to meet the school's graduation requirements.

If your teenager's grades or teacher indicates that it is needed, make sure that he or she gets extra tutoring after school. If your school does not provide after-school tutoring, contact your city mayor's office to locate programs run by community organizations.

Write letters to, call, or request a meeting with your state elected representatives to share your concerns and the need for reform. Visit www.congress.org to find contact information.

Contact the Public Education Network (www.publiceducation.org) to find an advocacy organization near you focused on high school reform.

Work with the Parent Teacher Association (www.pta.org) or another advocacy organization to develop or participate in a lobby day at the state capitol focused on high school education accountability and reform.

Write letters to, call, or request a meeting with your congressional representatives to share your concerns and the need for reform. Visit www.congress.org to find contact information.

Contact the Alliance for Excellent Education online at www.all4ed.org or Public Education Network at www.publiceducation.org to find a national advocacy organization focused on high school reform.

Join with an organization to participate in a lobby day at the U.S. Capitol focused on high school education accountability and reform.

(continued)

Target Audience	Local	State	National
Action Level			
	Contact your school district superintendent to find out whether the district has plans to implement high school reforms. Request immediate action if no initiative is planned.	Contact your chief state school officer to request more information about your state's plans for improving high schools. Visit www.ccsso.org to find contact information.	Contact the assistant secretary for communications and outreach at the U.S. Department of Education (www.ed.gov) to request more information about its plans for reforming high schools.
	Write an article for your local paper or community newsletter about your observations or experiences.	If there are not enough library, computer, or textbook resources in your child's school, ask your state legislators and chief school officer to seek more support for your high school and others like it. Visit www.congress.org and www.ccsso.org to locate your representatives and school officers.	Ask your congressional representatives to increase federal funding support for high schools.
	Start or become active in your school's parent education organization, the Parent Teacher Association (www.pta.org), or another local school group to get more resources to help your student and convince local members to champion high school reform.		Visit the Alliance for Excellent Education online (www.all4ed.org) to sign up for updates on national high school reform initiatives and congressional action alerts.
	Contact your local school board to get a meeting schedule. Attend meetings, and demand they give more attention to high school reform.		

	Although your local elected officials may not have direct responsibility for your area schools, request a meeting with, call, or send a letter to your mayor or city council members to discuss strategies for raising community awareness about high school reform.		
Concerned citizens	Visit www.schoolmatters.com to download your state's high school report cards. Write an article for your local paper or newsletter about your observations or experiences. Contact your local school board to get a meeting schedule. Attend meetings and demand they give more attention to high school reform.	Write letters to, call, or request a meeting with your state elected representatives to share your concerns and the need for reform. Visit www.congress.org to find contact information. Contact the Public Education Network (www.publiceducation.org) to find an advocacy organization near you focused on high school reform.	Write letters to, call, or request a meeting with your congressional representatives to share your concerns and the need for reform. Visit www.congress.org to find contact information. Contact the Alliance for Excellent Education (www.all4ed.org) or Public Education Network (www.publiceducation.org) to find a national advocacy organization focused on high school reform.

(continued)

Target Audience	Local	State	National
Action Level			
	Contact your school district superintendent to find out whether the district has plans to implement high school reforms. Request immediate action if no initiative is planned.	Join with an organization to participate in a lobby day at the state capitol focused on high school education accountability and reform.	Join with an organization to participate in a lobby day at the U.S. Capitol focused on high school education accountability and reform.
	Although your local elected officials may not have direct responsibility for your area schools, request a meeting with, call, or send a letter to your mayor or city council members to discuss strategies for raising community awareness about high school reform.	Contact your chief state school officer to request more information about your state's plans for improving high schools. Visit www.ccsso.org to find contact information for your chief state school officer.	Contact the assistant secretary for communications and outreach at the U.S. Department of Education (www.ed.gov) to request more information about plans for reforming high schools.
	Contact the Public Education Network (www.publiceducation.org) to find an advocacy organization near you focused on high school reform.	If there are not enough library, computer, or textbook resources in your local schools, ask your state legislators and chief school officer to seek more support for these and other high schools. Visit www.congress.org and www.ccsso.org to locate your representatives and school officers.	Ask your congressional representatives to increase federal funding support for high schools.
			Visit the Alliance for Excellent Education online (www.all4ed.org) to sign up for updates about national high school reform initiatives and congressional action alerts.

Advocacy organizations	Connect with an existing "P–20 council" (or ask your governor to establish one) that coordinates state education from prekindergarten through graduate education. Visit www.schoolmatters.com to download your state's high school report cards. Create score cards measuring the quality of high schools in your area. Publicize score cards and other information about local high schools to area residents and community groups by issuing a press release and distributing score cards at grocery stores, malls, banks, churches, and special events.	Organize a lobby day at the state capitol focused on high school education accountability and reform. Organize a letter writing campaign to state elected officials calling for high school education accountability and reform.	Organize a meeting with your congressional representatives when they are home in your district. Organize a letter writing campaign to the U.S. Congress calling for high school education accountability and reform. Ask your congressional representatives to increase federal funding support for high schools.

(*continued*)

Target Audience	Local	State	National
Action Level			
	Disseminate "Elements of Successful Schools" brochures to parents, PTA members, and other community advocacy groups to help them understand the features of a good school.	If there are not enough library, computer, or textbook resources in your local schools, ask your state legislators and chief school officer to seek more support for these and other high schools. Visit www.congress.org and www.ccsso.org to locate your representatives and school officers.	Visit the Alliance for Excellent Education online at www.all4ed.org to sign up for updates about national high school reform initiatives and congressional action alerts.
		Connect with an existing "P–20 council" (or ask the governor to establish one) that coordinates state education from prekindergarten through graduate education.	Organize a lobby day at the U.S. Capitol focused on high school education accountability and reform.

Educators and administrators	Visit www.schoolmatters.com to download your state's high school report cards.	Contact the Parent Teacher Association (www.pta.org) or professional organizations for educators to find out if they sponsor state lobby initiatives. If so, attend and support lobby initiatives focused on educating state elected officials about the need for stronger high schools.	Contact professional organizations for educators to find out if they sponsor federal lobby initiatives. If so, attend and support lobby initiatives focused on educating your congressional representatives about the need for stronger high schools.
	Research best practices and incorporate techniques into the high school or classroom setting.		Ask your congressional representatives to increase federal funding support for high schools.
	Visit schools and districts that have adopted or are undertaking significant high school reforms.		Visit the Alliance for Excellent Education online (www.all4ed.org) to sign up for updates about national high school reform initiatives and congressional action alerts.
	Pursue professional development opportunities that incorporate new thinking about high school curriculum and instruction.		
	If you work in the school, connect with your school district superintendent to share why high school reform is important. Request a districtwide in-service day highlighting best practices in high school reform.		

(continued)

Target Audience	Local	State	National
Action Level		If there are not enough library, computer, or textbook resources in your school, ask your state legislators and chief school officer to seek more support for your high school and others like it. Visit www.congress.org and www.ccsso.org to locate your representatives and school officers.	
		Connect with an existing "P–20 council" (or ask the governor to establish one) that coordinates state education from prekindergarten through graduate education.	

Business leaders		
Convene an ongoing business roundtable examining the performance of high schools in your city or town.	Convene an ongoing business roundtable examining the performance of high schools in your state.	Educate your congressional representatives about the relationship between quality high schools and workforce preparedness and the need for twenty-first-century secondary school reforms.
Establish partnerships with local high schools that provide internship opportunities, training resources, and other supports for schools, educators, and students.	Host a meeting with business leaders, the chief state school officer, and the governor to discuss how to achieve high school reform.	Ask your congressional representatives to increase federal funding support for high schools.
Sponsor an education leadership summit that brings together educators, administrators, parents, and community leaders to discuss and develop an action plan for high school reform.	Connect to, or create, a business-education partnership to advance school improvement.	Visit the Alliance for Excellent Education online (www.all4ed.org) to sign up for updates about national high school reform initiatives and congressional action alerts.
Host a meeting of local school district superintendents to find out if the district has plans to implement high school reforms.	Work with state officials to develop a plan of action to increase graduation rates and improve the skills of the state's workforce.	

(continued)

Target Audience / Action Level	Local	State	National
	Work with local officials and school district superintendents to coordinate high school curricula and activities with desired workforce skills.	Educate state elected officials about the relationship between quality high schools and workforce preparedness and the need for high school reforms. Connect with an existing "P–20 council" (or ask the governor to establish one) that coordinates state education from prekindergarten through graduate education.	
Elected officials	Visit high schools and talk with administrators, teachers, parents, and students about how high schools should be improved. Hold hearings highlighting effective high school reform efforts.	Hold hearings on effective high school reform efforts. Convene state business, education, and community leaders to highlight best practices and discuss educational reforms.	Hold hearings on effective high school reform efforts. Convene national business, education, and community leaders to highlight best practices and discuss educational reforms.

Convene local business, education, and community leaders to discuss best practices and how to implement educational reforms.

Develop and pass model legislation to strengthen high school education.

Develop and pass model legislation to strengthen high school education.

Connect with an existing "P–20 council" (or ask the governor to establish one) that coordinates state education from prekindergarten through graduate education.

Develop and pass model legislation to strengthen high school education.

Visit the Alliance for Excellent Education online at www.all4ed.org to sign up for updates about national high school reform initiatives.

1201 Connecticut Avenue, NW, Suite 901, Washington, DC 20036 • 202.828.0828 T • 202.828.0821 F • www.all4ed.org

Notes

Chapter One

1. National Commission on Excellence in Education, *A Nation At Risk: The Imperative for Educational Reform*, U.S. Government Printing. Office, Washington, D.C., 1983.
2. Wise, Mike. "We Got No Game: Poor Fundamentals Cost Americans a Shot at Gold." *Washington Post*, August, 2004, A01.
3. Lemke, Mariann et al. 2004. *International Outcomes of Learning in Mathematics Literacy and Problem Solving: PISA 2003 Results From the U.S. Perspective.* (NCES 2005–003). Washington, DC: NCES, U.S. Department of Education.
4. Organisation for Economic Co-operation and Development (OECD). *Programme for International Student Assessment(PISA) 2006: Science Competencies for Tomorrow's World.* Paris: OECD, 2007.
5. Educational Testing Service (ETS). *America's Perfect Storm: Three Forces Changing Our Nation's Future.* Washington, D.C.: ETS, Jan. 2007.
6. National Center for Education Statistics (NCES). Lee, J., Grigg, W., and Donahue, P. *The Nation's Report Card: Reading 2007*(NCES 2007-496). NCES, Institute for Education Sciences, U.S. Department of Education, Washington, DC: 2007.
7. Balfanz, R., McPartland, J. M., and Shaw, A. *Reconceptualizing Extra Help for High School Students in a High Standards Era.* Baltimore: Center for Social Organization of Schools, 2002.

8. Office of Vocational and Adult Education. *High School Reading: Key Issue Brief.* Washington, D.C.: U.S. Department of Education, 2002.

9. National Center for Education Statistics (NCES). *The Condition of Education 2004, Indicator 31: Remedial Coursetaking.* Washington. D.C.: NCES, U.S. Department of Education, 2004.

10. Adelman, C. *The Toolbox Revisited: Paths to Degree Completion from High School Through College.* Washington, D.C.: U.S. Department of Education, 2006.

11. Mundy, A. "Gates 'Appalled' by High Schools." *Seattle Times,* UNKNOWN Feb. 27, 2005.

12. National Center on Education and the Economy (NCEE). *Tough Choices or Tough Times.* Washington, D.C.: NCEE, New Commission on the Skills of the American WorkForce, 2006.

13. U.S. Department of Labor. *America's Dynamic Workforce.* Washington, DC: U.S. Department of Labor, 2006. Available online at HYPERLINK "http://www.dol.gov/asp/media/reports/workforce2006/ADW2006_Full_Text.pdf" http://www.dol.gov/asp/media/reports/workforce2006/ADW2006_Full_Text.pdf.

14. Barton, P.E. *What Jobs Require: Literacy, Education, and Training, 1940–2006.* Washington, D.C.: Educational Testing Service, 2002.

15. Hays, E., and Ingrassia, R. "Cmdr. Torpedoes School." *New York Daily News,* Nov. 1, 2002.

16. U.S. Department of Labor, 2006.

Chapter Two

1. Bridgeland, J., DiIulio, J., and Burke Morison, K. *The Silent Epidemic: Perspectives of High School Dropouts.* Seattle: Bill and Melinda Gates Foundation, 2006.

2. Bridgeland, J., DiIulio, J., and Burke Morison, K. *The Silent Epidemic: Perspectives of High School Dropouts.* Seattle: Bill and Melinda Gates Foundation, 2006.

3. Bridgeland, J., DiIulio, J., and Burke Morison, K. *The Silent Epidemic: Perspectives of High School Dropouts*. Seattle: Bill and Melinda Gates Foundation, 2006.

4. Gray, C., and Dunster, S. "Report: Nearly 1/3 of Public School Students Fail to Graduate." WCPO television, Cincinnati, Ohio (http://wcpo.com/news/2007/local/02/08/grad_rates. html).

5. Harlow, C. *Education and Correctional Populations*. (Special report.) Washington, D.C.: Bureau of Justice Statistics, U.S. Department of Justice, 2003).

6. Alliance for Excellent Education. "Saving Futures, Saving Dollars." (Issue Brief.) Washington, D.C.: Alliance For Excellent Education, Aug. 2006.

7. Harlow, C. *Education and Correctional Populations*. (Special report.) Washington, D.C.: Bureau of Justice Statistics, U.S. Department of Justice, 2003).

8. Levin, H. Belfield, C., Muennig, P., and Rouse, C. *The Costs and Benefits of an Excellent Education for All of America's Children*. New York: Teachers College, Columbia University, 2007.

9. Alliance for Excellent Education. "Saving Futures, Saving Dollars." (Issue Brief.) Washington, D.C.: Alliance For Excellent Education, Aug. 2006.

10. "College Enrollment and Work Activity of 2006 High School Graduates," 2007 Washington, D.C.: Bureau of Labor Statistics, U.S. Department of Labor.

11. "College Enrollment and Work Activity of 2005 High School Graduates," 2007 Washington, D.C.: Bureau of Labor Statistics, U.S. Department of Labor.

12. De la Cruz, B., and Russakoff, D. "Working Toward Success." (Video essay.) *Washington Post*, Feb. 16, 2007 (http://www .washingtonpost.com/wp-dyn/content/video/2007/02/16/ VI2007021601030.html).

13. U.S. Department of Labor, 2006.

14. ACT. *Reading Between the Lines: What the ACT Reveals About College Readiness in Reading*. Iowa City, Iowa: ACT, 2006.

15. Colvin, R. L. "Congratulations! You're About to Fail." *Los Angeles Times*, Jan. 2, 2005.

16. NCES. *The Condition of Education 2004, Indicator 31: Remedial Coursetaking.* Washington, D.C.: NCES, U.S. Department of Education, 2004.

17. Jenkins, D., and Boswell, K. *State Policies on Community College Remedial Education: Findings from a National Survey.* Denver, Colo.: Education Commission of the States, 2002.

18. NCES. *The Condition of Education 2004, Indicator 31: Remedial Coursetaking. (2004).*

19. National Center for Education Statistics [NCES] (2004). *The condition of education 2004, indicator 18: Remediation and degree completion. washington,* DC: U.S. Department of Education.

20. Alliance for Excellent Education. "Demography as Destiny: How America Can Build a Better Future," (Issue Brief), Washington, DC: Alliance for Excellent Education, Oct. 2006.

21. Alliance for Excellent Education. "Demography as Destiny: How America Can Build a Better Future," (Issue Brief), Washington, DC: Alliance for Excellent Education, Oct. 2006.

22. Metropolitan Life Insurance. *The Metropolitan Life Survey of the American Teacher: Are We Preparing Students for the 21st Century? The Metropolitan Life Insurance Company: New York, NY,* 2000.

23. Perkins, B. K. *Where We Teach: The CUBE Survey of Urban School Climate.* National School Board Association, Alexandria, VA, Mar. 2007.

24. AEE. "Paying Double: Inadequate High Schools and Community College Remediation." (Issue Brief.) Washington, D.C.: AEE, Aug. 2006.

25. Alliance for Excellent Education. "Demography as Destiny: How America Can Build a Better Future," (Issue Brief), Washington, DC: Alliance for Excellent Education, Oct. 2006.

26. Greene, J. *The Cost of Remedial Education: How Much Michigan Pays When Students Fail to Learn Basic Skills.* Mackinac Center for Public Policy, Midland, MI.: 2000.

27. National Association of Manufacturers (NAM). *2005 Skills Gap Report: A Survey of the American Manufacturing Workforce.* Washington, D.C.: NAM, 2005.

28. Alliance for Excellent Education (AEE). "Hidden Benefits: The Impact of High School Graduation on Household Wealth." (Issue Brief.) Washington, D.C.: AEE, Feb. 2007.

29. Goldstein, A. "Civic Involvement Tied to Education: High School Dropouts Unlikely to Vote." *Washington Post*, Sept. 19, 2006, A19.

30. Levin, Belfield, Muennig, and Rouse (2007).

31. Cutler, D., and Lleras-Muney, A. *Education and Health: Evaluating Theories and Evidence.* (Working Paper.) National Bureau of Economic Research. Cambridge, MA, July, 2006.

32. Levin, Belfield, Muennig, and Rouse (2007).

33. Alliance For Excellent Education, "Healthier and Wealthier: Decreasing Health Care Costs by Increasing Educational Attainment." (Issue Brief.) Washington, DC: Alliance for Excellent Education, Nov. 2006.

34. Rank, M. R., and Hirschl, T. A. "Likelihood of Using Food Stamps During the Adult Years." *Journal of Nutrition Education and Behavior*, Volume 37, Issue 3, 2005, 137–146.

35. Levin, Belfield, Muennig, and Rouse (2007).

36. Thornburgh, N. "Dropout Nation: What's Wrong with America's High Schools." *Time*, Apr. 9, 2006.

Chapter Three

1. Government Accounting Office. *Title I Funding: Poor Children Benefit Though Funding per Poor Child Differs.* Washington, D.C.: GAO, Jan. 2002.

2. Thornburgh (2006).

3. *A Prairie Home Companion with Garrison Keillor*, American Public Media, 2007. http://prairiehome.publicradio.org/about/.

4. Connell, J. "California Chief Warns of Achievement Gap." *Education Week*, Feb. 14, 2007. 26(23), 20.

5. U.S. Census Bureau. *U.S. Interim Projections by Age, Sex, Race, and Hispanic Origin*. Washington, DC: Author, 2004. <http://www.census.gov/ipc/www/usinterimproj/>

6. Balfanz, R., and Letgers, N. *Locating the Dropout Crisis: Which High Schools Produce the Nation's Dropouts? Where Are They Located? Who Attends Them?* Baltimore: Center for Social Organization of Schools, John Hopkins University, 2004.

7. National Center for Education Statistics (NCES), U.S. Department of Education. *The Condition of Education, 2004, Indicator 24*. Washington, D.C.: NCES, U.S. Dept. of Education, 2004.

8. Balfanz, R., and Letgers, N. *Locating the Dropout Crisis: Which High Schools Produce the Nation's Dropouts? Where Are They Located? Who Attends Them?* Baltimore: Center for Social Organization of Schools, John Hopkins University, 2004.

9. Eckholm, E. "Plight Deepens for Black Men, Studies Warn." *New York Times*, Mar. 20, 2006, Front Page (A1).

10. Meyer, D., Madden, D., and McGrath, D. *English Language Learner Students in U.S. Public Schools: 1994 and 2000*. Washington, D.C.: National Center for Education Statistics, U.S. Department of Education, 2004.

11. National Center for Education Statistics (NCES). Lee, J., Grigg, W., and Donahue, P. *The Nation's Report Card: Reading 2007*(NCES 2007-496). NCES, Institute for Education Sciences, U.S. Department of Education, Washington, DC: 2007.

12. Alliance for Excellent Education. "The High Cost of High School Dropouts: What the Nation Pays for Inadequate High Schools." (Issue Brief.) Washington, D.C.: Alliance for Excellent Education, Oct. 2007.

13. Vu, Pauline. "Lake Wobegon, U.S.A. — where all the children are above average." *Stateline.org*, January 31, 2007.

14. Data Interaction for Connecticut Mastery Test, 4th Generation. *State by District/School Report*(2007). http://www.cmtreports.com/.

15. Salzman, A. "No Child Left Behind? Hardly." *New York Times*, May 1, 2005.

Chapter Four

1. Balfanz and Letgers (2004).
2. Williams, J. "Thugs Rule School at Lafayette High." *New York Daily News*, Dec. 30, 2002.
3. New York State Department of Education. *Lafayette High School in New York City Geographic District #21 2004–05.* The University of the State of New York, April, 2006.
4. Allensworth, E., and Easton, J. *What Matters for Staying On-Track and Graduating in Chicago Public High Schools: A Close Look at Course Grades, Failures and Attendance in the Freshman Year.* Chicago: Consortium on Chicago School Research at the University of Chicago, University Publications Office, 2007.
5. Balfanz, R., and Letgers, N. "Closing 'Dropout Factories': The Graduation Rate Crisis We Know and What Can Be Done About It." (Commentary.) *Education Week*, July 12, 2006, 25(42).
6. Editorial Projects in Education. "Diplomas Count 2007: Ready for What? Preparing Students for College, Careers, and Life After High School." (Special issue.) *Education Week*, 26(40), 2007, 40–41.
7. Jerald, Craig. *Dropping Out Is Hard To Do.* The Center for Comprehensive School Reform and Improvement, Learning Points Associates, 2006.
8. New York State Department of Education, 2006.
9. New York State Department of Education, 2006.
10. New York State Department of Education, 2006.
11. The Broad Prize For Urban Education, http://www.broaprize. org/. The Broad Education Foundation. Los Angeles, CA: 2007.
12. Thornburgh (2006).
13. Swanson is now director of *Education Week's* EPE Research Center.
14. Greene, J. P., and Winters, M. *Public High School Graduation and College-Readiness Rates, 1991–2002,* New York: Manhattan Institute for Public Research, 2005.

15. Pinkus, L. *Who's Counted? Who's Counting? Understanding High School Graduation Rates*. (Report.) Washington, D.C.: Alliance for Excellent Education, 2006.

16. http://nces.ed.gov/programs/slds/.

17. Information on the nation's dropout factories comes from Balfanz and Letgers, 2004.

18. Orfield, G., Losen, D., Wald, J., and Swanson, C. B. "Losing Our Future: How Minority Youth Are Being Left Behind by the Graduation Rate Crisis." Harvard Civil Rights Project, Mar. 11, 2004.

19. Prince, C. D. "Missing: Top Staff in Bottom Schools." *School Administrator*, Aug. 2002.

Chapter Five

1. Biancarosa, G., and Snow, C. Reading Next: A Vision for Action and Research in Middle and High School Literacy. (Report to Carnegie Corporation of New York.) Washington, D.C.: Alliance for Excellent Education, 2004.

2. Hillocks, G. *The Testing Trap: How State Writing Assessments Control Learning*. New York: Teachers College Press, 2003.

3. Heller, Rafael and Greenleaf, Cynthia L. "Literacy Instruction in the Content Areas: Getting to the Core of Middle and High School Improvement." (Report) Alliance for Excellent Education. Washington, D.C.: 2007.

4. Tovani, Cris. "Do I Really Have To Teach Reading?" Portland, ME, Stenhouse Publishers, Feb. 2004.

5. Alliance for Excellent Education. "University Park Campus School, Worcester, MA," (Case Study) Washington, DC: Alliance for Excellent Education, Sept. 2005.

6. ACT. *Reading between the lines: What the ACT reveals about college readiness in reading*. Iowa City, IA: Author, 2006.

7. ACT. *Reading between the lines: What the ACT reveals about college readiness in reading*. 2006.

8. Kamil, M. *Adolescents and Literacy: Reading for the 21st Century.* (Report.) Washington, D.C.: Alliance for Excellent Education. 2003.

Chapter Six

1. Heckman, J. J. "Beyond Pre-K: Rethinking the Conventional Wisdom on Educational Intervention." *Education Week*, Mar. 19, 2007, 26(28), 40.
2. Balfanz and Letgers, "Closing Dropout Factories" (2006).
3. Abraham, A., and Creech, J. *Reducing Remedial Education: What Progress Are States Making?* Atlanta: Southern Regional Education Board, 2002.
4. Paley, A. R. "Test Scores at Odds with Rising High School Grades." *Washington Post*, Feb. 23, 2007. A1.
5. Paley (2007).
6. Bottoms, G. *Things That Matter Most in Improving Student Learning.* Atlanta: Southern Regional Education Board, 1999.
7. Bottoms, G., Hornig Fox, J., and New, T. *High Schools That Work Assessment: Improving Urban High Schools.* Atlanta: Southern Regional Education Board, 2000.
8. Hu, W. "To Close Gaps, Schools Focus on Black Boys." *New York Times*, Apr. 9, 2007.
9. Letgers, N., Balfanz, R., and McPartland. J. *Solutions for Failing High Schools: Converging Visions and Beyond.* Baltimore: Center for the Organization of Schools, Johns Hopkins University, Mar. 1, 2002.
10. Bridgeland, J., DiIulio, J., Burke Morison, K. 2006. *The Silent Epidemic: Perspectives of High School Dropouts.* Seattle: Bill and Melinda Gates Foundation, Mar. 2006.
11. Rossi, R. J., and Stringfield, S. C. *Education Reforms and Students At Risk.* (Prepared for U.S. Department of Education, Office of Educational Research and Improvement, Oct. 1996).

12. Gray, C., and Dunster, S. 2007. "Report: Nearly 1/3 of Public School Students Fail to Graduate." WCPO television, Cincinnati, Feb. 8, 2007.

13. See, for example, Ferguson, R., and Ladd, H. "How and Why Money Matters." In H. Ladd (ed.), *Holding Schools Accountable*. Washington, D.C.: Brookings Institution, 1996; Ladd, H., and Hansen, J. (eds.). *Making Money Matter*. Washington, D.C.: National Research Council, 1999; Sanders, W., and Rivers, J. *Research Progress Report: Cumulative and Residual Effects of Teachers on Future Student Achievement*. Value-Added Research and Assessment Center, University of Tennessee, Knoxville, TN: 1996

14. Achieve. *1999 National Education Summit Briefing Book*. Washington, D.C.: Achieve, 1999.

15. Ferguson and Ladd (1996).

16. Greenwald, R., Hedges, L. V., and Laine. R. D. "The Effect of School Resources on Student Achievement." *Review of Educational Research*, Fall 1996, 66(3), 361–396.

17. National Association of Secondary School Principals (NASSP). *Breaking Ranks II: Strategies for Leading High School Reform*. Reston, VA: NASSP, 2004.

18. Education Trust. *Gaining Traction, Gaining Ground: How Some High Schools Accelerate Learning for Struggling Students*. Washington, DC: Education Trust, Nov. 2005.

19. Education Trust, 2005.

20. Communities in Schools. *A National Educational Imperative: Support for Community-Based, Integrated Student Services in the Reauthorization of the Elementary and Secondary Education Act*. Alexandria, VA: CIS, 2007.

21. Communities in Schools, 2007.

22. Milliken, William. "Battling The Dropout Epidemic," The Huffington Post, Oct. 16, 2007.

23. http://www.qualityednow.org/statelegresource/conference 2005/session6-HSReform.pdf.

24. Grossman, K. N. "Top Principal Credits Training: CPS Hopes New Leaders Program Fills Void." Chicago Sun-Times, Apr. 15, 2007, A8.
25. Dolejs, C. *Report on Key Practices and Policies of Consistently Higher Performing High Schools*, National Center for Education Accountability. Washington, D.C.: National High School Center, Oct. 2006.
26. Dolejs, C. 2006.
27. http://www.qualityednow.org/statelegresource/conference 2005/session6-HSReform.pdf.
28. Quint, J. *Meeting Five Critical Challenges of High School Reform: Lessons from Research on Three Reform Models*. New York, NY: MDRC, May, 2006.
29. Institute for Student Achievement (ISA). "The ISA Seven Principles," http://www.isa-ed.org/.
30. NASSP, 2004.

Chapter Seven

1. U.S. Department of Education, History. http://www.ed.gov/about/overview/fed/role.html.
2. ACT. *Reading Between the Lines: What the ACT Reveals About College Readiness in Reading*, Iowa City, Iowa: ACT, 2006.

Chapter Eight

1. Balfanz and Letgers (2004).

References

Abraham, A., and Creech, J. *Reducing Remedial Education: What Progress Are States Making?* Atlanta: Southern Regional Education Board, 2002.

Achieve. *1999 National Education Summit Briefing Book.* Washington, D.C.: Achieve, 1999.

ACT. *Reading Between the Lines: What the ACT Reveals About College Readiness in Reading,* Iowa City, Iowa: ACT, 2006.

ACT. *Crisis at the Core: Preparing All Students for College and Work.* Iowa City, Iowa: ACT, 2005.

Adelman, C. *The Toolbox Revisited: Paths to Degree Completion from High School Through College.* Washington, D.C.: U.S. Department of Education, 2006.

Allensworth, E., and Easton, J. *What Matters for Staying On-Track and Graduating in Chicago Public High Schools: A Close Look at Course Grades, Failures and Attendance in the Freshman Year.* Chicago: Consortium on Chicago School Research at the University of Chicago, University Publications Office, 2007.

Alliance for Excellent Education. "Elements of a Successful High School: Advocacy Action Matrix." Washington, D.C.: Alliance for Excellent Education, 2006.

Alliance for Excellent Education (AEE). "Reading for the 21st Century: Adolescent Literacy Teaching and Learning Strategies." (Issue Brief.) Washington, D.C.: Alliance for Excellent Education., Jan. 2004.

Alliance for Excellent Education. *Tapping the Potential: Retaining and Developing High-Quality New Teachers.* Washington, D.C.: Alliance for Excellent Education, 2004.

Alliance for Excellent Education. "Teacher Attrition: A Costly Loss to the Nation and to the States." (Issue Brief.) Washington, D.C.: Alliance for Excellent Education, Aug. 2005.

Alliance for Excellent Education. "Healthier and Wealthier: Decreasing Health Care Costs by Increasing Educational Attainment." (Issue Brief.) Washington, D.C.: Alliance for Excellent Education, Nov. 2006.

Alliance for Excellent Education."Paying Double: Inadequate High Schools and Community College Remediation." (Issue Brief.) Washington, D.C.: Alliance for Excellent Education, Aug. 2006.

Alliance for Excellent Education. "Reading and Writing in the Academic Content Areas." (Issue Brief.) Washington, D.C.: Alliance for Excellent Education, June 2006.

Alliance for Excellent Education. "Saving Futures, Saving Dollars: The Impact of Education on Crime Reduction and Earnings." (Issue Brief.) Washington, D.C.: Alliance for Excellent Education, Aug. 2006.

Alliance for Excellent Education. "Hidden Benefits: The Impact of High School Graduation on Household Wealth." (Issue Brief.) Washington, D.C.: Alliance for Excellent Education, Feb. 2007.

Alliance for Excellent Education. "The High Cost of High School Dropouts: What the Nation Pays for Inadequate High Schools." (Issue Brief.) Washington, D.C.: Alliance for Excellent Education, Oct. 2007

Alliance for Excellent Education. "University Park Campus School, Worcester, MA," (Case Study) Washington, D.C: Alliance for Excellent Education, Sept. 2005.

Alliance for Excellent Education. "Demography as Destiny: How America Can Build a Better Future," (Issue Brief.), Washington, D.C.: Alliance for Excellent Education, Oct. 2006.

Alliance for Excellent Education with assistance from Goodwin Liu. 2007. *8th Grade Reading, 2007*. Washington, D.C.: Alliance for Excellent Education. *··VT and DC are excluded from this graph as the data is not disaggregated by grade level. 2006 data is used for the following seven states: HI, NE, NC, NJ, OR, TN, and WI as 2007 data is not available by grade level. Chart is based on the best data available at the time of publication.*

Alliance for Excellent Education. "Graduation Rates: Independent (CPI) vs. State-Reported," (Graph.) with data from Klemick, E. *Implementing Graduation Rate Accountability Under NCLB.* Bethesda, MD: Editorial Projects in Education Research Center, 2007. Available online at: http://www.edweek.org/media/ew/dc/2007/40policy-2.pdf.

Balfanz, R., and Letgers, N. *Locating the Dropout Crisis: Which High Schools Produce the Nation's Dropouts? Where Are They Located? Who Attends Them?* Baltimore: Center for Social Organization of Schools, Johns Hopkins University, 2004.

Balfanz, R., and Letgers, N. "Closing 'Dropout Factories': The Graduation Rate Crisis We Know and What Can Be Done About It." (Commentary.) *Education Week*, July 12, 2006, 25(42).

Balfanz, R., McPartland, J. M., and Shaw, A. *Reconceptualizing Extra Help for High School Students in a High Standards Era.* Baltimore: Center for Social Organization of Schools, Johns Hopkins University, 2002.

Barton, P. E. *What Jobs Require: Literacy, Education, and Training, 1940–2006.* Washington, D.C.: Educational Testing Service, 2000.

Biancarosa, G. and Snow, C. E. *Reading Next: A Vision for Action and Research in Middle and High School Literacy.* (Report to Carnegie Corporation of New York.) Washington, D.C.: Alliance for Excellent Education, 2004.

Bottoms, G. *Things That Matter Most in Improving Student Learning.* Atlanta: Southern Regional Education Board, 1999.

Bottoms, G., Hornig Fox, J., and New, T. *High Schools That Work Assessment: Improving Urban High Schools.* Atlanta: Southern Regional Education Board, 2000.

Bridgeland, J., DiIulio, J., and Burke Morison, K. *The Silent Epidemic: Perspectives of High School Dropouts.* Seattle: Bill and Melinda Gates Foundation, 2006.

Carey, K. *One Step from the Finish Line: Higher College Graduation Rates Are Within Our Reach.* Washington, D.C.: Education Trust, 2005.

"College Enrollment and Work Activity of 2006 High School Graduates," 2007 Washington, D.C.: Bureau of Labor Statistics, U.S. Department of Labor.

Colvin, R. "Congratulations! You're About to Fail." *Los Angeles Times*, Jan. 2, 2005.

Communities in Schools. *A National Educational Imperative: Support for Community-Based, Integrated Student Services in the Reauthorization of the Elementary and Secondary Education Act.* Alexandria, VA: CIS, 2007.

Connell, J. "California Chief Warns of Achievement Gap." *Education Week*, Feb. 14, 2007, 26(23), 20.

Cruz, B., and Russakoff, D. "Working Toward Success," Washingtonpost.com, Feb. 16, 2007 (http://www.washingtonpost.com/wp-dyn/content/video/2007/02/16/VI2007021601030.html).

Cutler, D., and Lleras-Muney, A. *Education and Health: Evaluating Theories and Evidence.* (Working Paper.) National Bureau of Economic Research. Cambridge, MA, July, 2006.

Communities in Schools. *A National Educational Imperative: Support for Community-Based, Integrated Student Services in the Reauthorization of the Elementary and Secondary Education Act.* Alexandria, VA: CIS, 2007.

Data Interaction for Connecticut Mastery Test, 4th Generation. *State by District/School Report* (2007). http://www.cmtreports.com/

Dolejs, C. *Report on Key Practices and Policies of Consistently Higher Performing High Schools*, National Center for Education Accountability. Washington, D.C.: National High School Center, Oct. 2006.

Eckholm, E. "Plight Deepens for Black Men, Studies Warn." *New York Times*, Mar. 20, 2006. A1.

Editorial Projects in Education. "Diplomas Count 2007: Ready for What? Preparing Students for College, Careers, and Life After High School." (Special issue.) *Education Week*, 26(40), 40–41.

Education Trust. *Gaining Traction, Gaining Ground: How Some High Schools Accelerate Learning for Struggling Students*. Washington, D.C.: Education Trust, Nov. 2005.

Educational Testing Service (ETS). *America's Perfect Storm: Three Forces Changing Our Nation's Future*. Washington, D.C.: ETS, 2007.

Ferguson, R., and Ladd, H. "How and Why Money Matters." In H. Ladd (ed.), *Holding Schools Accountable*. Washington, D.C.: Brookings Institution, 1996.

Goldstein, A. "Civic Involvement Tied to Education: High School Dropouts Unlikely to Vote." *Washington Post*, Sept. 19, 2006. A19.

Government Accounting Office (GAO). *Title I Funding: Poor Children Benefit Though Funding per Poor Child Differs*. Washington, D.C.: GAO, 2002.

Gray, C., and Dunster, S. "Report: Nearly 1/3 of Public School Students Fail to Graduate." WCPO-TV, Cincinnati, Feb. 8, 2007 (http://wcpo.com/news/2007/local/02/08/grad_rates.html).

Greene, J. *The Cost of Remedial Education: How Much Michigan Pays When Students Fail to Learn Basic Skills*. Midland, MI: Mackinac Center for Public Policy, 2000.

Greene, J., and Winters, M. *Public High School Graduation and College-Readiness Rates, 1991–2002*. New York: Manhattan Institute for Public Research, 2005.

Greenwald, R., Hedges, L., and Laine, R. "The Effect of School Resources on Student Achievement." *Review of Educational Research*, Fall 1996, 66(3). 361–396.

Grossman, K. N. "Top Principal Credits Training: CPS Hopes New Leaders Program Fills Void." *Chicago Sun-Times*, Apr. 15, 2007. A8.

Harlow, C. (Special Report.) *Education and Correctional Populations*. Washington, D.C.: Bureau of Justice Statistics, U.S. Department of Justice, 2003.

Hays, E, and Ingrassia, R. "Cmdr. Torpedoes School," *Daily News*, Nov. 1, 2002.

Heckman, J. J. "Beyond Pre-K: Rethinking the Conventional Wisdom on Educational Intervention." *Education Week*, Mar. 19, 2007, 26(28), 40.

Heller, Rafael and Greenleaf, Cynthia L. "Literacy Instruction in the Content Areas: Getting to the Core of Middle and High School Improvement." (Report) Alliance for Excellent Education. Washington, D.C.: 2007.

Hillocks, G. *The Testing Trap: How State Writing Assessments Control Learning*. New York: Teachers College Press, 2003.

Hu, W. "To Close Gaps, Schools Focus on Black Boys." *New York Times*, Apr. 9, 2007.

Institute for Student Achievement (ISA). "The ISA Seven Principles," http://www.isa-ed.org/.

Jenkins, D., and Boswell, K. *State Policies on Community College Remedial Education: Findings from a National Survey*. Denver: Education Commission of the States, 2002.

Jerald, Craig. *Dropping Out Is Hard To Do*. The Center for Comprehensive School Reform and Improvement, Learning Points Associates, 2006.

Joftus, S., and Maddox-Dolan, B. *New Teacher Excellence: Retaining Our Best*. Washington, D.C.: Alliance for Excellent Education, 2002.

Kamil, M. *Adolescents and Literacy: Reading for the 21st Century*. (Report.) Washington, D.C.: Alliance for Excellent Education, 2003.

Ladd, H., and Hansen, J. (eds.). *Making Money Matter*. Washington, D.C.: National Research Council, 1999.

Lemke, Mariann et al. *International Outcomes of Learning in Mathematics Literacy and Problem Solving: PISA 2003 Results From the U.S. Perspective*. (NCES 2005–003). Washington, D.C.: U.S. Department of Education, National Center for Education Statistics, 2004.

Letgers, N., Balfanz, R., and McPartland, J. *Solutions for Failing High Schools: Converging Visions and Beyond*. Baltimore: Center for the Organization of Schools, Johns Hopkins University, 2002.

Levin, H., Belfield, C., Muennig, P., and Rouse, C. *The Costs and Benefits of an Excellent Education for All of America's Children*. New York: Teachers College, Columbia University, 2007.

Metropolitan Life Insurance. *The Metropolitan Life Survey of the American Teacher: Are We Preparing Students for the 21st Century? The Metropolitan Life Insurance Company*. New York, NY: 2000.

Meyer, D., Madden, D., and McGrath, D. *English Language Learner Students in U.S. Public Schools: 1994 and 2000*. Washington, D.C.: National Center for Education Statistics, U.S. Department of Education, 2004.

Milliken, William. "Battling The Dropout Epidemic," The Huffington Post, Oct. 16, 2007.

Mundy, A. "Gates 'Appalled' by High Schools," *Seattle Times*, Feb. 27, 2005.

National Association of Manufacturers (NAM). *2005 Skills Gap Report: A Survey of the American Manufacturing Workforce*. Washington, D.C.: NAM, 2005.

National Association of Secondary School Principals (NASSP). *Breaking Ranks II: Strategies for Leading High School Reform*. Reston, VA: NASSP, 2004.

National Center for Education Statistics (NCES). *The Condition of Education 2004, Indicator 31: Remedial Course-Taking*. Washington, D.C.: NCES, U.S. Department of Education, 2004.

National Center for Education Statistics. *Long-Term Trends: Reading*. Washington, D.C.: NCES, U.S. Department of Education, 2004.

National Center for Education Statistics (NCES), U.S. Department of Education. *The Condition of Education, 2004, Indicator 24*. Washington, D.C.: NCES, U.S. Dept. of Education, 2004.

National Center for Education Statistics (NCES). Grigg, W., P. Donahue, and G. Dion. *The Nation's Report Card: 12th-Grade Reading and Mathematics 2005* (NCES 2007-468). NCES, Institute for Education Sciences, U.S. Department of Education, Washington, D.C.: U.S., 2007.

National Center for Education Statistics (NCES). Lee, J., Grigg, W., and Donahue, P. *The Nation's Report Card: Reading 2007* (NCES 2007-496).

NCES, Institute for Education Sciences, U.S. Department of Education, Washington, DC: 2007.

National Center for Education Statistics (NCES). Shettle, C. et al. *The Nation's Report Card: America's High School Graduates* (NCES 2007-467). NCES, Institute for Education Sciences, U.S. Department of Education, Washington, D.C.: 2007.

National Center on Education and the Economy (NCEE). New Commission on the Skills of the American Workforce. *Tough Choices or Tough Times.* NCEE, Washington, D.C.: 2006.

National Commission on Excellence in Education. *A Nation At Risk: The Imperative for Educational Reform,* U.S. Government Printing. Office, Washington, D.C.: 1983.

New York State Department of Education. *Lafayette High School in New York City Geographic District #21 2004–05.* The University of the State of New York, April, 2006.

Office of Vocational and Adult Education. *High School Reading: Key Issue Brief.* Washington, D.C.: Office of Vocational and Adult Education, U.S. Department of Education, 2002.

Orfield, G., Losen, D., Wald, J., and Swanson, C. "Losing Our Future: How Minority Youth Are Being Left Behind by the Graduation Rate Crisis." *Harvard Civil Rights Project,* Mar. 11, 2004.

Paley, A. "Test Scores at Odds with Rising High School Grades," *Washington Post,* Feb. 23, 2007. A1.

Perkins, B. *Where We Teach: The CUBE Survey of Urban School Climate.* Alexandria, VA: National School Board Association, 2007.

Pinkus, L. *Who's Counted? Who's Counting? Understanding High School Graduation Rates.* (Report.) Washington, D.C.: Alliance for Excellent Education, 2006.

Prince, C. "Missing: Top Staff in Bottom Schools." *School Administrator,* Aug. 2002.

Quint, J. *Meeting Five Critical Challenges of High School Reform: Lessons from Research on Three Reform Models.* New York, NY: MDRC, May, 2006.

Rank, M. R., and Hirschl, T. A. "Likelihood of Using Food Stamps During the Adult Years." *Journal of Nutrition Education and Behavior,* 2005, 37(3), 137–146.

Rossi, J., and Stringfield, S. *Education Reforms and Students At Risk.* Washington, D.C.: Office of Educational Research and Improvement, U.S. Department of Education, 1996.

Salzman, A. "No Child Left Behind? Hardly." *New York Times,* May 1, 2005.

Sanders, W., and Rivers, J. *Research Progress Report: Cumulative and Residual Effects of Teachers on Future Student Achievement.* Value-Added Research and Assessment Center, University of Tennessee, Knoxville, TN: 1996.

Sherraden, M. *Assets and the Poor: Implications for individual accounts and social security*. (testimony). St. Louis, MO: Center for Social Development, 2001.

The Broad Prize For Urban Education, http://www.broaprize.org/. The Broad Education Foundation. Los Angeles, CA: 2007.

Thornburgh, N. "Dropout Nation: What's Wrong with America's High Schools." *Time*, Apr. 9, 2006.

Tovani, Cris. "Do I Really Have To Teach Reading?" Stenhouse Publishers, Portland, ME: Feb. 2004.

U.S. Census Bureau. *U.S. Interim Projections by Age, Sex, Race, and Hispanic Origin*. Washington, DC: Author, 2004. <http://www.census.gov/ipc/www/usinterimproj/>.

U.S. Census Bureau. *Income, Poverty, and Health Insurance Coverage in the United States: 2005*. Washington, D.C.: U.S. Government Printing Office, 2006.

U.S. Department of Education. History. http://www.ed.gov/about/overview/fed/role.html.

U.S. Department of Education. *Educational and Labor Market Performance of GED Recipients*. Washington, D.C.: National Library of Education, 1998.

U.S. Department of Labor. *America's Dynamic Workforce*. Washington, DC: U.S. Department of Labor, 2006. Available online at "http://www.dol.gov/asp/media/reports/workforce2006/ADW2006_Full_Text.pdf".

Vu, Pauline. "Lake Wobegon, U.S.A. — where all the children are above average." *Stateline.org*, Jan. 31, 2007.

Williams, J. "Thugs Rule School at Lafayette High." *New York Daily News*, Dec. 30, 2002.

Wise, Mike. "We Got No Game: Poor Fundamentals Cost Americans a Shot at Gold." *Washington Post*, Aug. 2004, A01.

The Author

Bob Wise became president of the Alliance for Excellent Education in February 2005. Under his leadership, the Alliance has continued to build its reputation as a respected authority on high school policy and to advocate for reform in America's secondary education system, working to ensure that all students graduate from high school prepared for success.

Since joining the Alliance, Wise has become a sought-after speaker and advisor on education issues. He has advised the U.S. Department of Education and frequently testifies before the U.S. Congress. As governor of West Virginia from 2001 to 2005, he fought for and signed legislation to fund the PROMISE Scholarship Program, which has helped thousands of West Virginia students remain in the Mountain State for college. He also established a character education curriculum in all state schools and created the Governor's Helpline for Safer Schools. During his administration, West Virginia saw a significant increase in the number of students completing high school and entering college.

In 2001, he proposed salary bonuses for teachers who achieve National Board Certification, which helped triple the rate of certified teachers in the state. Education Week's 2004 Quality Counts report gave West Virginia the highest cumulative grade of all fifty states. As governor, Wise was the first West Virginian to chair the Southern Governors' Association.

From 1983 to 2001, he served in the U.S. House of Representatives representing the second district of West Virginia; he aggressively worked to preserve federal financial aid for students to attend college. For several terms, he was a member of the Democratic Party Leadership team, as a regional whip and as a whip-at-large. Committee assignments during these eighteen years included Transportation and Infrastructure, Government Reform and Organization, Education and Labor, and Budget. Among his notable congressional accomplishments are the Chemical Right to Know legislation, the Wise Amendment to the Clean Air Act, and first-ever federal Mental Health Parity legislation.

Wise also serves on the Public Education Network's board of directors and is an advisory committee member for a number of organizations, among them the Campaign for Educational Equity, Editorial Projects in Education, and the National High School Center, which is funded by the Office of Elementary and Secondary Education and the Office of Special Education Programs and housed at the American Institutes for Research. He also serves on the board of directors of C-Change, which works to eliminate cancer as a major public health risk at the earliest possible time.

Governor Wise earned a bachelor's degree from Duke University in 1970 and a J.D. from Tulane University College of Law in 1975. He recently earned a black belt in Tae Kwon Do. He and wife Sandy live in Washington, D.C., with their two children.

Index